AF343509

THE FILES OF THE IMPOSSIBLE
Crimes and Disappearances

Geoffrey Claustriaux

THE FILES OF THE IMPOSSIBLE
Crimes and Disappearances

Foreword by Bob Bellanca

It's been 10 years since I created BTLV, the #1 medium for mystery and the unexplained, and I've been asked to write prefaces on numerous occasions. Only once did I accept, because I thought the author's work was incredibly serious in a world that isn't often serious enough. For the same reason, I agreed to write the preface to the book you're holding in your hands. Geoffrey Claustriaux has a gift for blending fact and fiction like no one else, and that's what I liked about it.

The brilliant idea behind this book is to have imagined what the main protagonists and victims of the stories told here said to each other. Who wouldn't have liked to hear the conversations of the main protagonists of the great criminal, paranormal and mysterious cases? The cinema has understood this and has often ventured into this territory. Literature, on the other hand, is less familiar with this approach, or at least more clumsy.

Geoffrey Claustriaux takes us beyond the facts, opening the door to complicated human relationships. Because that's what it's all about. What drives one man to murder another? Or to keep the two hands of his poor victim as a trophy? Why do people disappear without ever being found? How can we explain the total disappearance of a colony on Roanoke Island, North Carolina, over 400 years ago? What were the last exchanges, the last words, the last decisions of all these people who met a tragic fate?

This book shows us that there's a fine line between mystery and the paranormal. Geoffrey Claustriaux skilfully plays with us, sometimes hinting at the beginnings of an explanation, which remains speculative, as he likes to remind us. To tell you the truth, I'd love to be in your shoes and discover, as you will, these incredible stories... A word of advice: don't turn off the light...

The *Smiley Faces* folder

1

"May God have mercy on you," says the masked woman to the young man tied up in front of her.

His tone is calm and collected, but there's a hint of anger in his voice. The *smiley face* painted on his mask draws a chuckle from the young man.

This mask stinks. That chick's got bad breath!

This absurd, nonsensical thought would have amused him had he not been suspended upside down, facing the Hudson, his hands and feet tied to a railing by a plastic bracelet. Snot drips from his nose, accumulating in his nostrils without his being able to wipe or blow it out. His head is spinning, the result of the gallons of alcohol he and his friends had imbibed at McSwiggan's Pub earlier in the evening. The biting, icy cold gnaws at his skin.

Matthew Genovese, before finding himself tied to the pier at Jersey City's Pier A Park like a dangerous animal, had led a life of alcohol, sex and, occasionally, drugs. Wall Street *trader* by day, party boy by night, the *golden boy* hadn't made just any friends over the past year. Unfazed by the human woes brought on by finance, he didn't hesitate to trigger bankruptcies before capitalizing on other, more valiant companies. *If it's not me, it'll be someone else,"* he often repeated to himself to justify the profits he made from these transactions. His parents, far from wondering where they had gone wrong, when they had made a mistake in his upbringing, supported his greedy approach, all the more so as Matthew never missed an opportunity to share it with them through gifts of all kinds.

The young man shivers. Death transpires from the wet sand and brown seaweed that has dried on the rocks. The darkness teems with inexplicable sounds, sometimes amplified by the immensity of the river. His eyes misty with alcohol, Matthew risks a glance back. Three masked people stare back at him, all wearing the same smiling *smiley* face. They seem to be chatting. Finally, one of them moves away from the group to spray-paint the *smiley* symbol on a rock, while the smaller one, the one who'd already spoken to him, approaches again. Matthew grimaces. His wrists ache, and the sea-salt-laden air doesn't help. He tries to free himself, but cannot. The first wave hits his forehead, soaking his already damp hair.

He knows what awaits him. Like the rest of the U.S., he's heard about the masked killers who prey on college students and recent graduates, reeling at the details of each new murder. Tonight, he's their whipping boy. Tomorrow, in the newspapers, his name will appear in bold letters over a photo of himself, probably from his Facebook account. *A Wall Street* golden boy *drowns. Accident, suicide or murder?*

"Please," he stammers. I didn't hurt anyone. I don't deserve this.

The masked woman doesn't answer.

"I don't make the rules," adds Matthew, almost plaintively.

A second wave, bigger than the first, washes over his nose. He suffocates, then coughs and spits. The masked woman takes a step back to avoid getting her shoes wet. Matthew stares in horror at the watery horizon unfolding upside down before him. The water has become his sky, Manhattan a carpet of lights. He contorts to free his hands, but only succeeds in skinning his wrists. He grimaces. A third wave drowns his face before receding. He coughs again, expelling the salt water from his mouth as best he can.

"What do you want from me?" he finds the strength to shout. Punish me for being a *trader*? I've always respected the law!

His question is purely rhetorical; he's dealt with people of the same ilk before, including a rather vindictive man. Except that, on that occasion, it had ended in a bar brawl and the certainty that you couldn't argue with "those people".

"Is that why you're doing this? You're going to kill everyone on Wall Street?"

He could honestly think of no other explanation for his situation: these people were either jealous of his social status or had suffered the consequences of his actions. It's one or the other, since otherwise he's always behaved in an exemplary fashion—apart from the odd evening screw-up, but nothing that would justify killing him. He then realizes with horror that no motive has ever been established for the homicides perpetrated by the masked people.

Matthew's arms begin to go numb. A diffuse pain creeps into his back muscles. He winces, unable to prevent another wave from filling his nose and mouth. This one takes longer to recede. He holds his breath. Finally, the Hudson decides to give him another minute's reprieve.

Something moves in the darkness, a metallic glint reflects the moon. For a moment, Matthew believes in the appearance of a savior, the advent of an incredible *deus ex machina*. His torturers will be apprehended and sent to prison, while he returns home, pours himself a whisky and thinks about how to grow his assets.

But this reflection is only the consequence of the empty paint can, thrown into the distance by one of the masked acolytes. His savior has vanished into thin air, and there's nothing left to save him from drowning.

The sensation of water pouring into his lungs is indescribable, fiery and icy at the same time, like the bite of a polar wind. He suffocates, trying to scream as the second, more intense and devastating wave of pain surges through his nervous system. The water forced his cry to the back of his throat. Her burning chest hurts like hell and feels like it's about to burst. Vertigo grips him, the lack of oxygen begins to take its toll, but he struggles to stay conscious. Struggling to reach the top, that's what he's always done. A series of obscure, shapeless, vaporous thoughts run through his mind. *Flashes* and snatches of memory flash before his eyes. His body is a dying shell. He feels a stranger to himself. For a second, he thinks he sees himself from the outside, lying on the sand in his $1,000 suit, as if his soul is trying to extricate itself from this moribund carcass.

Matthew shakes with all his limbs. Yet he's no longer cold. He stares absently at the bottom of the water. His lungs release the last bubbles of oxygen, the last vestiges of life now leaving his body.

2

Putrefied bodies, blood and wasted lives, Inspector Kevin Gannon can't take it anymore. Fifteen years he's been working on his own on the case that the press has dubbed the "*Smiley Face* Murders"[1], without managing to apprehend the culprit(s). Worse still, he still has no clue as to their appearance, let alone their identity. He attributes no less than forty-five homicides to these assassins, but he doesn't doubt for a moment that the real number is much higher. It's just that we still haven't identified all the crimes, because, as the many bloggers who are passionate about this theory have pointed out, the *Smiley Face Killers* didn't leave a single clue at the crime scenes, apart from a smiling face painted near the bodies.

Gannon and his sidekick Anthony Duarte, also a retired detective, have been tearing their hair out for almost two decades to support their theory. For a while,

---

1. The murders of smiling faces.

they even suspected that the murderers might be revenge cops, given their elusive nature. For them, each new corpse feels like a frustrating return to square one. In fact, they've come to harbor the distinct impression of chasing chimeras that leave only a bloody trail in their wake. Time and again, they've been dismissed as cranks because their theories haven't been proven. Officially, the forty-five deaths they attribute to the masked killer(s), and almost all the others, have been classified as accidental deaths due to alcohol-related drowning, or even suicide. The FBI and several police organizations investigated the deaths and concluded that no link could be established between the cases. The Center for Homicide Research[2] went so far as to publish an exhaustive report entitled *Drowning the Smiley Face Theory*[3] listing eighteen reasons why the theory doesn't hold water, including the fact that *smiley* faces are a very common form of graffiti and that murder by drowning is extremely rare.

Sitting in front of his living room table, piled high with thousands of photocopies made in the run-up to his retirement, Gannon feels pitiful, incompetent, despite a career rich in arrests of all kinds. He consults his watch. Forty minutes to go before Duarte arrives for their weekly tune-up. He has time to go over the case a thousand times. He may have missed something the previous 999 times...

The first file in the pile bears the name Patrick McNeill, traced in blue marker on the flap by the light hand of Dr. Lee Gilbertson. It was the discovery of his body on April 7, 1997, when a teenager stumbled upon it near the entrance to New York harbor, that set the wheels in motion. The boy had sneaked out to smoke a bag of weed stolen from his older brother, but what he saw, wedged between the rocks, far exceeded the sensations he'd come for. He ran home, shouting to anyone who would listen that he'd just found the bloated corpse of a homeless man. A police team led by Anthony Duarte had arrived on the scene about fifteen minutes after the teenager's mother had contacted the NYPD. Gannon arrived twenty minutes later, his raincoat billowing behind him like a superhero cape. He found Duarte kneeling beside the body, his hands encased in latex gloves so as not to compromise any possible clues.

"What have we got?"

"Patrick McNeill, 21, a student at Fordham College, had responded to Duarte by cracking his neck stiffened by a prolonged uncomfortable position. He was last seen drinking with friends in a Manhattan bar nearly two months ago."

---

2. Homicide Research Center.
3. Drown out the smiley face theory.

"Were you able to contact the family?"

"His best friend. He says Patrick was seen in the bar bathroom throwing up just before he left."

"Where exactly did it happen?"

"At Dapper Dog."

"I know this bar. It's about twenty kilometers from here. Do you think he had too much to drink, fell into the East River and the current drifted the body here?"

"Possibly, but that's for the experts to determine."

Unfortunately, the experts hadn't been able to determine anything at all. *Death by drowning* had been their official conclusion and, from the outset, it had not fully satisfied Gannon and Duarte. However, it was only much later, at the end of 2006, nine years after the fact, at a meeting with Dr. Lee Gilbertson, that they finally had the opportunity to place the homicide in the realm of "possible, even probable".

Douglas Lee Gilbertson, professor of criminal justice and *gang* specialist at Staint Cloud State University, was approaching fifty. His graying hair was cut very short, military style, and his skin was visibly prone to sunburn. He must have been blond before turning gray. His favorite pastime was getting together with his friends on weekends to walk in the forest and venture into the remotest corners of nature. That morning, he would certainly have preferred to lose himself in an unexplored region of the Appalachians rather than face two detectives to whom he had planned to demonstrate their ineffectiveness in the country's most terrible serial murder case. That's why he took a swig of coffee before entering their office.

"Gentlemen," he nodded.

On Gannon's desk, he placed a chronologically arranged stack of folders. At the top was the folder for Patrick McNeill.

"I know you're doing your best," he added, "but I'm afraid you've missed something in all this business.

"Dr. Gilbertson, thank you for coming," replies Duarte, whose voice is colored with annoyance. Get to the point. On the phone, you told me you had new information on a number of closed investigations.

"That's right. There are a lot of aspects to cover in these cases, I'm aware, but it would seem that you've overlooked a few. To summarize my research, details of which you'll find in these binders, we currently have fifteen victims."

"On what do you base this assertion?"

"I'm coming to that."

From Patrick McNeill's folder, he took out a series of documents, including photos he had taken himself. On one of them, a weathered *smiley face* was fading on a rock. Traces of blue paint were still visible.

"As you know, Patrick was last seen drinking with friends at the Dapper Dog bar in Manhattan on February 17, 1997. Later, he was seen by passers-by staggering through the streets, bumping into parked cars and vomiting. I was able to retrace his steps. Patrick started walking south on Second Avenue from 92nd Street."

"We've also come to this conclusion," said Gannon.

"That's right. But did you know that a double-parked vehicle, occupied by a man and a woman, was observed following Patrick down Second Avenue? A witness reported to me that Patrick had fallen to the ground a little while later, and that the vehicle following him then stopped and waited for him to get up. When Patrick started walking south again, the vehicle resumed following him."

"What do you mean?" said Duarte, suddenly interested, eyebrows furrowed.

"I was able to recover part of the plate number, but not enough to identify the vehicle."

"Interesting, but a little thin," commented Gannon.

"Wait a minute. I questioned the NYPD harbor unit that patrols the river daily and, according to them, Patrick's body should never have been recovered there given the currents. Patrick had to be removed, taken to the mouth of the harbor and dumped there. What's more, he was wearing only his jeans, underwear and socks. I find it hard to believe that he would have removed most of his clothes before jumping into the East River, especially in February."

"We thought the alcohol had made him delirious."

"Ah! Let's talk about alcohol! According to your report, Patrick was recovered with a blood alcohol level of 0.16. The human body naturally produces alcohol after death, during decomposition. Considering that he was supposed to have been in the water for almost two months, his BAC must have increased by 0.04 due to post-mortem alcohol production. This means that his actual BAC, when he entered the water, was probably closer to 0.12, or about 6 drinks. That's not much for a young man of his size. Nor is it consistent with the kind of behavior he exhibited in the bar's restroom or outside right after that. If that was his actual blood alcohol level, then something else made him sick that night."

This time, the two inspectors had nothing to reply. Gilbertson took the opportunity to continue his presentation.

"As you know, since you were present, Patrick was recovered on his back, which is extremely unusual for drowning cases, especially for an individual of his height and weight—as your experts pointed out in their report. Most drowning victims are found floating or lying on their stomachs. Exceptions occur when a victim is obese or the water is rough, but a river could not have tipped him over in this way. In short, Patrick's body position was incompatible with the usual criteria for drowning."

Thoughtfully, Gannon leaned over his desk to take hold of the document Gilbertson was holding, then dropped back into his seat, his eyes riveted to the paper.

"Finally," concludes the professor, "the autopsy revealed a pattern around the neck consisting of numerous regularly spaced vertical lines."

"The coroner attributed this to the brush in which the body lay," objected Duarte.

"For my part, I see ligature marks."

"And what's this?" asked Gannon, grabbing the photo of the *smiley face* sprayed in blue paint.

"I photographed it a few yards from where you found Patrick."

"What's so special about this graffiti? There are hundreds just like it all over the docks."

"On its own, it's nothing special, I grant you. But in relation to..."

Gilbertson opened several files in quick succession.

"... Brian Welzien, 21, disappeared in 2000 in Chicago. Todd Geib, 22, disappeared in 2005 in Casnovia, Michigan. And last but not least, Lucas Homan, 21, missing in 2006 from La Crosse, Wisconsin."

Each time, Gilbertson took out a photo of a *smiley face* spray-painted on a wall or rock.

"This, gentlemen," he announced peremptorily, "is proof that we're dealing with the same individual or group of individuals."

Gannon and Duarte exchanged puzzled glances, filled with doubts as to the veracity of this theory. They couldn't have known, of course, that these doubts would be violently swept away a few months later.

Sitting in the living room of his house in West Roxbury, a suburb of Boston, Gannon nonchalantly smoked a cigarette, looking out at the city beyond the window. He'd picked up this bad habit after his ex-wife told him she wanted a divorce. Time and again, he'd tried to get rid of it, but the stress of work, and especially the *Smiley Faces* affair, had always prevented him from doing so. Mr. Clayborne, owner of the premises and husband of the woman who discovered William Hurley, glared at him but didn't dare ask him to stop stinking up his clean interior. Clearly, he wasn't the one to bring home the money or the one to wear the pants.

"Are you sure we still need to question Margaret?" he said to the two detectives sitting on his sofa. It's already been done this morning and, to be honest, she's feeling a bit shaken up by it all.

"Sir, we welcome any help you can give us in our investigation. Perhaps she saw something, some detail that could help us. The smallest thing, even if it seems insignificant to you, is likely to help us. So yes, we need to talk to her."

Gannon's little monologue had the desired effect, as Clayborne—not without a final sigh—called his wife. She sluggishly descended from their bedroom and settled into the armchair opposite the policemen. Dressed in a pair of jogging bottoms that were certainly too baggy, with her gaze lost in a haze, this usually confident and vivacious woman set about answering the policemen's questions in a monotone voice.

"Thank you for agreeing to talk to us, Mrs. Clayborne," began Gannon. "We know this is difficult for you, but unfortunately it's very important. Please start by telling us what you saw, without leaving out any details. We already know the main points, but we need to hear it from you."

With her head turned towards the window, she told us once again that she had gone for a run along the Charles River, which she did every morning. In the distance, the TD Garden stadium dominated the landscape. She hadn't passed anyone on the way, and there was no sign that she'd come across a crime scene.

"It was 5:30 a.m. when I arrived in the vicinity of Nashua Street Park," she explains. "I like to go running early, it's quieter and gives me energy for the whole day."

"I know you said you didn't notice anything, but let me insist: there really isn't anything that made you tick?" intervened Gannon. "Anything unusual, the first thing that comes to mind."

The young woman massaged her temples, at first surprised by the question, then an indefinite expression appeared on her face, as if a buried memory had inadvertently resurfaced.

"Well… (She hesitated for a moment) Now that you ask, it's true that just before I came upon the body in the park, I noticed a *smiley face* painted on one of the tree trunks. I'd forgotten about it. Is it important?"

Duarte flinched. At his side, Gannon felt a surge of excitement, but tried not to let it show.

"Maybe more than you think," he says in a measured tone. Please continue.

"I was about to turn back when I noticed something between the bushes at the edge of the bank. I got closer and saw that it was a man lying down. At first I thought he was homeless—it's not uncommon to come across the homeless in the park— but then I noticed he was wearing a Marine Corps jacket, so I got even closer, and that's when I saw that… that he… (She coughed to regain composure) … Well, that his skull was bashed in. I immediately called 911, and that was that. Can I go back to bed now? I've got a big meeting tomorrow, I'd like to get some rest."

Gannon nodded in agreement. Then the investigators got up to leave the house, not without Duarte taking the trouble to leave his card with Mr. Clayborne, as he always did in case anything came back to the witness. Mr. Clayborne escorted them to his doorstep and waited for them to get into their car before closing it. *Good riddance,* he thought. *Hope never to see you again.* If the case was indeed over for him and his wife—despite occasional reminders of his status as a witness—it was unfortunately far from over for Detectives Gannon and Duarte… and for the future victims of the *Smiley Face Killers.*

*

At 8 a.m. the next morning, Gannon arrived at the police station fresh as a daisy. The trip to Boston and back had exhausted him, so much so that he had slept like a baby—a first since his divorce. After greeting his colleagues, he poured himself his usual morning coffee, before settling in at his desk. The mountain of paperwork that accumulated there seemed never to diminish, and he sighed at the thought of spending hours signing forms when that wasted time could be spent tracking down S.F.K.'s (the abbreviation now used for *Smiley Face Killers*). Just as he was about to begin his tedious paperwork, Duarte suddenly appeared.

"Kev, S.F.K. *briefing* in five minutes."

Happy to put off his pile of paperwork for a few minutes, he made his way quietly to the meeting room. Duarte was already there, along with Gilbertson and the last member of their team, Mike Donovan, who took the floor to open the meeting. He gestured to Duarte, who turned off the lights and pressed a button on the remote control he was holding. Behind him, on the meeting room's large screen, appeared a photo depicting a scene that Gannon knew well, and for good reason: the corpse of William Hurley.

"As you know, this young man's lifeless body was discovered yesterday morning by a woman named Margaret Clayborne. He has been identified as William Hurley, who went missing a week ago after attending a Boston Bruins game at TD Garden stadium. He reportedly left the stadium at half-time to meet his fiancée, Claire Mahoney, but when she arrived at the venue, she didn't see him arrive. She claimed that William had asked her to pick him up early, explaining that he was tired from his long day at work."

"What was his profession?" asked Gannon.

"Gardener."

While on the phone with Claire, Hurley warned that his cell phone battery was low; when she asked for his exact location, someone behind him shouted "99 Nashua Street", just before the line went dead.

"Did someone shout?"

"Claire assumes she was on speakerphone."

Donovan pressed his remote control and the shot changed to a close-up of William Hurley's head, puffy from his extended stay in the Charles River.

"The victim suffered blunt trauma to the head, left eye and back of the leg. Boston police speculated that Hurley, in an intoxicated state, had walked from the stadium to the river's edge, where he slipped into the water. Surveillance footage from outside the stadium captured Hurley staggering and struggling to maintain his balance. However, the toxicology report revealed that while Hurley had a low level of alcohol in his blood, traces of GHB, the date-rape drug, were also found in his system and his cell phone was damaged. At first glance, it seems obvious that this murder was perpetrated by the S.F.K. The modus operandi and the crime scene are entirely consistent with their habits."

The image changed again. A *smiley* face spray-painted on a tree trunk appeared. The face, composed of a circle, two lines for the eyes and a semicircle for the mouth, was strangely monstrous in its simplicity.

"We can conclude that this is the fifteenth alleged victim of these bastards."

"It's awful," Gilbertson couldn't help but blurt out.

The others took no notice. Donovan continued:

"As usual, we haven't collected any clues about the area where the body was found, but that's hardly surprising given that it's not the scene of the crime."

"Damn it," grumbled Gannon.

Of course, he was accustomed to this lack of information, since the bodies drifted for days before being found, offering no indication of where they had been dumped.

"It's worth noting, however, that William Hurley fits the profile, reinforcing the idea that the killer(s) are targeting a specific type of person. For the record, the victims are all young men either attending university or having left shortly before. They generally get good grades and have high career aspirations. They are athletic, popular, white and almost always drinking with friends shortly before their disappearance. Some of them were openly homosexual. This consistency among the victims supports our theory that a person or group is behind their deaths."

"We know all that," grumbled Duarte.

"I was just stating the facts," Donovan justified himself.

"I know," sighed Duarte. It's just that... let's say I'm fed up with not having any leads to explore.

"You're not the only one, believe me."

"Speaking of which," Gilbertson interjected, "I've come up with a theory I'd like to discuss with you."

"The spittoon is yours," said Donovan as he sat back down.

The professor took his place in front of the screen.

"I think what we're dealing with is much larger than we had originally envisaged. I think there could be over a thousand people involved, divided into 'cells' in twelve to fifteen different cities. I can see from your skeptical expressions that this assertion needs to be substantiated. Very well, then. My hypothesis would explain how some of the identified victims disappeared on the same day, in different cities. I also believe that the actual number of victims is much higher than we assume.

"How much do you think?"

"Difficult to determine with certainty, but several hundred, certainly. As you know, my speciality is the study of criminal groups, and to my mind all the signs point to an organized small group. My theory is that this murderous *gang* has been around for some time. Membership of this group could change over the years, as some members age or die, and others are recruited."

"If you're right, this coordinated approach would also contribute to confusion in police investigations," Donovan pointed out.

"That's right. Our guesses usually involve a single perpetrator, and we'd be baffled if different people were involved, especially if they have no connection with the victims. I note that the S.F.K. has become more active in recent years. In my opinion, this is due to the fact that law enforcement agencies have not taken them seriously, and the group therefore feels safer and confident in its ability to kill with impunity."

"What do you mean, 'law enforcement didn't take them seriously'?" offended Duarte.

"Relax, Anthony," Gannon tempered, "you know very well what Gilbertson means. Apart from us and some of the unofficial media, who cares? Everyone denies its existence."

"Serial murder is hard work," continued the professor. "It involves selecting a target, watching over them, kidnapping them, choosing a place to commit the deed and then, eventually, staging the disappearance or constructing a credible scenario. The most prolific serial killer on record is Luis Garavito, who has confessed to killing 140 people. If we're right, the *Smiley Face Killers* put Garavito to shame. I've compiled a database that identifies a total of 335 victims based on crime scene profiles and characteristics. It should be noted that these are "possible" victims—there is no way of proving that these deaths are related, at least for the time being. The circumstantial evidence, however, is compelling. The victims in the database have many features that suggest they spent a lot of time out of the water before being discovered, and many post-mortem examinations show similar toxicological reports."

"Incredible," gasped Gannon. "When did you find the time to do all this?"

"My work? That's my whole life," smiled Gilbertson, alluding to the fact that he didn't own a wedding ring, lived alone and didn't see anyone apart from his students.

"What does this *gang* want?" asked Donovan. "What's their objective?"

"I confess that their motives escape me a little. There's nothing in their victims' past to justify such an act."

"Some were even accused of sexual assault," observes Gannon.

"Absolutely, but it's only a minority, and their numbers are proportionally equal to those of the rest of the population."

"Others were notorious racketeers, and still others were into drugs," Gilbertson added.

"What if we were dealing with a group organized around a common cause?" suggested Duarte.

"What do you mean?"

"Let's imagine we're talking about a kind of secret society to which people wanting to take revenge on students who have harmed them in one way or another can join."

"Expand."

"I'm astonished that the targets were only students, and that drowning was the cause of death. Why drowning? There are quicker and more effective ways of eliminating someone. What's more, if this were an organized gang, making the bodies disappear would have been easy. But no, each time they decided to leave the body where it was, indicating its location with a *smiley face*. Why did they do this?"

"Do you think they want to send a message to all academics?"

"More like a warning: behave yourself, because we're watching you."

Donovan groaned aloud.

"If you're right, we'll never be able to stop them," he whined in the manner of a plaintive child.

"It's going to be complicated," admits Gannon, "but not impossible. If we manage to infiltrate the group or identify one of its members, or even find out how they communicate, the house of cards could collapse."

<h1 style="text-align:center">4</h1>

Gannon thinks back to these words as he closes the file on Dakota James, the latest victim and the only one perhaps to have been targeted twice. As reported by *The Daily Beast*, the young man had contacted his friend Shelley on December 15, 2016. It was late and James was very drunk after a night out at a bar. He seemed upset about something. When she tracked him down, she saw a visibly confused James walking towards an SUV parked on the wrong side of the street. Shelley intervened and brought James home safely.

Five weeks later, James disappeared. Once again, he was out drinking with friends. Forty days after his disappearance, his body was found floating in the Ohio

River. Gannon and Duarte discovered graffiti of a smiling face nearby, as well as clues suggesting that James had been drugged and strangled before drowning. The coroner, however, disagreed, deeming his death accidental. If Gannon and Duarte were right, it meant that the killer(s) had been thwarted in their evil plans—and seen by a witness—but had nevertheless continued to wait for an opportunity to murder Dakota James, proof of their determination as much as their arrogance.

Gannon sighs as he rebuilds his stack of files, at the top of which sits the folder bearing Patrick McNeill's name. Five more minutes before Duarte arrives for their weekly tune-up. It will be their last. Gannon intends to tell him he's giving up. Since 2007, he has distanced himself from the police and set up his own agency, GD Investigations, in collaboration with Duarte, Gilbertson and Donovan, so that he could devote himself fully to investigating the *Smiley Face Killers*, but ten years on, despite the accumulation of files and the database developed by Gilbertson, they are still nowhere to be found and the agency is beginning to falter. Funds are dwindling dangerously, and Gannon has even had to mortgage his house. The coroner's refusal to consider Dakota James' death suspicious was the last straw. Despite this, Gannon can't blame him, and for good reason: there has always been a fundamental disconnect between law enforcement and forensic science professionals. Duarte is quick to point out that both the coroner and the police expect the other to provide evidence of homicide, and as a result, these cases simply end up being pushed aside by more urgent investigations. Evidence of homicide is never officially collected, and everyone simply accepts that the drowning was accidental. But this time, enough is enough. They may not have been able to provide proof, but the body of evidence is enormous and should have been enough to launch an official investigation.

What's more, there's a good reason why it's so difficult to produce real evidence of the murders coordinated by the S.F.K.: they use the *Dark Web*, that network of sites parallel to the Internet, to organize themselves. Gannon and his colleagues had managed to get close to one of these *websites*. They had been given an address, but when they accessed the site, they were confronted with a request for a password and a request to turn on the camera so that the site administrators could verify their identity. As a result, they had backtracked, thereby signing the death warrant of their investigation, even if they didn't know it yet. Their chance had passed, a chance that would never come again. They had approached the sun and, like Icarus, had burnt their wings. Never again would they soar so high, for the team had subsequently spent another two years in vain, except to count the dead.

"Yep," mumbles Gannon as he rises from his chair and heads for the window to observe New York, the city that never sleeps. Time to hang up.

A tear beads at the corner of his eye. He feels he's abandoned all the families to whom he promised answers. So he shakes his head, clinging to the image of the distant city, the throbbing echo of fifty years of accumulated fatigue, and the beginnings of a state that resembles peace. Then he smiles because he knows he's right. He's entitled. He has the right to rest.

The facts

Is Elgin man's death the work of the 'smiley face' killer?

BY HARRY HITZEMAN
hhitzeman@dailyherald.com

Stephany Welzien knows her only child is dead.

What the Elgin woman doesn't know is what happened to her son before he died.

Brian Welzien, a 21-year-old finance major at Northern Illinois University, was last seen by friends outside a Chicago hotel in the early morning hours of Jan. 1, 2000, sick after drinking too much.

The former soccer player's body washed up on a Lake Michigan beach in Gary, Ind., about 2½ months later.

The manner in which he drowned was undetermined and authorities speculated he somehow wandered into the icy water.

Brian's mother disagrees.

"In my heart, I know he didn't get into the water himself. Somebody else was responsible," she said last week.

Welzien and others may soon have answers if a theory of two retired New York police detectives holds true.

A larger scheme?

Detectives Kevin Gannon and Anthony Duarte, part of a four-man team called Nationwide Investigations, have investigated the disappearances of more than 40 other young men in the Great Lakes region. They all share

See CAUSE on PAGE 10

An article from The Daily Herald, dated May 8, 2008 (@Newspapers.com)

When 24-year-old William Hurley calls his girlfriend Claire Mahoney on the evening of October 8, 2009, all he wants to do is go home. The Navy veteran, who had attended a Boston Bruins game, asked Claire to pick him up early, explaining that he was tired from his day's work. A few minutes later, Claire arrives at the rendezvous point, but Hurley is nowhere to be found. Six days later, his body is found in the Charles River, and the cell phone he used to make the last call is found broken nearby. Hurley's death is eventually classified as an undetermined drowning, the police declaring that they have found no evidence of foul play.

Yet those close to Hurley—including Claire Mahoney—dispute these claims, pointing out that her cell phone was damaged, that her injuries indicate blunt force trauma and that a toxicology report revealed high levels of GHB, commonly known as the date-rape drug.

Hurley is not the first young man to die under suspicious and highly controversial circumstances. More than a decade before Hurley's disappearance in Boston, Fordham College student Patrick McNeill vanished after stumbling out of a bar on New York's Upper East Side. McNeill was missing for over a month before his body was found floating in the East River, and his death was declared—like Hurley's—to be an undetermined drowning.

Several alleged victims, including William Hurley, top right (©Oxygen.com)

Fordham student is dead

Body washes ashore in B'klyn

Golden knives sever 6 fire chiefs

New York Daily News article, April 8, 1997 (@Newspapers.com)

Kevin Gannon, one of the detectives who investigated the McNeill case, disagrees with the official ruling on the young man's death and promises the deceased's parents that he'll find answers for them. More than 20 years later, he's still trying.

Hurley and McNeill were part of what Gannon, now retired, Anthony Duarte, a former NYPD detective, and Lee Gilbertson, a criminal justice professor, called an "epidemic" of college-educated young white men who disappeared at parties with friends before being found lifeless in nearby rivers. Like Hurley's death, most of these cases were considered accidental or undetermined drownings, and many were attributed to alcohol consumption. But since 2008, Gannon, Duarte and Gilbertson have been claiming that these deaths are the work of a *gang-like* organization—dubbed the *Smiley Face Killers* because of the happy-face graffiti found at some of the alleged crime scenes.

The three investigators (©Dr. Lee Gilbertson)

According to these three men, the victims didn't drown accidentally, but were targeted, kidnapped and murdered by dangerous criminals who are still at large and continue to kill. The detectives believe these crimes are motivated by jealousy and reflect a coordinated effort to prey on men the killers consider privileged— whom Gannon refers to as "the best of the best". It's this ongoing threat, with new deaths matching the profile every year, that keeps the *Smiley Face Killers* theory alive.

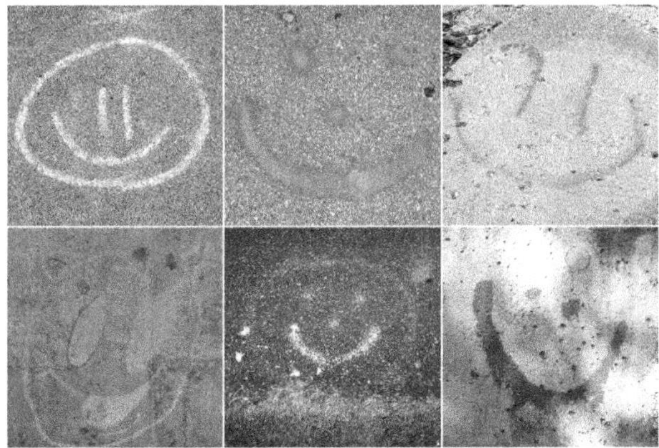

Some smileys found near crime scenes

According to Gannon, Duarte and Gilbertson, their evidence is not merely circumstantial. Above all, the trio point the finger at the decomposition chronologies. "The absence of decomposition on the bodies is inconsistent with the period during which the victims disappeared," explains Gannon. Dakota James, for example, disappeared for forty days, but decomposition of his body appears to have lasted only around three days, as did Todd Geib, who disappeared for twenty-one days, but whose decomposition lasted around two and a half. Gannon also notes that the presence of terrestrial insects and the absence of bloating suggest that the victims died on dry land and not in the water.

Detectives also noted the presence of GHB in 99.9% of cases. Gannon, Gilbertson and Duarte believe that the forensic results prove that the victims were drugged before being abducted, then murdered and placed in water. In addition to similarities in the victims' profiles and the circumstances of their disappearance and

An article from the Detroit Free Press, July 5, 2005, about Todd Geib (©Newspapers.com).

SUSPICIOUS DEATH

Missing man's body is found floating in lake

The body of a man who had been missing for three weeks was found Saturday floating in a lake in rural **Muskegon County.**

Results of an autopsy conducted Sunday on Todd Geib, 22, of **Casnovia** were incomplete. The case has been labeled a suspicious death investigation, the Muskegon Chronicle reported.

Geib's body was found Saturday in Ovidhall Lake in Casnovia Township, 25 miles east of Muskegon. He was last heard from on June 12 at an outdoor party about half a mile from the lake and 1½ miles from his house.

A female acquaintance told police that Geib called her on his cell phone about 12:50 a.m. to say he was lost. "I'm in a field," were the last words she heard him say. More than 1,500 people helped search for Geib.

By the Associated Press

death, they have also spotted thirteen symbols, including *smiley face* graffiti, in the vicinity of what they believe to be the crime scenes.

Perhaps the most chilling detail, however, is that many bodies appear to have been staged. As the police write in the book they have published based on their theories, Case Studies in Drowning Forensics, one example is the body of Tommy Booth, who disappeared in January 2008. His body was found two weeks later, face down, with his arms carefully crossed beneath him. Sticks had been driven into the soft earth in strategic places to hold his body in place, making it very clear that his body had been deliberately posed and placed there.

Smiley-face murder theory put to test

Graffiti found near man's body

By **STEPHANIE FARR**
farr.s@phillynews.com
215-854-4225

THOMAS BOOTH worked as a "first-class drywall finisher," but the 24-year-old's true passion was art, his mother recalled.

"He was very artistic," Barbara MacKay-Bush said this week. "That's why I think he did drywalling, because to get it perfect was artistic to him."

Oddly, it's a piece of art — graffiti featuring a simple, ominous smiley face — that has MacKay-Bush and police speculating about Booth's drowning in January in a creek behind Bootlegger's Bar in Ridley Township.

Found near where Booth is believed to have entered the shallow creek, the smiley face has raised concern that his death may have been the work of a network of serial killers that two former New York City detectives believe is responsible for at least 40 similar deaths spanning more than a decade.

Last week at a New York City news conference and on "Good Morning America," retired officers Sgt. Kevin Gannon and Det. Anthony Duarte discussed their theory that a group of killers target and drown white, college-age men.

In at least a dozen of the 40 deaths in 11 states they're investigating, the retired officers said that graffiti including a smiley face was found near where the victim is believed to have entered the water.

Detective Sgt. Scott Willoughby of Ridley Township police, one of the lead investigators on Booth's case, was watching "Good Morning America" as part of his daily ritual last week when he caught the segment.

"I was shocked at all the similarities I had," he said.

At the township police station, Willoughby rattled off the likenesses between Booth's case and the 40 cases in the Midwest and Northeast that the detectives have identified: Booth was a white male between 18 and 25, between 5 feet 8 and 6 feet, and between 150 and 200 pounds. He drowned after a night of drinking at a college bar and he had no visible signs of trauma. When his body was found, he had his money, ID card and wallet but not his cell phone.

And there was the smiley face — replete with a crown — painted below the back deck of Bootlegger's, where Booth is believed to have entered the creek.

Timothy Kephart, a Gloucester County native who is the founder and president of Graffiti Tracker

See **THEORY** *Page 49*

A Philadelphia Daily News *article about Thomas Booth (©Philadelphia Daily News)*

In 2008, after a decade of undercover investigation by Gannon and Duarte, the FBI took an interest in the case. Their conclusion was simple: they found no link between the deaths, and most of the drownings were in fact accidental.

In 2010, the Center for Homicide Research also conducted an in-depth study of *Smiley Face Killers* and concluded that it was nothing more than a conspiracy theory.

A documentary series, *Smiley Face Killers: The Hunt for Justice,* was drawn from these events, as well as a film entitled *Smiley Face Killers.*

SAM GRAVES
6th District, Missouri

1513 Longworth House Office Building
Washington, DC 20515
(202) 225-7041

113 Blue Jay Drive, Suite 100
Liberty, MO 64068
(816) 792-3976

201 South 8th Street, Suite 2
St. Joseph, MO 64501
(816) 233-9818

Congress of the United States
House of Representatives
Washington, DC 20515–2506

August 6, 2008

Honorable Robert S. Muller
Director
Federal Bureau of Investigation
935 Pennsylvania Avenue, NW
Washington, DC 20535

Dear Director Miller:

Recent press reports indicate that there is new evidence that may link the drowning of numerous college-aged men across the country. It is clear that the FBI must work with local law enforcement to follow-up on new leads and evidence.

I am aware that the FBI investigated this matter some time ago, but I respectfully request that the FBI reopen its investigation in light of new evidence. Several college-aged men have drowned, including as many as 12 from Wisconsin, and all of these tragic deaths may be linked.

Thank you for your attention to this matter. I look forward to hearing from you.

Sincerely,

Sam Graves
Member of Congress

A letter from U.S. Congressman Sam Graves, asking FBI Director Robert S. Mueller to look into the case

The opinion of 1st Commissioner Maillard of the Brussels Judicial Police - Division in charge of crime against property and people.

First and foremost, and this applies to all the cases in this book, it should be pointed out that I have obviously not had access to the case documents, that I have not been out in the field, and that it is not my intention to encroach on the work of my counterparts, or even to point out any shortcomings. My reflections are based solely on the elements gathered by Geoffrey for this book and which he asked me to analyze from my professional point of view, no more and no less. I have no doubt that my colleagues on the other side of the Atlantic and elsewhere have done their utmost to solve these crimes.

With that out of the way, let's move on to the famous *Smiley face murder theory*.

When there are too many coincidences, you have to start wondering, because it's quite obvious that it's not logical. William Hurley calls Claire to pick him up, but he's not at the rendezvous point, even though he's tired and wants to go home.

The high levels of GHB found in his system, as revealed by the toxicology report, are very significant. Add to this a damaged cell phone and injuries indicative of blunt force trauma.

Then, we realize that this case is not unique, but that other similar cases could resemble Mr. Hurley's case. What's more, smiley faces are drawn close to the scene.

And finally, two policemen and a professor of criminal justice come together to try and find an explanation.

Obviously I don't have the whole file in front of me, so I can only talk about how I would have done it myself.

1/ Telephony

In a case like this, it's worth doing some research into telephony, such as:

- Cross-reference the telephone numbers marked on the pylons at the scene of the incident for the various cases and extract the common numbers. Then research these numbers. Are there any known persons among the holders of these telephone numbers?

- Study the contacts of the various victims to see if there are any common contacts.

- Check with the operator, for each victim, to find out what the victim's last calls were.

2/ Stolen items

- It is not clear from Geoffrey's evidence whether any items or assets were stolen in the process.

- If any cards have gone missing, check that no withdrawals have been made. Some terminals have built-in cameras that can provide images of the people making withdrawals.

3/ The GHB trail

In my opinion, GHB is not an easy product to obtain. An investigation in this direction could shed some light on the matter.

4/ *Modus operandi*

- As the *modus operandi* is not common, it is always interesting to list all similar incidents over a large enough area to see if there is an epidemic of similar incidents.

- If this is the case, a timeline is important in order to determine the frequency with which events are committed, and the route taken by the perpetrator(s). From there, the tedious work of searching for camera images, etc., begins.

- This *modus operandi* bears a strong resemblance to a case where a trucker/router was killing victims all over America along his trucking journey. The fact that decomposition does not correspond to immersion in water could be due to freezing in a refrigerated truck. But this remains pure supposition.

5/ Neighborhood survey and cameras

- Once again, it's important to get out in the field and see the crime scene for yourself.

- It should be pointed out that you have to go to the place where the events are supposed to take place to meet the people who are there at the time.

- Recording camera images is essential.

The Eilean Mòr file

1

To the west of the Scottish Highlands emerges the archipelago of the Outer Hebrides, home to the Flannán Islands, named after a 6th-century abbot, Flannán mac Toirrdelbaig, who built a stone chapel on the largest of them, the beautiful and mysterious Eilean Mòr. Shepherds once flocked here to graze their sheep on the rich pastures covering these otherwise desolate lands. Yet none of them would have agreed to spend the night here, even in exchange for a case of whisky. And if you'd asked them the reason for such a hostile attitude, they'd probably have replied in something like the following terms: "'Are damned, these damned islands. Haunted by the spirits and beings of the little people". They would then have recited the name of each island in a litany akin to a conjuration of some absurd evil spell: "*Eilean Taighe, Soray, Sgeir Tomain, Eilean a' Gobha, Roaireim, Bròna Cleit, Eilean Mòr*".

Towards the end of the 19th century, as English maritime trade expanded, many ships ran aground on the reefs of the Flannán Islands, which sailors soon nick-named *the Seven Huntresses* for their propensity to leave no survivors. In 1895, the Northern Lighthouse Board announced that a lighthouse would be built on Eilean Mòr to reduce the number of goods and men lost.

However, the birth of the lighthouse was a painful affair, as all the equipment had to be transported up steep cliffs from ships facing the tumultuous waters of the Atlantic. To put it bluntly, the region was unfit for human habitation, as it was completely exposed to the violent gusts from the north. Yet this did not prevent the Flannán Islands lighthouse from lighting up the ocean sky for the first time on December 7, 1899.

Four men, all retired sailors, were then hired to operate it and become the antidote to the desolation reigning over Eilean Mòr.

2

Thomas Marshall is fifty-four years old, lives from odd jobs since he stopped going to sea, and has two daughters. One is studying to be a teacher at Strathclyde

University and the other is a housewife in Portree. He has three grandchildren. He describes his current relationship with his wife as "distant but cordial".

He asks, catching his first glimpse of the lighthouse standing proudly like a white arrow atop Eilean Mòr: "Do you think we'll sleep well in there?"

He has to shout to drown out the noise of the *Hesperus* supply ship's engine, which is the only way in and out of the archipelago. I reply that it should be fine, also shouting. Our living space has been built on the downward slope of the ridge. We should be fine.

"The reason I ask," he adds, "is because I can't sleep. I've tried every trick and plant there is, including poppies and opium, with the sole result of ending up in a cell for indecent exposure. I just wanted to take a piss, but the bitch opened her door just then and found herself face to face with... the beast. I don't need to draw you a picture."

I don't answer that. When I ask him about his insomnia and how long he's been suffering from it, he hardly needs to think.

"Eighteen months," he replies immediately. "Ever since my wife ran off with that damn salesman. He's the kind of well-coiffed, clean-cut guy you always want to slap. Oh, I don't blame her, I've spent my life at sea. So when I had to stop, I had a hard time, let's say, finding my feet in my new life. In short, it fried my brain. I went into what the doctors call "emotional delirium".

Behind me, I hear McArthur sigh in annoyance. Marshall's incessant flow of words seems to displease him greatly. For my part, I find it rather fascinating. Mentally, I take note of the most interesting elements with the intention of writing them down later. My ambition is to write a novel, but the subject still eludes me. So I decide to dig a little deeper and ask Marshall what kind of delirium he's talking about.

"I count things."

"What things?"

"All sorts of things. The number of street lamps between my house and the West Highlands Bar... and when they're on, I count them twice, because I find it safer to check. Necessary, actually. My steps. The number of steps on the stairs. To board the *Hesperus*, I had to go up and down exactly sixty-one. I can also tell you that we passed twenty-six men in hats and fifteen ladies. I tried to count the gloves once, but ran out of luck. It was a bit ridiculous. I came across a penguin. Not the kind of penguin on an ice floe, no, a guy whose arm stopped at the elbow. So he was only wearing a glove, you see. It ruined the rest of my day, and the next night I couldn't sleep, because odd numbers are bad luck. Do you know that..."

A wave higher than the others prevents him from finishing his sentence. He coughs up the salt water that has rushed into his wide-open mouth.

"Ugh, filthy water!"

"You'd better get used to it," McArthur warns him. "From now on, you're going to eat fleet until you're blue in the face."

"Pfff. Can't wait to roll over in a month!"

"Isn't it six weeks until Ducat comes to replace you? I objected."

"Ah, shit! You're right. Six weeks... it's gonna be a long fucking time!"

His eyes then glide from the top of the lighthouse to its base, where the living quarters have been built, then up the path to a stone footbridge overlooking the choppy water below.

"Well, this is going to be gay. Hope you guys like poker."

I tell him I'm an avid reader. I also write, when inspiration strikes, just as I scribble charcoal drawings. I hope this breathtaking view will stimulate my muse over the coming months. I'm not much for games.

"As for me, I like solitude," says McArthur. "Once I'm here, you'll only see me at mealtimes. The rest of the time, I like to be left alone."

Marshall doesn't insist: McArthur is known throughout Scotland as a seasoned sailor and a solid brawler whom it's not really advisable to antagonize.

"Yep, it's gonna be gay," Marshall sighs.

I turn my attention back to the island that will become my new home. *Home sweet home.* My wife passed away two years ago. I don't have any children and, since my knee gave out on me, I haven't had any work either, which is why I didn't hold back when the Northern Lighthouse Board offered me the job of lighthouse keeper. I'd have been mad not to. My knee may be gone, but I've still got all my wits about me, and I certainly don't want people to be able to say of me that "old Joseph Moore is going senile". They already think I'm a scholar because I'm interested in a lot of things they've never heard of and don't even know exist. For example, in Gaelic, Eilean Mòr means "Big Island". Yet it's only about eight acres in size (or three hectares), with a single road linking the east and west quays to the lighthouse, a path leading to the ruined chapel and another to the concrete promontory, itself dominated by a crane left there in case of need when the place was built.

"I estimate its length at 300 metres," says Marshall as we approach the island from the southeast, zigzagging between the reefs. "Its width is 100 meters at most. I count six menhirs on the western tip and seventeen rocks outcropping around the jetty. I also see…"

"Okay, we get it," interrupts McArthur. "And if you don't shut up, I'm gonna throw you overboard."

The captain of the *Hesperus*, a brave fellow by the name of James Harvie, announces that we're about to dock. He slows down as we approach the eastern pontoon, allowing me to get a better look at the chapel, whose roof has long since disappeared, and the amazing circle of menhirs that Marshall spotted. I find the coincidence amusing. Two months earlier, I'd been reading up on these standing stones, scattered all over Scotland, in the hope of finding a sufficiently solid subject for my book. I learned that they were installed by early settlers over 10,000 years ago. But what is their significance and why do they exist? This truth remains shrouded in mystery, even if ancient folklore has its share of explanations. For example, the iconic menhirs of Calanais, located on the Isle of Lewis, just a stone's throw from Eilean Mòr, are known as *Na Fir Bhrèige*, "the false men". Legend has it that they embody the petrified souls of a bygone age, giants turned to stone after refusing to convert to Christianity. Some sailors also whisper by the fire in the evening, when the children are in bed, that a ghostly figure haunts these stones at sunset on the day of the summer solstice.

Elsewhere, on the Isle of Arran, it is said that fairies once sat on the mountain and threw pebbles onto the moor below. As they hit the ground, the pebbles turned into huge stones and formed the six circles of Machrie Moor. These menhirs are known to produce inexplicably strong emotions. Pagans venerate them as sacred sites, while at the Brodgar circle in Orkney, people wait patiently for visitors from outer space to arrive.

The roar of the engine fades, as do the vibrations that shake the hull of the *Hesperus*. Captain James Harvie docks his ship safely at Eilean Mòr's wooden pontoon, then unloads the food crates and wishes us a pleasant stay.

"Gentlemen, I'll see you in a fortnight," he announces before setting sail again. "Until then, take care."

In fact, the *Hesperus* is scheduled to bring us mail and supplies twice a month, and to rotate with the fourth man at the same time. However, the first rotation is not scheduled for another six weeks, when James Ducat will relieve Thomas Marshall.

Six weeks is more than enough time to get to know each other and discover the secrets of this three-hectare island.

3

Eilean Mòr can be circumnavigated in less than half an hour if you're in a hurry—Marshall's current record is twenty-seven minutes. Naturally, there are few distractions on this rock lost in the middle of the sea and, as he had announced on the boat, McArthur spends most of his time on his side, resting or drinking. Underneath his bear-like exterior, however, lies a great shyness, which explains his celibacy and almost exclusive affection for cats. This is what I discovered when I chatted with him during meals.

We don't get together until suppertime, just before dusk, when our night's work is about to begin and the 140,000 candles in the lighthouse lamp need to be inspected, changed and lit.

As planned, James Harvie brings us a few letters and three crates of food every fortnight. So we have to prepare for his arrival, stacking the empty packages on the east quay, unwinding the mooring cables, etc., a tedious job, but hardly less so than on a ship. I joined the merchant navy to earn a living, but my real passion, as I've already pointed out, is writing. After the death of my wife (and despite my recalcitrant knee, which was almost as painful as my widowhood), I spent most Sundays wandering around the Northern Highlands, blackening whole pages in my notebook. Unfortunately, inspiration always eluded me.

For the record, I live—or at least used to live—in Fort Augustus, having grown up in Aberdeen.

Curiously, this area in central Scotland is where I did my best sketches: Dundreggan, Whitebridge, the River Findhorn... These were the most... inspired sketches. I even tried to start three novels there, but met with just as many failures. Do you want me to tell you, as a simple amateur? I think writing is a much more difficult art than most people realize. It's logical to think that, provided you have good spelling and a keen sense of grammar, which you can learn in any school class, you're capable of writing a book. A blank sheet of paper, a pencil, and all that's left to do is to let the words sink in, to *piss off the page* as some rather vulgar writers say. Except that's not how it works. Technique is important in writing, just as it is in painting, photography or cooking, but… The soul, the emotion, that's what's most important in a work of art. And that's precisely what I lacked when I arrived on Eilean Mòr. I could write, and quite well at that, without false modesty, but my texts didn't reflect any deep-seated desire, any visceral need to be expressed, which made them beautiful shells, yes, but empty shells of meaning.

I digress. After three months on this island, I still haven't written a single line. Yet I seem to have detected a subject that tickles my imagination.

Yesterday, during my evening stroll, I passed the chapel to find myself, without paying much attention, standing in front of the circle of menhirs dominating the western tip of Eilean Mòr. We had just finished inspecting the candles, and the lighthouse was illuminating the Flannán at full speed. Dusk was falling. The sun was a red ball of gas, slightly flattened at the top, with its base flirting with the ocean horizon. There were hardly any waves, yet their rumble reached me in the evening silence. Not a seagull was laughing. Around the menhirs, the grass had burnt for a dozen meters.

I seem to have wavered. Not because of the beauty of the spectacle, although it was obviously magnificent—imagine a sunset seen from the crest of an island lost in the Atlantic—but because everything in front of me seemed blurred, without contours, as if I were in a state bordering on hallucination and had abused the opiates dear to good Thomas Marshall. The six menhirs towered above me, the largest measuring around two and a half metres, the smallest just under one and a half metres, the others in between. I remember approaching the first one, but it's like remembering a dream when it's already begun to dissipate with the morning mist. Except that it wasn't a dream. I could feel the ocean breeze caressing my skin, the humidity sticking my hair to my forehead, beading on the metal buttons of my jacket.

I stopped near the nearest, highest rock. At first I thought they were carved human faces, tortured faces, laughing faces, anguished faces, but then I realized they were horse heads covered in seaweed. For a minute, time seemed to stand still, the seagulls to freeze in mid-air. Then the luminosity shifted as the sun suddenly resumed its slow decline behind the horizon, and I realized that what I had taken to be sculptures were in fact a succession of natural hollows and bumps, which the lighting had shaded so as to give them a vaguely recognizable shape. I had just become an insidious victim of my imagination, and realized that it was an effect of isolation combined with the enormity of the ocean stretching out before me. So I launched into a long burst of laughter, supposed to dispel the fear that had fleetingly inhabited me.

It's not what I think today, but today it's too late.

I returned to the lighthouse and recounted my misadventure to my companions, who were quick to laugh at me. I confess I accepted their mockery with good grace, having found myself ridiculous. Today, however, we're laughing less. Marshall has just returned, claiming that there are now nine menhirs on the western point, and if there's one thing he can be trusted to do, it's count. We leave the lighthouse. In the distance, I can see the point of six stones. I ask him if he's taken too many sleeping pills this morning.

"Very funny, Moore. Check this out."

He hands me his spyglass. I grab it and ask what I'm supposed to be looking at.

"Menhirs, you hansom cab driver."

"It's okay, you don't have to insult me."

I look through the telescope and... nine menhirs. I must be dreaming. I rub my eyes, make sure I can see six spikes in the distance, then put the spyglass back on my eye. Nine. Nine *bloody* menhirs, arranged in a rough circle a few metres from the ruined chapel. They seem to be undulating slightly, indulging in a joyful dance. My head starts to spin; I think back to the horse heads and fear grips me. Of course, I'm familiar with the myth of the *Kelpies*, the water monsters that prowl the remote lochs and rivers of Scotland, luring unsuspecting victims to the water's edge with the aim of drowning them without mercy. I don't see any truth in it, but all I want to do is get the hell out of Eilean Mòr as soon as possible. Otherwise, the relief won't arrive for another three days. What's more, I have the feeling that if I leave, something terrible will happen.

4

I left, came back, left and came back again, but no cataclysm swept the island. My comrades haven't fallen ill, none of them have gone mad. At best, Ducat is beginning to find time slowing down. The menhirs are always there, sometimes six, sometimes nine. We're used to it. Over the years, we've attributed this curious phenomenon to a defect in the telescope, or to an optical phenomenon caused by the deviation of light beams due to the superposition of layers of air at different temperatures. In short, we think it's a mirage. Well, I say "we", I should rather say "them", my fellow sufferers. For my part, I believe that there's something *in the middle of* the standing stones, in the middle of the circle they form, whether by chance or by will, and that *it's* watching me through the veil of reality, never taking its eyes off me. For this... *thing* has eyes. Don't ask me why or how I know, but I'm convinced. Eyes as black as the Atlantic when a storm approaches. I know it's just a lighting effect, like when I thought I could make out tortured human faces on the surface of menhirs, but I also know there's more to it than that. I've always had a rational mind, even back in the days of the merchant navy when other sailors claimed to see monsters in the midst of the storms we traversed; my mind has never failed me. Why should it be any different today? Solitude doesn't explain everything.

I'm sure the others are feeling it too. Ducat is wasting away by the day, McArthur is drowning in the bottle and Marshall is counting more and more things, down to the most insignificant. I wouldn't mind knowing that two hundred and thirty-three ants swarm at the top of the anthill near the pier, and that he takes between 8,622 and 9,248 steps every day—never an odd number, it's bad luck. For a year now, thanks to us, the lighthouse's reassuring light has been guiding ships through the icy, tumultuous waters. In fact, we've grown so close that we've become, if not friends, good business colleagues. Even McArthur began to find our company "not so unpleasant", to the point of bringing us back a bottle of Craigellachie[4] after one of his vacations. It lasted three days.

It's fair to say that the atmosphere on Eilean Mòr is pretty decent, even if the inevitable frictions, inherent as much in the isolation as in the constant promiscuity of three men, do break out from time to time. One of them has just come to an end. It's December 6, 1900, and my turn to be repatriated to the continent.

"Happy to be going ashore?" asks Captain Harvie as he maneuvers the *Hesperus* between the Flannán reefs.

I tell him yes, before adding that you might not say so, but it's a bit lonely sometimes.

"Lonely? How so?"

---

4. Scotch whisky.

"It's hard to explain. It's more an impression than an established fact... We often have the impression of being alone in the world on this rock, you know? As if a catastrophe had engulfed the rest of the planet and we were the last survivors of civilization."

"I know what you mean. I sometimes feel the same way at sea."

"I doubt it, James," I murmured, looking up at the circle of menhirs disappearing in the distance. "I doubt it very much."

5

Captain Holman can't understand why he feels so uncomfortable. It's December 15, 1900, and his ship, the SS *Archtor*, is en route from Philadelphia to the port of Leith; a routine voyage for Holman and his crew. It's almost midnight and the Flannaán Islands are only six miles to the south. However, where there should be light, there is only darkness. And the furious screeching of birds. Once again, Captain Holman feels that sense of unease and terror. He knows something is wrong. Standing on deck, he scans the horizon for the lighthouse.

At the same time, Roderick MacKenzie is standing at Gallan Head, on the Isle of Lewis, watching the ocean for Eilean Mòr's light. He himself is a gamekeeper on Lewis, but the Northern Lighthouse Board also pays him £8 a year to watch the lighthouse signals through his telescope. Yet he hasn't seen the light since December 7, now eight nights in a row. At first, he attributed this to bad weather, sea mist, fatigue, but tonight he has the feeling that something bad is happening in the distance, something terribly bad.

It's no different on the beach at Loch Roag, where I stroll tirelessly until I'm ready to head back to the island, staring at the Flannán, trying in vain to fight the anguish that's gnawing at my insides. It's inconceivable to me that neither Ducat, Marshall nor McArthur thought of switching on the lighthouse light. Something terrible has happened to them, I'm convinced, and my thoughts wander to the most improbable suppositions, all linked to the menhirs. I wish I could find out for sure, but I'm not due to leave for Eilean Mòr for another five days, and James Harvie is currently in another sector. Five days of torturing my mind.

I finally board the *Hesperus* on December 21st. The captain greets me with a mixture of pleasure and apprehension. We both know that something is wrong. The weather, which has been very calm recently, changes abruptly and a storm breaks shortly after we leave port. Given the situation, Harvie decides to stay at sea to lose as little time as possible. He seems convinced that time is running out. For three days, the *Hesperus* cruises off the Hebrides, and it's only on December 24 that the sea gods finally deign to allow us to approach Flannàn. I'm alarmed to see that the 140,000 candles in the lighthouse are out. Harvie raises a flag to signal our arrival. No response from the lighthouse. The foghorn sounds several times, then the captain sets off a flare. Still no response. All is deathly quiet on the island. However, the strong winds continue to prevent us from docking. Impatience overcomes me, making me delirious. I talk of menhirs, of creatures lurking in the shadows of the circle, so much so that James Harvie has to threaten to take me ashore to calm me down.

We still have to wait two days for the *Hesperus* to approach the pontoon in complete safety. Nothing has been prepared for our arrival. On the jetty, we see neither packing crates nor mooring cables. The repeated blasts of the fog siren do not draw anyone out of the lighthouse. I inform the captain of my intention to disembark, but he doesn't stop me; it's like trying to prevent a hungry wild beast from pouncing on a quarter of meat.

I immediately noticed an absurd detail: the menhirs had disappeared. In their place, all that remains is the circle of burnt grass.

I start up the steps to the lighthouse—I know there are forty-three of them, a bad number. As I look up, I see three black birds at the top of the tower, and as we stare at each other, they rise noiselessly, fly out to sea and disappear. A shiver of anguish shakes my spine.

The lighthouse door is hermetically sealed, but not locked. I push it open cautiously. The silence assaults me. I enter and call out. No answer. All is cold and empty. On a shelf, the clock is stopped. In the kitchen, plates, cups and cutlery have been washed and put away. The fire is out, the ashes in the fireplace cold to the touch.

I hesitate to go upstairs and check the rooms. I've seen dead bodies before, more than I'd like to, but none that could have been me. Because, I'm convinced, if something has happened to my comrades in my absence, it can only be a coincidence. Had I been present, I too would have died. I can't bring myself to go up alone, so I return to the pier and ask Captain Harvie for help. He agrees to come up with me.

Fearing what we'll find behind the closed doors, we hesitate for a moment before entering. Through the window, I can see the circle of burnt grass where the menhirs once stood, and almost feel invisible eyes watching our every move. I dismiss this idea with a wave of my hand and take a long breath before entering the first room, that of James Ducat. There's no sign of life here, any more than in the others. The lighthouse is absolutely empty, but everything is tidy and in order. The lamp wicks have been cleaned and trimmed, and the tanks are filled with oil and ready for use. The last entry in the register was made on December 15.

I notice only one unusual thing: two of the three oilskins, and as many pairs of boots, are missing. For a moment, a sudden impulse makes me want to leave Eilean Mòr, to get away from its deafening silence, and never return. Captain Harvie brings me back to my senses with a proposal to search the island, which I reckon shouldn't take more than an hour. We discover no trace of the missing persons, but notice a few clues that lead us at first to believe that the mystery has been solved. The west dock was badly damaged by a hurricane. The mooring ropes are gone, and the iron railing along the sidewalk is deformed. The lifebuoy is also gone.

On the concrete promontory, we notice that ropes are hanging down from the crane. I'm astonished, because these ropes are usually stored much higher up, in a trunk installed in a recess thirty meters above sea level, i.e. far upstream. Could it be that a storm with waves over thirty meters high has battered the island and swept away the chest, causing the ropes to fall onto the crane? Did it also sweep away my comrades and the menhirs? It's an easy explanation, but I find it implausible, not only because such giant waves are extremely rare, but also because the experienced lighthouse keepers Ducat, Marshall and McArthur wouldn't have been foolish enough to venture onto a jetty in the middle of a storm, and even if they had, all three oilskins, not just two, would have been missing. At worst, two would have died, but the third would have lived to tell the tale. The regulations were very clear on this point, stipulating that in the event of wild weather, a keeper should always remain on duty *inside the lighthouse.*

Very worried, we return to the tower to examine the register. It's our last hope of finding out what's happened. It's Marshall's custom to keep it in my absence. His style is cold and dry—he's not a writer at all—yet from his brief sentences emerge glimpses of the nameless terror that has overtaken the three men isolated on this rock.

Here's what we read:

December 12th. Gale from north-quarter-northwest. Stormy sea. Isolated by the storm. 9pm. Never seen such a hurricane. Very high waves, breaking on the lighthouse. Everything in order. Ducat irritable.

Harvie and I exchange a puzzled look. Indeed, on December 12, no storm was reported on the Isle of Lewis, 60 miles away. The remark about Ducat seems plausible to me, given his scowl over the last few months.

The sequel was written at midnight on the same day.

The storm is still raging. The wind doesn't let up. Isolated, we can't get out. We hear suspicious rumblings from the menhirs. A ship passes, sounding its foghorn. I can see the cabin lights. Ducat is quiet. McArthur cries. Shadows in the rain.

Once again, we looked at each other in amazement. Had some strange storm, unheard of elsewhere, swept across the island? But above all, what nervous extremity had seasoned sailor Donald McArthur reached to weep? We resume our reading.

December 13. The hurricane continued throughout the night. The wind is blowing west-quarter-northwest. We hear repeated thuds. 3 series of 2, every 111 seconds. I counted. Ducat quiet. McArthur prays. Yesterday McArthur was crying, today he's praying!!!! A hole has appeared in the middle of the circle of menhirs. It looks like the blows are coming from there.

Midday. The day is gray. Me, Ducat and McArthur prayed.

I declare, amazed, that I have never seen any of my comrades pray. It couldn't have been their fear of hurricanes, as they'd all faced gargantuan storms in their years of sailing. Harvie asks me about the hole in the menhirs. I reply that I don't know anything about it, as a quick glance out the window shows us that the ground here is intact.

Nothing was entered on the December 14 page. Why not? Would Ducat and McArthur have gone to the west quay and been taken away by a blade? It seems more likely to me that they went out in calm weather, once the hurricane had passed, to inspect everything.

All that remains on the register are a few sentences, dated December 15.

1pm. Storm over. Calm sea. We are in God's hand. Hole is calling us. He who lives beyond the menhirs asks for an audience.

My fingers scroll through the following pages almost in spite of myself. Feverishly, I search for other words that would invalidate the horrible hypothesis forming in my mind, but this hope vanishes in vain.

Out of the corner of my eye, I catch a glimpse of the golden reflection of the spyglass, which has rolled under a piece of furniture. I bend down to pick it up, then, as I hold it in the palm of my hand, a doubt comes over me. Could it be that...? I raise the binocular and look in the direction of the circle of burnt grass. There they are, all new and proudly standing on the western ridge. They seem to be laughing at me. I *know* they're laughing at me. And behind the veil of reality, *it* smiles, as I seem to make out the faces of the missing on the surface of the three additional menhirs.

6

Investigation revealed that, on the night of December 15, the steamer *Archtor* had sought to dry out on Eilean Mòr, but had been forced to abandon the attempt because the lighthouse was out, and as Roderick MacKenzie, based at Gallan Head, reports, had been out since December 7. It's safe to assume that by then my companions had already disappeared.

Some talk of murder, uncontrollable temper, perhaps fueled by drink, or isolation, or madness. So, according to a widely accepted supposition among the general public, one of the three went mad, murdered his two comrades and committed suicide. I can't believe it. All the hammers, knives and axes remained where they belonged. Of course, the assailant might have used a stone as a weapon. He would have thrown the bodies of his companions into the sea, and then himself into the water. Honesty leads me not to reject this hypothesis out of hand, but it seems highly improbable for a number of reasons, both personal and empirical.

Others wonder about the ancient legends about the island, the menhirs, the ruined chapel and the burials that have been there since the time of the Druids. Was Marshall seized by religious madness? Did he have visions? Did the furious hurricane mentioned in the register exist only in his mind? After all, the damage to the western quay may have been caused by the storm that delayed the *Hesperus*.

Some disappearances are so astounding that we have no choice but to put forward supernatural explanations. According to a number of specialists, whose names should be withheld here to avoid damaging their reputations, there are "empty spaces" in the visible world, a kind of "wormhole" through which animate—or inanimate—objects can enter a world adjacent to our own, where they are no longer seen or heard. In such cavities, there is absolutely nothing. It is a void so absolute that it cannot be artificially reproduced. In such cavities, light does not propagate; no sound can be heard; nothing can be felt. None of the conditions required to activate our senses are possible. A man trapped in such a universe can neither see nor be seen; neither live nor die, because life and death are processes that can only occur where there is force. But in these empty spaces, no force exists."

I hope with all my heart that my comrades don't wander into such a place. And, above all, that they don't find themselves in the company of *the one who lives beyond the menhirs.*

The facts

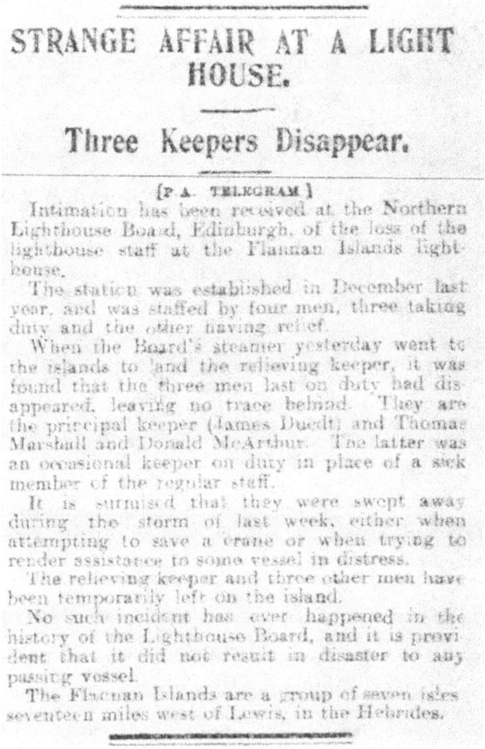

STRANGE AFFAIR AT A LIGHT HOUSE.

Three Keepers Disappear.

[P. A. TELEGRAM.]

Intimation has been received at the Northern Lighthouse Board, Edinburgh, of the loss of the lighthouse staff at the Flannan Islands lighthouse.

The station was established in December last year, and was staffed by four men, three taking duty and the other having relief.

When the Board's steamer yesterday went to the islands to land the relieving keeper, it was found that the three men last on duty had disappeared, leaving no trace behind. They are the principal keeper (James Ducdt) and Thomas Marshall and Donald McArthur. The latter was an occasional keeper on duty in place of a sick member of the regular staff.

It is surmised that they were swept away during the storm of last week, either when attempting to save a crane or when trying to render assistance to some vessel in distress.

The relieving keeper and three other men have been temporarily left on the island.

No such incident has ever happened in the history of the Lighthouse Board, and it is provident that it did not result in disaster to any passing vessel.

The Flannan Islands are a group of seven isles seventeen miles west of Lewis, in the Hebrides.

An article from the Northants Evening Telegraph, December 27, 1900 (©The British Library Board)

Located off the Western Isles of Scotland, the Eilean Mòr lighthouse was commissioned on December 7, 1899, to provide guidance to sailors navigating off the Scottish coast. Four men were assigned to operate it full-time. But in December 1900, its light suddenly went out. A small ship passing by noticed the malfunction and immediately reported it to the maritime authorities.

A few days later, Joseph Moore, the keeper on leave, returns to the island, but finds no trace of his colleagues supposedly living in the lighthouse. The gate is closed, the ashes in the chimney are cold and there's nothing to suggest a recent human presence. Two of the three oilskins are missing. The logbook kept by Thomas Marshall indicates that the three men faced a major storm, yet no storms have been reported in the area.

From left to right: Thomas Marshall, James Ducat, Donald McArthur and Superintendent Robert Muirhead. This is the last known photo of the missing men.

Telegram from the captain of the Hesperus sent on December 26, 1900

A terrible accident has occurred in the Flannán. The three keepers, Ducat, Marshall and the occasional man, have disappeared from the island. When we arrived this afternoon, there was no sign of life on the island. We fired a rocket, but when there was no response, we docked Moore, who went up to the station, but found no guards there. The clocks were stopped and other signs indicated that the accident must have happened about a week ago. Poor guys, they must have been blown over the cliffs or drowned trying to tie down a crane or something.

As night fell, we couldn't wait to find out what had happened to them. I left Moore, MacDonald, the buoy captain, and two sailors on the island to keep the [lighthouse] *light on until you made other arrangements. I will not return to Oban until I hear from you. I have repeated this message to Muirhead in case you are not at home. I shall remain at the telegraph office tonight until it closes, if you wish to telegraph me.*

Captain, HESPERUS

Letter from Joseph Moore, assistant keeper, who was to take over at the lighthouse.

Mr,

It is with deep regret that I wish to inform you of the very sad affair that has unfolded here over the past fortnight, namely the disappearance of my two lighthouse keeper colleagues, Mr Ducat and Mr Marshall, as well as the occasional keeper, Donald McArthur.

As you know, the changeover took place on the 26th. On that day, as on other relief days, we arrived to drop anchor in the Flannán Islands, but not seeing the lighthouse flag flying, we thought they hadn't seen us arrive. The boat's foghorn was blown several times, always without response. Finally, Captain Harvie thought it prudent to launch a boat and send a man ashore, if possible.

I was the first to disembark, leaving Mr. McCormack and his men on the boat until I returned from the lighthouse. I went upstairs, and when I reached the front door, I found it locked. I then went to the front door leading to the kitchen and storeroom, found it also closed, but the kitchen door itself was open. Entering the kitchen, I looked at the fireplace and saw that the fire hadn't been lit for a few days. I then entered room after room, finding the beds empty as they had left them in the early morning.

I didn't take the time to look any further, as I knew only too well that something serious had happened. I rushed to the landing. When I got there, I informed Mr. McCormack that the place was deserted. He came himself, accompanied by a few men, to make sure, but unfortunately, the first impression was all too true. Mr. McCormack and I went to the lighthouse room, where everything was in order. The lamp was cleaned. The fountain filled. The blinds on the windows, etc. We left and re-boarded the steamer. On arrival, Captain Harvie ordered me to return to the island in company with Mr. McDonald (the buoy captain), A. Campbell and A. Lamont, who were to accompany me until timely help arrived.

We went ashore and made our way to the lighthouse room, where we lit the fire in good time that night and every night since. The following day, we scoured the island from end to end, but still saw nothing that could tell us what had happened. Nothing seems to have been damaged at the landing stage to indicate that they were taken from there. The ropes are all in their respective places in the shelter, exactly as they were left after the changeover on the 7th.

On the west side, it's a bit different. We had an old box halfway down the track to hold the mooring ropes, as well as the equipment, and it's gone. It seems that some of the ropes have been washed away and are scattered on the rocks near the crane. The crane itself is intact.

The metal railings along the passageway, connecting the railway to the pathway leading to the landing, were torn from their foundations and broken in several places, as were the railing around the crane and the railing used to secure the mooring rope for the boat, which were completely washed away. Now, there's no indication that this is where the poor men lost their lives, only that Mr. Marshall had his seaman's boots and oilskin on, and Mr. Ducat had his seaman's boots on too. He had no oilskin, only an old waterproof coat, and he disappeared. Donald McArthur left his coat behind, which shows, as far as I know, that he went out in his shirt. He never used any other coat on previous occasions, only the one I'm referring to.

Mr. J. Moore,
Assistant lighthouse keeper,
Flannán Islands lighthouse
December 28, 1900

The investigation begins shortly afterwards and continues for days, without success. The guards are gone, never to return.

Report submitted by Robert Muirhead, Superintendent, January 8, 1901

On receipt of Captain Harvie's telegram of December 26, 1900, reporting that the three keepers of the Flannán Islands, namely James Ducat, senior keeper, Thomas Marshall, second assistant, and Donald McArthur, occasional keeper (replacing William Ross, first assistant, on sick leave), had disappeared and must have been blown over the cliffs or drowned, I made the following arrangements with the secretary for the temporary operation of the station.

James Ferrier, senior keeper, was transferred from Stornoway lighthouse to Tiumpan Head lighthouse, and John Milne, senior keeper at Tiumpan Head, was sent to take temporary charge of the Flannán Islands. Donald Jack, the second assistant, was also sent to the Flannán Islands, the intention being that these two men, together with Joseph Moore, the third assistant on the Flannán Islands, who was ashore when the accident occurred, would provide service until permanent arrangements could be made. I also went to the Flannán Islands where I was landed, along with Milne and Jack, early on the 29th.

Having satisfied myself that everything connected with the lighthouse was in good order and that the men ashore would be able to maintain the lamp, I set out to determine, if possible, the cause of the disaster and also took statements from Captain Harvie, Mr McCormack, the second mate of the HESPERUS, *Joseph Moore, third assistant keeper of the Flannan Islands and Allan MacDonald, buoy master.*

The HESPERUS *arrived at the Flannan Islands with the intention of carrying out the regular relief around noon on Wednesday December 26 and, as no signal was shown and none of the usual preparations for landing had been made, Captain Harvie sounded the steam whistle and siren to attract the attention of the keepers. When this had no effect, he fired a rocket, which also elicited no response, and a boat was launched, then sent ashore to the east landing with Joseph Moore, assistant keeper, on board.*

When the boat reached the landing, as there was still no sign of the guards, the boat reached the landing and, with some difficulty, Moore managed to jump ashore. When he went up to the station, he found the front and outer doors closed, the clock stopped, no lights on and, looking into the rooms, he found the beds empty. He then became alarmed and ran back to the ship to inform Mr. McCormack, and one of the sailors managed to jump ashore and, with Moore, carried out a thorough search of the station, but found nothing. They then returned to the ship and informed Captain Harvie, who told Moore he would have to return to the island to maintain the lighthouse pending instructions, and asked for volunteers from his crew to help.

He replied in the affirmative, and two sailors, Lamont and Campbell, were chosen along with Mr. MacDonald, the buoy master, who was on board, who also offered his services, which were accepted, and Moore, MacDonald and these two sailors were left in charge of the lighthouse while Captain Harvie returned to Breasclete and telegraphed an account of the disaster to the secretary.

The men remaining on the island carried out a thorough search of the station and discovered that the last inscription on the slate had been made by Mr Ducat, the main keeper, on the morning of Saturday December 15th. The lamp was adjusted, the oil fountains filled, the lens and cogs cleaned, proving that the work of the 15th had been done. The pots and pans had been cleaned and the galley tidied up, showing that the man who acted as cook had finished his work, proving that the men disappeared on the afternoon when it was learned (after the news of the disaster had been published) that Captain Holman had passed the Flannán Islands on board the steamer ARCHTOR at midnight on the 15th, but had not been able to observe the light although he is convinced that he should have seen it.

On Thursday and Friday, the men did a thorough search around the island, and I walked the grounds with them on Saturday. Everything was in order at the east landing, and the ropes that had been coiled and stored there at the end of the relief on December 7 were all in place, the lighthouse buildings and everything at the stations were in order. Because of the height of the sea, I couldn't get down to the berthing place, but I did get down to the crane platform 70 feet above sea level. The crane originally erected on this platform had been washed away last winter, and the crane installed this summer was found to be unharmed, the boom lowered and secured to the rock, and the canvas, covering the wire rope of the barrel, securely lashed around it, and there was no evidence that the men had done anything to the crane. The mooring ropes, derrick ropes and crane handles, together with a wooden box in which they were kept, were fixed in a crevice in the rocks 70 feet from the rail terminus and some 40 feet higher than the crane platform, a total of 110 feet above sea level, had been washed away, and the ropes were scattered in the rock crevices near the crane platform and entangled between the crane legs, but they were all wound up, no spools having been found loose. The iron railings around the crane platform and between the rail terminus and the concrete steps of the west landing were displaced and twisted. A large block of stone, weighing over 20 quintals, had been dislodged from its position higher up and transported downstream, and left on the concrete path leading from the rail terminus to the top of the steps.

A lifebuoy attached to the railings along this path, for use in an emergency, had disappeared, and at first I thought it had been removed for use, but on examining the ropes by which it was attached, I found that they had not been touched, and as pieces of canvas adhered to the ropes, it was obvious that the force of the sea pouring through the railings had, even at this great height (110 feet above sea level) torn the lifebuoy from the ropes.

When the accident occurred, Ducat was wearing sea boots and a raincoat, and Marshall was wearing sea boots and an oilskin, and as Moore assures me that the men only wore these items to get off at the landings, they must have intended, when they left the station, to get off at or near the landing.

After a careful examination of the location, railings, ropes, etc., and after weighing all the evidence I was able to obtain, I am of the opinion that the most likely expla- nation for the men's disappearance is that they all went down in the afternoon of Saturday, December 15, in the vicinity of the western landing stage, to secure the box with the mooring ropes, etc., and that a roll of unexpected magnitude rose on the island, then a great mass of water rising higher than where they were washed over them, and washed over them, and that a roll of unexpected magnitude rose on the island, then a great mass of water rising higher than where they were fell on them, carrying them away with unresisting force.

I have considered and discussed the possibility that the men were swept away by the wind, but, as the wind was from the west, I am of the opinion, in spite of its great strength, that the most probable explanation is that they were swept away by the waters, for, if the wind had caught them, it would, by its direction, have blown towards the top of the island and I am certain that they would have managed to throw themselves ashore before reaching the top or front of the island.

At the end of my investigation, on Saturday afternoon, I returned to Breasclete, reported my findings to the secretary and visited the widows of James Ducat, the senior janitor, and Donald McArthur, the occasional janitor.

I should mention that, as Moore was naturally very upset by this unfortunate event and seemed very nervous, I left A. Lamont, deckhand, on the island to go to the lighting room and keep Moore company when he's on watch for a week or two.

If this nervousness doesn't leave Moore, we'll have to transfer him, but I hesitate to recommend it, as I'd like to have at least one man who knows the station's work.

The commissioners appointed Roderick MacKenzie, gamekeeper at Uig, near Meavaig, to keep a daily watch for any signals that might be emitted from the rock, and to note each night whether or not the lighthouse had been seen. As it was obvious that the lighthouse had not been lit from December 15 to 25, I decided to meet him on Sunday morning to find out what he had to say on the subject. He was away from home, but I found his two sons, aged about 16 and 18—two very intelligent boys of the gamekeeper class, and who actually performed the task of watching the signals— and had a conversation with them about it, and also examined their register. From the December entry, I found that the lighthouse itself had not been visible, even with the aid of a powerful telescope, between December 7 and 29. The light was seen on

---

December 7, but not on December 8, 9, 10 or 11. It was seen on the 12th, but not again until the 26th, the night Moore turned it on. MacKenzie said (which I've since verified) that lights sometimes can't be seen for four or five consecutive nights, but he was concerned about not seeing it for such a long period and, for two nights before its reappearance, asked the natives for help to see if it could be spotted.

If the watch had been kept by an ordinary lighthouse keeper, as at Earraid for Dubh Artach, I believe the man ashore would have realized sooner that something was wrong and, although it would not have prevented the lamentable event from occurring, it would have enabled steps to be taken to have the lighthouse relit sooner. I would recommend that the signalman be advised that in future, if he fails to observe the light when in his opinion, given the state of the atmosphere, he should see it, he should be instructed to inform the Secretary, so that action can be considered.

In conclusion, I would like to express my deep regret at seeing such a disaster befall the guardians of this service. I knew Ducat and Marshall intimately, and the occasional McArthur, well. They were chosen, on my recommendation, for the lighting of so important a station as the Flannán Islands, and as I always endeavour to obtain the best possible men for the establishment of a station, as the success and satisfaction of a station depends largely on the keepers present at its installation, this in itself indicates that the Board has lost two of its most efficient keepers and an able occasional keeper.

I cohabited with the keepers for over a month in the summer of 1899, when they all worked hard to keep the station lit before winter, and, working with them, I appreciated the way they went about their work. I visited the Flannán Islands during the handover on December 7, and I have the melancholy memory of being the last person to shake their hands and say goodbye.

Robert Muirhead
Superintendent
January 8, 1901

Some time later, the lighthouse was put back into service, with new keepers taking over until 1971, when it was automated.

The unsolved mystery of the three men's disappearance has captured the public imagination and inspired numerous artists and writers, as well as a film starring Gerard Butler, *Keepers*, released in 2018.

The opinion of 1st Commissioner Maillard of the Brussels Judicial Police - Division in charge of crime against property and people.

Of course, it's very difficult to speculate on a case that's over 100 years old, without the complete file and a visit to the site. Let's take a look at the evidence we have.

December 1900: the Eilean Mor lighthouse is extinguished and three lighthouse keepers disappear from the island.

A major storm would be the most plausible reason, as several indicators point in this direction:

- no trace of fighting in the lighthouse dwellings;
- the ashes in the chimney are cold;
- the lighthouse entrance door is closed;
- the door to the kitchen and storeroom is also closed;
- the beds are empty and just as they left them in the early morning.
- the landing stage is left intact on the east side.

On the west side, on the other hand, some damage can be seen, such as:

- an old box used to hold the mooring ropes has disappeared, along with the equipment. Some of the ropes were found scattered on the rocks near the crane, which remained intact;
- on the landing side, a great deal of damage can be seen. Several metal railings have been washed away or broken in several places;
- Two of the guards had their sailor boots on, and were wearing coats or oilskins. Only one of the men was without his coat (perhaps because he had rushed out to help his comrades).

Just because no thunderstorms were reported in the area doesn't mean there couldn't have been another meteorological phenomenon leading to such damage and the deaths of these three men.

Too much damage remains inexplicable apart from the consequences of a violent meteorological phenomenon.

Now, it would have been interesting to question the ship captains who approached the island during this period to find out what the weather was like at the time.

Another question to ask, so as not to leave anything to chance: was there any smuggling or other illicit traffic in the vicinity of the lighthouse, which could have led to the disappearance of all three men at the same time? They may have witnessed the events.

Because, in very bad weather, I can't imagine that the three keepers would have gone out without precaution, leaving the lighthouse abandoned, knowing that this was their main mission and that procedure required one of them to remain inside.

The Panama dossier

Groping in the dark, Lisanne Froon's cold fingers find her Canon PowerShot camera at the bottom of her backpack, between two pairs of sunglasses, a passport, a half-used bottle of water, two bras and two cell phones, both permanently switched off. The camera *flash*, inadvertently triggered, dazzled her eyes, making her wince. All around her, the jungle of Panama is filled with noises, each more frightening than the last, but she has long since moved beyond terror to resignation.

Trembling, she turns the Canon's rear dial and activates its "video" mode to begin her confession, vaguely lit from the side by the moon filtering through the trees.

*

I don't know where to start...

[Lisanne whispers, clearly afraid of attracting attention. Her reddened eyes indicate advanced fatigue and, most certainly, repeated crying. Numerous scratches dot her face. Her features are drawn. She looks weary, exhausted].

My name is Lisanne Froon, I'm 22 years old and I have a degree in applied psychology from the University of Deventer, in the Netherlands, but I didn't grow up there, as I'm from Amersfoort, like my friend Kris Kremers. For as long as I can remember, I've been reading and watching videos from around the world, with a passion for animals and nations, as well as mysteries and legends. It's this passion that has driven me to travel a lot, especially in Europe, but two years ago I conceived the idea of visiting Panama to perfect my Spanish and experience volunteering with underprivileged children. I didn't want just a vacation, but a real trip, with meaning behind it. I mentioned it to my best friend, Kris Kremers, who was immediately very enthusiastic. Kris is...

[Lisanne pauses for a moment, then resumes.]

Kris was a very open, creative and responsible person. She had just finished her studies in cultural and social education when we flew in. As for me, people describe me as more reserved, but cheerful, optimistic, intelligent and passionate about volleyball.

[She crushes a tear with the back of her hand. She's shaking, maybe from cold, maybe from fear. The camera battery shows only 10% charge left].

I'm recording this video for my parents and Kris's parents, so that they know what happened to us. I also implore anyone who finds this camera to please pass it on to the Dutch authorities.

We left the Netherlands on March 15 from Schipol, Amsterdam's international airport. It wasn't a direct flight, as we had a four-hour stopover in Houston. After this long wait, we were finally able to fly to San José, Costa Rica. Once there, we were picked up by a couple who drove us to our hostel. It was around 10 pm. I remember Kris exclaiming "What a trip!", and I couldn't agree with him more. With jet lag, we'd spent the last twenty-four hours awake in transport, anxious to land in a country that was completely foreign to us. Yet we slept like babies that night, overcome by exhaustion and emotion.

The next day, we took a bus to Panama. Kris was daydreaming and kept repeating, "If the job gives us time, we'll see the beauty of this country, it's so exciting. Now the journey has really begun!" Poor thing, if she'd only known…

[Lisanne rubs her eyes, probably to keep another tear from falling].

At around 6:30 p.m., we finally arrived in the Bocas del Toro archipelago. The journey had not been easy. At the border, we had to pay for a stamp that should normally have been free. That's how things work here… Anyway, it didn't dampen our enthusiasm.

Our program was simple: for ten days or so, we'd be taking Spanish classes in Bocas del Toro, then off to Boquete, before being picked up by our host family. There, we would work with a lady called Aura, as volunteers with children. On April 26, game over, goodbye everyone, back to the Netherlands.

At first, everything went according to plan. We started our Spanish course on Isla Colon, the main island of the Bocas archipelago, where we met Bas and Edwin, Dutch like ourselves. We quickly became good friends. Later, we met Mart, also Dutch. The five of us had a great time together, then Mart left for Panama City as part of his travel plan. For our part, we set off for Boquete. Unlike the journey to Bocas, this one went off without a hitch, although we had to get off the bus early, as the school was actually in Alto Boquete, the outlying part of town. It was a bit strange, as it seemed to be in the middle of nowhere.

Our host family picked us up, and I have to admit that the first few days were pretty complicated. It was hard to adapt to a foreign family, whose habits you don't know and with whom it's difficult to speak Spanish. I cried several times. The transition from our vacation to life with a local family was a real pain for me. I was clearly naive to think I could handle it, because it was exactly the kind of situation I can't handle. I missed my parents, I felt like a child who can't separate from her mother. To be honest, I saw this stage in Boquete as a kind of initiation test to help me feel better about my life. But here I was failing miserably.

Kris, on the other hand, was solid and confident.

[Lisanne pauses. She turns her head as if she's heard a noise in the jungle behind her. Then, after about fifteen seconds, she faces the camera again. The battery shows 8% charge].

On the way to meet Aura, we were quite nervous and excited. We were expecting her to recognize us since she was supposed to be expecting us, but instead we were confronted with a very unfriendly lady, rude and not at all friendly or welcoming. She told us that she wasn't expecting us so soon, that we weren't welcome until the following week. Outraged and disappointed, we went to the school to ask for an explanation, but none was forthcoming. The school found Aura's attitude strange, since our project had been planned and the dates fixed for several months. Having a week to spare, we asked Marjolein, the school employee, if there were any other projects available. Unfortunately, she couldn't get hold of the person in charge, so, while we were waiting to make ourselves useful, we decided to visit the region and booked an excursion, with a guide named Feliciano, to the hot springs of La Caldera, two days later.

But I didn't feel like waiting that long to start exploring the area, so I suggested to Kris that we get a head start. I remember writing on Facebook that we intended to walk around Boquete, then hike near the forests surrounding the Barú volcano, on the El Pianista tourist trail. We'd heard a lot about El Pianista since we arrived in Panama, that it was a must-do. On the other hand, we had been warned not to stray far from the marked trail, as two girls alone in the jungles of Panama...

[Lisanne pauses to make a face.]

We weren't really alone when we started our walk, however, as Blue, a husky dog, accompanied us. No wonder. In fact, this dog belongs to the restaurant "Il Pianista", which can be found at the entrance to the trail, and is accustomed to accompanying hikers. As proof of his routine, Blue took the lead and regularly turned towards us, as if to make sure we weren't going the wrong way.

After a while, we took a break. Blue, perhaps the friendliest dog I've ever met, stopped too. He refused our food, but his good constitution suggested that his owners fed him very well. He kept us company for another half-hour, then turned back as we headed for the Mirador, the mountain summit.

[Lisanne clutches her head in her hands and begins to sob. Then she pulls herself together, wipes her face and continues talking].

We should have stopped there, we'd been warned it could be dangerous, but I wanted to prove to myself that I could overcome my fears. So I insisted we continue past the Mirador. Forgive me, Kris, I didn't realize how much we were prey of choice.

After a few hours, we realized that we had no idea where we were, so we turned back, which only made things worse. We'd never been very good at orientation, relying mainly on our maps and phones, but when we tried to check our position on Google Maps, we found that we'd been out of contact with the telephone network for some time. We still tried to call 112, each in turn, but to no avail. The weather was fine, and for the rest of the day we wandered around in the blazing sun, hoping to come across another traveler or to reach the El Pianista trail. All in vain. We were beginning to despair of the uniformly green horizon.

After a while, as night fell and teemed with terrifying sounds, we decided to stop. We found a spot where the vegetation was less dense and settled there, back to back, so as to be able to observe the surroundings and prevent a possible attack by a wild beast. But it didn't fail, we were overcome by fatigue and fell asleep in less than an hour.

The next morning, we tried again to call 112, then 911, but network coverage was still too remote. We hoped that Feliciano, who was supposed to guide us to the source of the Caldera, would be concerned about our absence and alert the authorities. That's why we didn't move too much from our position.

Our sleep, though short, was deep. In fact, it was the rain that woke us up. We then realized that we had half sunk into a mud puddle that extended around us over a vast circular area, with us at its center. We had obviously fallen asleep in a clearing.

[Lisanne pauses. She gives the impression of hesitating to continue her story, as if for fear of sounding stupid. Finally, she chooses to go through with it. The Canon's battery shows 5% charge].

The sun was still shining, but the sky seemed to be getting darker. For several hours, we sat thinking in the shade of the trees that protected us from the sun. As the day wore on, the muddy ground became less damp. It seemed to dry and harden. That night, we barely slept. The next day, after turning on our phones once again in search of a signal, we set off again, but the jungle seemed different. The trees were more... menacing, the noises more muffled and frightening.

After a few hours, we came across a river, which lifted our spirits considerably, at least at first, as Kris and I disagreed on whether to go up or down. We didn't have to choose: our attention was drawn to a huge object standing a few hundred meters from our position. It was a pyramid-shaped temple. The sight of it sent shivers down my spine. I sensed that it was different from other constructions in the area. I'd visited Mayan temples before and this one seemed… different. It's hard to say why, but as I watched it intently, strange sensations came over me—anxiety, repulsion… I clearly didn't want to go, but Kris insisted, and as I had no rational argument against it, I finally gave in. After all, maybe it was a tourist spot and we could find some help there. Besides, it was about to get dark.

The temple was huge and we had a feeling it was very old, especially as jungle covered a good half of it. We should have been wary, especially as we'd heard about the Conejos, a tribe of blind, nocturnal cannibals feared by the locals. We thought it was just a legend. Even the guide, Feliciano, shrugged and laughed when we mentioned it.

[Lisanne bursts into tears again. The crisis lasts more than a minute. She takes a long breath to regain her composure. The Canon battery reads 3%].

We never imagined for a moment that the temple could be their home. As soon as night fell, they emerged from the pyramid's various porticoes. Their eyes were white, like animals that would live in darkness all year round. Despite this, they chased us through the jungle. We did what we could to evade them, lighting ourselves with our cell phones, then with the camera flash, but they got Kris, and they almost got me too.

Then, out of luck…

[She takes the Cannon and points it at her leg. It's shattered, its fractured tibia piercing her skin. Blood soaks her dirty sock and the ground beneath her. The battery shows 2% charge].

I want to tell my parents that I love them, that I miss them. I'm so sorry… I just wanted to do something good with my life, make myself useful, be a good person…

[Her voice chokes on a sob, the emotion too strong. The next moment, a creak of branches turns his head. The battery goes to 1%. Then white shadows emerge from between the trees and pounce on the young woman, pulling her against her will. The Canon falls to the ground, rolls several dozen centimetres and finally comes to rest between two roots. The image of a blue backpack fills the screen, while in the background Lisanne Froon's screams fade into the night. 0%. Shadows and silence close in on the jungle of Panama].

The facts

A long article from Mannen Magazine, published on November 28, 2019 (©Juan Perea y Monsuwé)

In April 2014, Kris Kremers and Lisanne Froon, two Dutch tourists, disappeared while hiking in the jungles of Panama. The two girls, who had just finished their studies, had been planning the six-week trip for months.

The first two weeks were spent sightseeing, and on March 31, they headed for Boquete, a small town on the Costa Rican border. There, they moved in with a host family for a month, and were supposed to give lessons to pupils at a local school, but the housekeeping didn't keep up, and their "first day" was postponed for a week. To kill time, they decide to explore the mountains bordering the village.

A panel in Panama

On April 1, as announced on Facebook, they set out to climb the Mirador, the highest point of an easy trail nicknamed "El Pianista" for its colored stone steps reminiscent of a piano keyboard. The serious stuff is saved for the next day. In fact, the young women have already secured the services of an uncertified guide by the name of Feliciano, for an even more challenging hike.

But on April 2, the guide didn't see his clients arrive, so he decided to go straight to their home. The host family indicated that they had not returned since the previous day. The Panamanian police were contacted. This marked the start of an intensive search, which unfortunately yielded no results.

On April 6, Dutch investigators arrived, accompanied by tracking dogs and the families of the missing girls, who offered $2,500 for any information leading to the recovery of Kris and Lisanne. To no avail. The families left Panama some time later without knowing more about the fate of their daughters.

It was only on June 14, more than two months after the disappearance of the two friends, that investigators announced that Lisanne's blue backpack had been found. A young woman from a nearby village made the find nine kilometers from the trail used by the two girls, on the banks of the Culebra River, known as the "Snake River". She swore to the authorities that the bag had not been there the day before. Curiously, the object is in perfect condition, as are its contents, despite the fact that May and June are among the rainiest months in Panama. Inside were two bras, two cell phones, two pairs of sunglasses, a half-empty bottle of water, a Canon PowerShot camera, Lisanne's passport and 88.3 US dollars.

Investigations focused on the cameras' memory cards. Among the dozens of photos, the police identified two distinct periods. The first series, of *selfies* and landscapes, ends with photo number 508, taken on April [1] at 1:58 pm. It shows Kris looking back at the camera, all smiles, perched on a rockery by the water.

Photo 508

The second period curiously begins with photo 510, as if 509 had been erased after the fact. Of the hundred or so photos that follow, the spatio-temporal framework changes drastically: it's pitch-dark, and the photographer is in the middle of the jungle. The data indicate that this second series of photos was taken entirely between 1 a.m. and 4 a.m. on the night of April 7 and 8, 2014, a week after

The Files of the Impossible

photo 508. This one-week "gap" remains a real mystery, as does the content of these latest photos. Barely three of them are usable. One shows Kris's red hair, photographed from behind; the second reveals a ditch; the third, branches with orange plastic bags hanging from them.

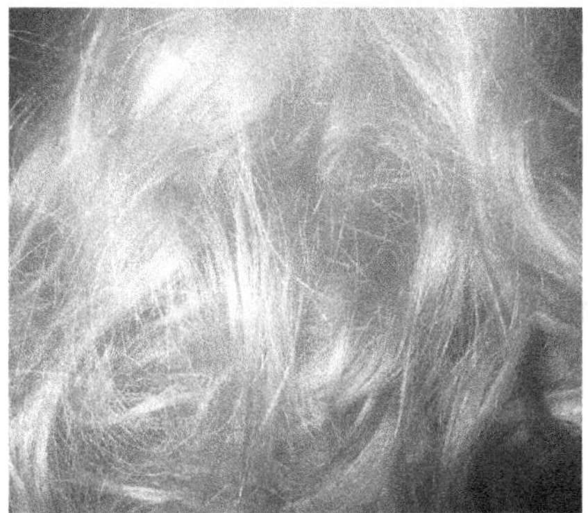

These strange photos, and their surprising dating, have given rise to countless speculations. Were the girls trying to light themselves with flashlight? Were they trying to mark a spot so they could return to it later? Was one of them injured and now unable to move, or even worse?

Examination of the phones suggests a physical problem for Kris or Lisanne. On April 1, at 4:39 p.m., Kris' mobile tried to call 112, the European emergency number. Twelve minutes later, it was Lisanne's turn to try. Over the next few days, both phones made numerous unsuccessful attempts to call this number and the American 911 number. Investigators claim that the two phones activated the base station signals several times without the young women, clearly unaware of the occasion, trying to make a call.

Lisanne's cell phone battery gave up the ghost on April 4 at 5:56 a.m., while Kris's didn't shut down for good until seven days later, on April 11.

The discovery of the backpack re-launches the investigation, and soon Kris's denim shorts are found on the banks of the Culebra River. Then, nine days after the discovery of Lisanne's bag, a handful of bones put an end to the families' last hopes: Kris's pelvis and a rib; Lisanne's femur and tibia, as well as her right foot, still stuck in her hiking boot.

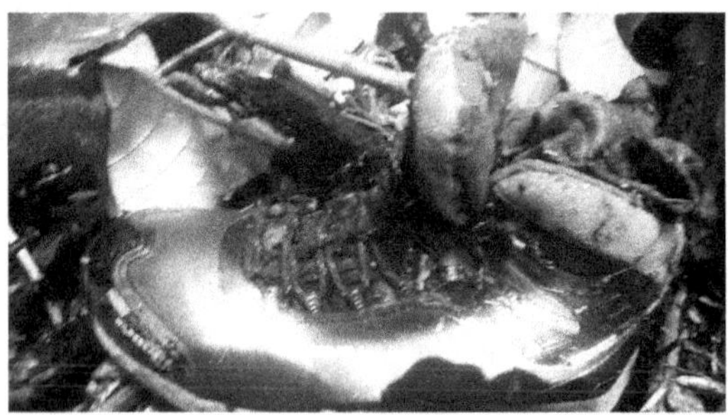

Lisanne's shoe

The autopsy revealed numerous fractures on the foot, the result of an extreme impact, perhaps a fall from a great height. For this reason, the Panamanian police did not open a criminal investigation: they postulated that the hikers had wanted to cross a "monkey bridge" (i.e. a bridge consisting of a simple cable stretched between two banks and supported by two ropes) and that they had fallen, the river scattering the bones.

However, there are still many grey areas in this affair, such as the seven-day gap between the two series of photos, or the disappearance of photo 509. What's more, the state of the backpack raises questions. After two months in the middle of rain, heat, humidity and animals, it would inevitably have retained the after-effects of this environment.

Several tourists who have taken the same route as the girls say it's impossible to get lost. Could Kris and Lisanne have been followed by a predator? Suspicion fell on guide Feliciano, a man known to surround himself with female tourists and make advances towards them during expeditions. Some even believe that he may have manipulated elements when he found himself alone in the girls' room. However, there is no evidence to incriminate him.

The Files of the Impossible

Various hypotheses have been put forward over the years: an accident, an unfortunate encounter with organ or drug traffickers, a sexual predator or even a mythical cannibal tribe (the Conejo Indians), but the case remains unsolved for the time being.

The backpack and its contents

In November 2022, journalist Mariana Atencio travelled to Boquete to reinvestigate, and said: *"In the course of our investigation, we uncovered cases of government corruption, possible drug trafficking, and even hints of organ and human trafficking. Without revealing too much, I can tell you that my life was directly threatened, something that had never happened to me before, even when I was covering cartel-related violence in Mexico or the repression of demonstrations in China or Cuba.*

In investigating what happened to Kris and Lisanne eight years ago, we uncovered more than 50 cases of missing women and girls in the same 65-kilometer corridor in Panama. Feminicide—the extreme violence and murder of women because of their gender—is so widespread in Latin America that it has been called a "phantom pandemic" by the United Nations".

The opinion of 1st Commissioner Maillard of the Brussels Judicial Police - Division in charge of crime against property and people.

I would like to remind you that I have not had access to the documents in the file, that I have not been in the field, and that it is not my intention to encroach on the work of my Panamanian counterparts, or even to point out possible shortcomings. I am relying solely on the information gathered by Geoffrey in the course of writing this book, to offer some food for thought.

So here we have a case of the disappearance of two Dutch tourists during an excursion into the jungles of Panama in April 2014.

Feliciano Track

We can already think about investigating the name Feliciano, who surely knew about the two girls' excursion the day before the one they had planned together. It is quite plausible that he himself advised the girls.

So, in the first instance proceed to interview Feliciano to find out his schedule for 01/04/2014. If he is in possession of a cell phone, research his movements on that day. Check if he has an alibi for the day. Who says he wasn't with the two girls that day too?

As the two girls planned their trip, check whether the highlight "El Pianista" was scheduled or not.

Also check whether Feliciano has a criminal record. Why is he uncertified?

How much were they planning to pay him?

Dutch investigators on descent

They arrived on April 6, which was not long given the paperwork problems and authorizations that slow down investigations. What's more, they were accompanied by tracking dogs, but found nothing.

A reward of $2,500 is offered for information, but they get nothing. Yet this is a lot of money for the inhabitants of the small town of Boquete.

Bag discovered 06/14/2024 (one and a half months after disappearance)

This bag, in perfect condition, still contains many objects to be exploited:

- if it had been a thief, the camera and money would probably not have been found, along with the two cell phones and sunglasses;

- these elements are important, and fingerprinting and DNA research had to be carried out in order to identify a possible suspect;

- sunglasses are also present. You have to ask yourself whether these are prescription glasses or not;

- the hearing of the young woman from the neighboring village must also be arranged to find out more about the place and time of the discovery, and also when the woman passed by the day before, since she claims that the bag was not there the day before;

- then, it would be interesting to proceed to the demarcation of the phones in order to know, if it's possible, the last pointing place of each GSM. Of course, in the jungle, there may be no way of searching;

- nine kilometers separate the path taken by the girls and the place of discovery. Who goes that way? Who could have taken the same route? A neighborhood survey is highly recommended. Why is this bag where it is?

Canon Powershot photos of one of the girls

First period:

- everything seems to be going well until 01/04 at 1:58 pm;

- selfies and landscapes can be researched to determine the places visited and retrace the girls' journeys;

- In the last photo, the girls are at the water's edge. Location is everything.

Second period:

- photo 509 deleted. Now that there is a way to restore data, it would be interesting to try. Now, who never deletes a photograph that has failed or that they don't like? The second possibility is that it has been erased by someone else, hence a DNA search on this object;

- as for the series of photographs taken between 1 a.m. and 4 a.m. on the night of April 7 to 8, 2014, it's much more intriguing, knowing that the camera was found in the bag intact on April 14, 2014 ;

- Again, a more careful analysis and restoration of this series of photographs should be attempted;

- In all three photographs, you can see that the flash was used, as they are clear for photographs taken in the middle of the night. Was it to light the way? If they had been removed, the authors would have been able to see the flash, so it seems unlikely to me.

Laptop analysis

- Analysis of the cell phones clearly shows that one or both of the girls had a physical problem or were lost. If they'd been kidnapped, I'm guessing the kidnappers wouldn't have left their mobile phones with them.

- Both phones have activated base stations without the two young women making a phone call. Who keeps looking at their mobile phone? And how long did this contact with a pylon last?

- However, it would be interesting to retrace the route of the GSM boundary markers to see the path taken by the two girls. Then, go down to the field and follow this route to try and understand the logic behind the movement.

Discovery of bones and denim shorts

- The discovery of some of the girls' bones puts an end to the search, especially as a foot is found in a shoe, which would tend to prove an accident.

- In addition, the autopsy revealed several fractures in the foot.

- Try to find out how the girls were dressed when they set off on their morning excursion. Were shorts worn or not?

In conclusion, I'd be tempted to go for an accident, but the element of the bag found intact is indeed rather disturbing.

The Yuba City missing persons case

1

"Step on it, Doc! They're right behind us!" shouts Ted Weiher as the "Doc" in question, Jack Madruga by full name, his hands clenched on the steering wheel of his Mercury Montego, tries to maneuver the car transformed into an unmanageable liner by its five occupants.

A few hours earlier, the little band of friends had attended the basketball game between UC Davis and the Chico State Wildcats at Chico University's Art Acker Gymnasium (UC Davis won 98-86). With the sound of the players' soles on the floor, sometimes drowned out by the cheers of the crowd, none of them could have imagined that they would find themselves entangled in this surreal situation.

"Take a left this time!" bellowed Bill Sterling, which made Gary Mathias wince, as he didn't appreciate being yelled at.

"But... this isn't our road," protests Jack Huett.

"I know, but look!"

The blinding headlights of a red pickup truck swoop down on them from Highway 70, the logical route back to Yuba City.

"How did they get to the 70? They were behind us ten minutes ago..."

"No idea, but with these guys, you can expect anything," retorts Madruga.

"I told you we should have taken the 99," grumbles Mathias.

"All right, shut up if you're going to say things like that, it won't help us!"

There were actually two expressways to the Marysville-Yuba City area: Highway 70, leading directly to Marysville, and the California 99 State Route. While some preferred the slightly shorter 99, Jack "Doc" Madruga always opted for the Madruga always opted for the 70, arguing that "the pavement was better and his sweetheart's tires deserved it".

"Go ahead, Doc, take the exit!" cries Sterling, clutching the door handle.

"Hang in there, guys."

With a dreadful screech of tires, the Mercury forks north-west as best it can, leaving the 70 and setting off down the kilometers of the 162 Oroville-Quincy freeway towards the Plumas forest.

"What the hell are we doing here?" whines Ted Weiher, who has always been the most emotional of the group, curled up in the passenger seat.

"Are they still behind us?" asks Doc Madruga, ignoring his comrade's intervention.

"I don't see them anymore," replies Jack Huett, grabbing one of the *snacks* he bought after the game at Behr's Market in Chico.

"Can I have one?" asks Madruga, without taking her eyes off the road.

With a hand shaking with nervousness, Huett tosses him an industrial burrito, which lands in his lap. Madruga snatches it up and, after opening the wrapper with an angry flick of her teeth, gobbles down the Mexican specialty in two mouthfuls.

"I think we've annoyed her a bit," Gary Mathias laughs, watching through the car door window as the moon is reflected on the calm waters of Lake Oroville in the distance.

"Who?" asks Huett.

"The Behr's Market employee. Didn't you notice how she glared at us?"

"Ah that... I guess she was anxious to get home and wasn't happy to see five guys show up just before closing time, ha! ha!"

"Nevertheless, she remained courteous," observes Weiher, who has regained his composure.

Silence falls again in the Mercury, barely disturbed by the purr of the engine.

"So, guys, what do we do?" Sterling finally asks. "Because we're heading for Bidwell Bar Bridge, and we can't go on like this."

"What do you suggest?" replies Madruga. "Turn back?"

"It doesn't sound so crazy to me. I feel like we've lost them."

But no sooner has he uttered these words than a pair of headlights dissipates the night in their wake, dazzling Madruga who has to look away from his rear-view mirror with a grimace.

"Damn it!"

The next instant, a violent impact almost sends the Mercury tumbling to the side of the road. Luckily, Madruga's army-acquired reflexes enable him to keep his darling on the asphalt. The red van has caught up with them. For a moment, Sterling finds it curious that their pursuers—bald, black-clad men with a pudgy look on their faces—are traveling in such an inconspicuous vehicle. But he doesn't have time to think about it any further, as the van is already bearing down on their rear bumper.

"Go for it! Weiher, whose panic has caused him to sink back into his seat."

With his foot to the floor, Madruga passes the few Oroville crossroads without slowing down, then flies over the Bidwell Bar Bridge that spans the lake and, finally, the Canyon Creek Bridge that marks the end of civilization as much as the beginning of the wilderness. A few dozen meters behind them, the engine of the red van seems to have reached its limits, as the distance separating the two vehicles increases with each passing minute. Not enough, however, to put the five out of reach, especially as the road steepens towards the mountains.

The snow appears on the side of the road, first in small, scattered piles, then in increasingly long strips until it forms a uniform carpet.

"Where are we now?" worries Mathias.

"We've just passed Whispering Pines Chapel," Sterling replies.

"What do you know?"

"Well… I saw the sign, smartass."

"Guys, let's stay calm," moderates Madruga, who is also starting to get nervous from the stress.

His ordeal was not yet over, however, for after a few more kilometers, he saw the headlights of his pursuers fade abruptly in his rear-view mirror, causing him to grit his teeth… and at the last second, turn left onto a winding, unmarked, gently sloping road that winds its way through bare trees.

"What are you doing?" worries Weiher, surprised by the maneuver.

"I wasn't thinking," Madruga apologizes. "Does anyone know where this road leads?" he then asks, as the branches whip around the Mercury's body and he slows down to zigzag between the holes.

"I think there's a campsite down the road called Rogers Cow Camp," Sterling replies. "We passed it earlier."

"How do you know that?"

"My father took me to the area for a fishing weekend a few years ago, but I didn't really like it and never wanted to come back."

"Fuck, couldn't you have said that earlier?"

"Sorry, I didn't think of that! In case you haven't noticed, it's hard to think straight these days."

"Is there a house where we can take refuge?" asks Weiher, full of hope.

"To call it a house would be to do too much honor to this ruined shack," retorts Sterling in a tone of amusement, "but yes, we could lock ourselves in and call for help."

"Do we have enough fuel to get there?"

A quick glance at the dashboard tells Madruga that the gauge is still half-full, so he hastens to reassure his friend.

"Don't worry, Ted, we'll get there long before my darling drops us."

"Super."

In the process, Madruga looks up from his rear-view mirror and sees Huett.

"Jack, can you see them?"

He turns around, squints in the hope of improving his night vision, but to no avail. The night is too dark, it's been too long, and the lack of light in the trees makes it impenetrable. The moon's reflection on the surface of the snow barely disturbs the darkness.

Suddenly, a jolt shakes and rocks the car, bringing it to a halt.

"What's going on?" alarms Weiher, his voice trembling.

"I think we've crashed into a snowdrift," grumbles Madruga. "Damn, that's going to scratch my paint!"

"Sorry about your bodywork, Doc, but I think we've got a more pressing problem," says Huett.

"Yeah, you're right... Still can't see anything?"

"No, but I have a feeling they're not far off."

"Shit!"

Madruga jerks the door open; the others shiver as the icy cold fills the cabin, accompanied by the distant murmur of an engine noise.

"It's them! Come on, guys, move it!"

"Weiher replies in the same tone, gazing anxiously at the tall trees bathed in night."

"We cross the forest." Jack said there was a camp nearby.

"In the middle of the night? You're crazy! We're going to die!"

" You've got a better idea?" spits Madruga, whose eyes glide over the path they've just climbed, from where the purr of the red van's engine swells. "You've seen what these guys are capable of! If you want to wait for them here, that's your choice, but I'll take my chances!"

The other three passengers are content to watch the exchange in silence, but they all know that there's no other way out of their situation: escape or death. And the sooner Weiher realizes this, the better.

"Fuck...," concludes the latter, opening the passenger door. "I hope you know what you're doing."

2

The snow slows their progress. Of course, they're not equipped for such an environment. All of them are wearing short-sleeved shirts, light jackets, jeans and sneakers—clothing unsuited to high mountain temperatures, to say the least. Weiher and Mathias try to bundle up with a blanket from the Mercury's trunk, but the wind keeps lifting the fabric, turning it into a useless cape three-quarters of the time. A few yards ahead of them, Madruga helps Huett along, while Sterling leads the way as an improvised guide.

It's not snowing, which is the only good news of the evening.

"I think it's this way," announces Sterling with aplomb, even though, deep down, he hasn't a clue and knows full well that they should have reached the campsite a while ago.

But he can't tell his friends. Such a revelation would lead them to despair, despair to abandonment, and abandonment to death.

"Come on, guys, let's keep up the pace!"

Of course, they'd like to slow down a bit, give themselves a few minutes' rest, but the light of the flashlight that occasionally filters through the trees behind them reminds them at regular intervals that their pursuers still haven't given up the chase.

"Maybe we should go and talk to them," Weiher suddenly suggests.

"To tell them what?" retorts Madruga. "That we didn't see anything? That we won't recognize them?"

"We can promise them we won't tell anyone!"

"Stop it, Sterling cuts him off, these guys are military, NSA agents or worse... Our word won't be good enough for them. Liquidating us is the only way they can be sure we won't talk. Besides, have you seen where we are? They don't even have to go to the trouble of finding a secluded spot to stash our corpses!"

"But even if we did talk, no one would believe us," Weiher whines. "They must know!"

"These guys aren't military," Madruga interjects. "I've been in the army, so has Gary, and I can assure you that nobody dresses like that. Those black clothes aren't uniforms, not even for *black ops* guys[5]."

---

5. *Black ops* are clandestine operations carried out by governments or (para)military organizations.

"I agree with Doc. I'd say they were agents of a government organization, like the CIA or FBI, but more secretive," adds Mathias.

"*Men in black*[6]?" risk Huett. "I've heard rumors about them. It's said that they often come to visit observers of a UFO phenomenon shortly after the fact, even if these witnesses haven't told anyone else about it."

"Do you think that's what we saw earlier? A UFO?"

"I don't know what we saw. Do you? After all, you touched it first!"

Mathias takes a breath, then allows himself half a dozen seconds to think before answering. The images of the evening flash before his eyes once again: the UC Davis victory, the trip back to the car, the stop at Behr's Market and finally the… meeting, as it must be called.

It was around 10:30 pm. The Mercury Montego had just turned onto the highway when Huett drew the passengers' attention to a curious celestial body falling slowly and erratically from the sky.

"It looks like a parachute in distress," commented Sterling, before quickly realizing that it wasn't a parachute at all.

Driven by curiosity, the friends had followed the object's trajectory to the Teichert Ponds marshes along Golden State Highway, where they were greeted by an imposing glittering mass that Doc Madruga had described, in a voice barely more audible than a whisper, as "a bulging disk of quivering jelly about six feet in diameter, a foot thick in the center and an inch or two near the edge", filled with a crystalline substance that reflected moonlight.

"It looks like it's vibrating," Mathias remarked, more fascinated than frightened. "Look at these fine lines on its surface."

"Do you think we should call the cops? Weiher suggested. Or go back to Behr's Market?"

But none of his friends had replied, bewitched by the mass which radiated an astonishing crimson glow whenever the clouds blocked out the lunar light.

It was then that Mathias thought it acceptable to touch the thing.

"Stop it!" interposed Weiher, as panicked as ever. "Imagine if it gave you a space disease!"

"You're an idiot," Mathias laughed, plunging his hand into the heart of the gelatinous mass.

---

6. Men in black.

  The Files of the Impossible

Tiny globules had stuck to his fingers when he pulled her off, then evaporated, leaving behind only an odorless, colorless but sticky residue.

"Did you see that? That thing is crazy!"

"Guys, I think we're going to be rich!" enthused Madruga, placing one hand on Sterling's shoulder and the other on Huett's. "We're going to be rich!"

"Should we take him in?"

"We take it on board."

The five men then coordinated to lift the "disc", which appeared to be of rare lightness, as it hadn't even flattened the grass on which it had crashed. It required no effort to leave the ground. But as with the globules on Mathias' hand, it evaporated completely within fifteen minutes, leaving only vague, sticky furrows in the Mercury's trunk, which in turn disappeared.

"Well, fuck it then... We can say goodbye to the mountain of bills," commented a dejected Madruga, hands on hips.

"Nobody's going to believe us," Weiher lamented. "We're going to look like a bunch of lunatics."

"That's why we must never talk about it," Mathias spat. "I have no desire to return to an institution."

His friends knew what he was talking about, since Gary Mathias was known to the authorities for having been violent in the past and was considered by the people around him to be the most "disturbed" of the group, due to his schizophrenia.

"But if I take my medication, I'm able to function in society," he defended himself when he broached the subject of his pathology. That's all in the past.

And, indeed, he hadn't had a psychotic episode in ages.

Sterling remembers all this as the wind whips his face and hopes that this nocturnal escapade in the mountains won't awaken his friend's old demons.

In their wake, the flashlight's rays transform the lanky tree trunks into exuberant titanic phasms ready to crush the ants at their feet—the ants being, in this case, Sterling and his friends.

He then thought back to the arrival of the men in black in their curious red van. There was an inexplicable discrepancy here, as this vehicle seemed so unsuited to discreet operations. In any case, it had landed belly-down in the middle of the Teichert Ponds swamp just as the five of them were climbing back aboard the Mercury, both excited by their find and dismayed by its rapid disappearance. In no time at all, Madruga had stepped on the gas, leaving the van, which had not expected such a move on their part, in its wake, and had sped off down the Golden State Highway towards Yuba.

The rest was history: the van had caught up with them, jostled them, manhandled them and forced them to turn off towards the mountains. And now, shivering with cold and fatigue, they were making their way through a thick layer of snow towards a hypothetical campsite.

"Talk about a galley," Madruga grumbles through gritted teeth.

"Come on, guys, we're almost there!" reacts Sterling.

His words of encouragement would certainly have borne fruit had they not been punctuated by several gunshots—or at least gunshot—like detonations accompanied by a surprising metallic resonance.

"We're all going to die," Weiher gasps.

"Run!" shouts Huett.

Indescribable chaos ensues. In the darkness of the forest, the five friends collide, scream, fall as they try to escape, and end up scattered among the spasms.

3

Ted Weiher gets his feet caught in a gnarlier root than most and topples headfirst into a pile of snow. When he emerges, he doesn't know whether he's crying or just dripping little blocks of melted ice down his cheeks. Probably both. His skin and eyes tingle with the same intensity.

It's been fifteen minutes since he was separated from his friends. Or perhaps an hour? He's not sure, because time doesn't flow in the same way since the men in black targeted him and his friends; sometimes it speeds up, sometimes it seems to slow down, or even freeze completely. What Ted is certain of, however, is that he is not alone in these woods. Presences lurk between the trees to his right, to his left and even above him. But then again, he can't be sure, since he doesn't dare look up for fear of what he might see beyond the treetops. So he starts running breathlessly, straight ahead, avoiding the trunks, not always avoiding the branches that lacerate his face. Short of breath, breathing hard, he's forced to moderate his pace, giving one of the shadows a chance to swoop down on him. Ted has just enough time to throw a punch before impact.

"Fucking hell!" lets out the intruder, smashing his hindquarters on a patch of frozen snow.

He puts his hands to his aching nose.

"You definitely broke it!"

"Gary? Is that you?" stammers Ted.

"Fuck, yeah, that's me! Are you stupid?"

"Hey! Ho! I didn't know it was you! Just showing up out of the blue. I could have killed you, man!"

"Mouais, as if you could do it," Gary Mathias grunts, struggling to his feet.

"Have you seen the others?"

"No, not since we got separated. I heard several gunshots, but I didn't see anyone."

"Shit... You think we should go get them?"

"And how are you going to do that, in the middle of the night, without knowing where we are? No, I say the best thing to do is keep walking towards the camp. Eventually, we'll find it or come across a road that will lead us there. It's our rallying point."

"What if the others can't find it?"

"Well, in that case, we'll call the cops and come back for them when it's light out. But right now, our priority is to get to safety. There's nothing more we can do, and we'll freeze to death if we try."

"Yeah, you're right."

And so the duo resume their arduous journey to their only lifeline, Rogers Cow Camp. To no avail. Minutes become hours, sprinkled with distant gunshots that startle them and keep them alert.

The night stretches on and on.

Ted and Gary's forces are about to leave them when the trees finally decide to give way to a few moss-greened caravans. A rusted sign tells them that they've just discovered a forest service site that's been abandoned for some time, and that a little further on is another camp, but not the Rogers Cow, as the sign indicates the Daniel Zink campsite.

"What do we do?" asks Ted in a voice as hoarse as it is frazzled.

Gary considers the derelict hut, then assesses his own ability to continue climbing the mountain and estimates that it's close to absolute zero—or almost.

"Let's spend the rest of the night here," he suggests. "If we're lucky, the forestry services have left a telephone here."

Ted welcomed this suggestion as a blessing.

A broken window later and the duo slip inside the largest caravan, where they discover a space heater and a large stock of canned goods capable of feeding them for several weeks if necessary. Some are out of date, but most are still edible, so Ted cries with joy.

"Later, the tears," Gary urges. "Let's see if we can find a damn phone."

But if the forestry services neglected the food when they emptied the premises, they were careful to take all the electronic equipment with them, from the small television, whose rectangle still stands out on a shelf, to the computer that was supposed to be sitting on the desk, not forgetting, of course, the telephone.

"Well, at least we've got something to eat," says Gary, considering the cans lined up in the hanging cupboard. "Are you hungry?"

"A little," confesses Ted.

Gary opens two cans of *Baked Beans* and serves them. Cold.

"Could we turn on the heating?" suggests Ted, shivering from head to toe.

"Out of the question. The flame would be visible from the outside. We'd better keep a low profile, at least until dawn."

"All right, then. Then can we at least patch the hole in the window?"

"No, that would be too visible a sign of our presence. I'd even go so far as to say that a broken window is the best proof that we're not there."

"Oh yeah... Not stupid!"

"Thanks," smiled Gary, before grimacing as he swallowed a mouthful of his glazed beans. "Fucking disgusting! It's really because I'm starving."

"It's clear...," agrees Ted, whose gaze wanders over the caravan wall, then slides to the window before venturing into the distance. "It's still dark, but you can feel that day is dawning; its first light is beginning to storm the dark opacity."

"Just a few more hours and we'll be off to pick up the others," says Gary. "Let's get some sleep."

"Do you think this is a good idea? Shouldn't one of us be on guard duty?"

Gary thinks for a few moments, then admits that his friend is right.

"I'll take the first shift, you need to rest."

"You're very kind."

"You're welcome. I'm used to it. In the army, we often had to go through this kind of exercise. I could stay up all night tomorrow if I really had to."

"Let's hope it doesn't come to that," concludes Ted, curling up on the floor in a fetal position, his short coat as a blanket.

He tells himself that it will take him an infinite amount of time to fall asleep, that the adrenalin still coursing through his veins will prevent him from slipping into Morpheus' arms, but in reality, it only takes a handful of minutes for him to sink body and soul.

His dreams are shrouded in feverish atmospheres, haunted by strange bald humanoids and cannibalistic gelatinous masses. Despite this, his sleep proves to be deep and welcome. His awakening is all the more brutal.

When he opened his eyes, an intense white light flooded the caravan, submerging the furniture and transforming it into shadow puppets. His friend is gone. The cold rushes in through the gaping door.

"Gary?"

It's not his comrade who answers him, nor the silence, but bursts of distant voices. So Ted crawls over to the broken window and peers out. Gary is standing there, some thirty meters from the caravan, facing the appalling whiteness that covers even the first light of day. He's not alone; the men in black are there too.

"How many of you are in there?" asks one of them in a singularly monotonous, hoarse, almost metallic voice.

"It's just me, I haven't found my mates."

"They are no more."

"What do you mean?"

"They have left us."

"You killed them, didn't you?" Gary enunciates coldly.

"Their bodily envelope ceased to function."

In the caravan, Ted stiffens with anguish. The surprising language of the bald men terrifies him beyond belief. Unable to make the slightest movement, he slides under the window, where he remains prostrate, one elbow against the wall.

If I don't move, they won't see me. If I don't move, they won't see me...

Outside, the exchange becomes more heated. Gary raises his voice.

"You didn't have to kill them! he roared. I'll skin you for this!"

"We weren't interested in your friends, Monsieur Mathias," replied the man. "You're the only one who's been in contact with the *shogg'rlyeh*. That's why we're asking you to come with us. It could be dangerous for this planet if you stick around."

If I don't move, they won't see me. If I don't move, they won't see me...

Gary retorts that he's not going anywhere, the man replies that he has no choice and, in the process, a shrill howl erupts from the void, so loud that Ted is forced to cover his ears with both hands. The scream lasts only a handful of seconds, then fades away, along with the light. The mountain, like the caravan, becomes dark and silent again. The men are gone. So is Gary.

If I don't move, they won't see me. If I don't move, they won't see me...

Ted remains in this position for an hour, then two, then three. When he finally decides to move, his aching muscles, frozen by the cold, refuse to support him. So there he remains, on the floor, unable to move.

Nor does it react when night falls again, and still not when a new sun rises behind the treetops.

One day passes, then another and another. Hunger is at least as strong as thirst. Luckily, the snow has rushed in through the broken window and the open door, so he has plenty of water to lick up. He hasn't felt his fingers and toes for a long time, but he doesn't dare risk looking at them. He knows they're blue, or black. Either way, it's best to stay still.

If I don't move, they won't see me...

Were they government agents? Did they come from further away? From beyond the stratosphere? The idea seems preposterous, given their curious means of locomotion, but then again, who could blame extraterrestrials for choosing an ill-advised vehicle model? Of course, one might find it silly that interplanetary creatures should travel in vans rather than spaceships, but there could be a host of reasons for this, starting with a certain need for discretion or the need to conserve their precious fuel.

Ted can't stop thinking about it as his limbs go numb, rotting more and more. His urine no longer warms him; he hasn't peed in two days anyway. Death is not far off, he sees it, it's coming.

Maybe if I don't move, she won't see me...

The facts

Foul Play Suspected in Disappearance of 5

Continued from Third Page

ported the location of the men's car on Monday, Feb. 27, three days after their disappearance.

The 1969 Mercury sports coupe had been mired in 10-inch snow on a gravel recreational road northeast of Oroville, in Butte County's rugged Rogers Cow Camp area.

The site was at the 4,500-foot elevation, more than 2½ hours from Chico by car, and far off the direct auto route between Chico and Marysville.

The ranger had seen the car on Feb. 25 but had not considered it unusual, because many residents drive to the area on weekends to go skiing. He contacted officials after a missing persons bulletin had been issued.

According to Richard Stenberg, undersheriff for Butte County, there was no evidence of foul play at the car's location, nor were the car keys found, he said.

"The car was littered with candy wrappers, basketball programs, milk cartons, and other material indicating a good time," he said. "We found no trace of the men during a five-day search of the surrounding area."

But Melba Madruga insisted that her son, the car's owner, would not have driven up the isolated road at night, and would not have abandoned the car.

"I'm sure he would have come home directly from the game," she said. "There is no way he would have gone voluntarily into the mountains at night."

The relatives of Ted Weiher said that all five men planned to play in a special Olympics basketball game for the handicapped near Sacramento on Feb. 25.

Four of the men had practiced for the game in Sacramento two days earlier. "Ted wouldn't have missed

MISSING—Jack Huett, William Sterling, Jack Madruga, Theodore Weiher, Gary Mathias, from left.
AP Wirephoto

that game for anything," his mother said. "He had gone to the Special Olympics playoffs in Los Angeles last year and had gotten Sally Struthers' autograph. He even had his basketball clothes all laid out in his room."

Adding to the mystery, a Sacramento man apparently saw the

He told his wife he had seen a pickup truck behind the car.

Mercury coupe between 11 p.m. and midnight Friday, Feb. 24.

The man, Joseph Schons, had become stuck in snow while driving the mountain road to check his cabin, and suffered a heart attack while trying to push his auto back onto the road.

Schons told officials initially that he had seen two sets of headlights, one that of a pickup, come behind him about 11:30 p.m. as he lay in his car in pain, trying to keep warm.

He said he got out and yelled for help, but that the several persons parked about 20 feet behind him then drove away in one car.

This week, however, Schons admitted he was not certain about the second vehicle.

"I was half-conscious, not lucid, hallucinating and in deep pain," he told The Times Thursday.

"Whether I half-saw or half-imagined the second vehicle, I just don't know." But he said he was certain about seeing the Mercury.

Early Saturday morning, Feb. 25, Schons managed to walk eight miles back down the road to a mountain lodge where the manager drove him home. Schon's wife later took him to a local hospital.

Schons said he told his wife he had seen a "pickup" behind the car but does not remember now why he said that.

Imogene Weiher said that her son would have responded to a call for help. "Ted and Bill Sterling once helped a person get to a hospital who had overdosed on Valium," she said.

Regarding a possible pickup truck, a second person said she saw the five men in a red, 1950s-model pickup about 2 p.m. Saturday, Feb. 25 in the Brownsville area of Yuba County, about 40 miles northeast of Marysville.

The woman, who asked not to be identified, said the men were in front of Mary's Country Store in Brownsville, a small town more than an hour's drive over back country roads from Rogers Cow Camp, where the Mercury had been abandoned.

The woman did not report her information to sheriff's officers until Friday, March 3, after the reward poster was printed with pictures of the missing men.

Lt. Dennis Moore of the Yuba County sheriff's office said that he believes "she is a credible witness and we take her information seriously." A search this week has centered around the Brownsville area.

According to the woman, two men were in a pickup truck, two men were at the outside telephone booth and the fifth man was in the store.

"I noticed them because they didn't look from this (Brownsville) area," she said. "And you notice strangers around here, especially them with their big eyes and facial expressions."

The owner of the store, Carroll Waltz, also said he saw several of the

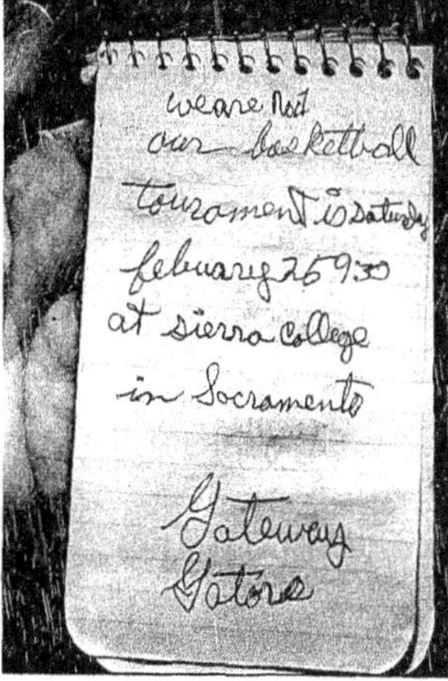

A FINAL WORD—The last entry in Ted Weiher's notebook diary.
Times photo

men on both Saturday, Feb. 25, and Sunday, Feb. 26.

"I'm pretty sure I saw (Weiher and Huett) buying burritos, chocolate milk and soft drinks," he said. "I can't be positive but I remembered after (the Brownsville woman) asked me whether I had seen the poster."

Dallas Weiher said his brother liked "to eat anything he could get his hands on" and that Huett was Ted's inseparable companion.

"So the store thing sounds logical, but everything else about the (Brownsville) story is completely out of character," he said.

The Yuba County sheriff's office said the woman identified Jack Huett as the man in the telephone booth.

Please Turn to Page 29, Col. 1

Article from the Los Angeles Times, *dated March 10, 1978 (©Los Angeles Times)*

It's February 24, 1978, around 10 p.m., and a Mercury Montego is rolling along the roads of Northern California. On board were five men: William "Bill" Sterling Sterling (29), Jack "Jackie" Huett Huett (24), Theodore "Ted" Weiher (32), Jack "Doc" Madruga Madruga (30) and Gary Mathias (25).

The five friends return from the town of Chico, where they attended a local university basketball game. Jack Madruga, an army veteran discharged from civilian life after a diagnosis of schizophrenia, is at the wheel, as he owns the car. He and his friends met at a day program for adults with disabilities, as they were all mildly mentally retarded, but that didn't mean they couldn't function in society; in fact, it was quite the opposite. They were considered highly functional, but could struggle to cope when placed in a stressful situation.

Shortly after the basketball game, the gang stop off at a roadside grocery store to stock up on snacks. 70 km separate them from the area where they live with their respective families, between Marysville and Yuba City. No one will ever see them alive again.

After Oroville, Madruga, rather than turning south, turns north towards the Plumas National Forest, and that's where we lose them.

BOLO issued by the Yuba County Sheriff's Department (©Yuba County Sheriff's Department)

Families raised the alarm as early as February 25, and a *United States Forest Service* (*USFS*) employee, William Burris, eventually found the Mercury on the evening of Tuesday February 28, on an unpaved road on the old Quincy road.

The Files of the Impossible

The car is near Rogers Cow Camp, at an altitude of 4,200 to 4,500 feet. The light-blue 1969 two-door Mercury Montego, California license plate XQG831, is about 1 hour and 15 minutes' drive from Chico, in the opposite direction from where they would have had to go home, and high up in the mountains of the Plumas National Forest.

The Mercury is parked in the middle of the road and seems to be stuck in a snowdrift. Temperatures here are well below zero.

Five slightly retarded men vanish without a trace

MARYSVILLE, Calif. (AP) — Five slightly retarded men who vanished without a trace more than a week ago are the objects of an intensive hunt in a snowy wilderness rated as some of the roughest country in California.

"We don't know what happened to them — we've a real mystery on our hands," declared Yuba County Undersheriff Jack Beecham, who said multiple murder is one possible explanation.

If the missing men became confused and wandered into the forest, not much hope is held for their survival, said Sheriff Jim Grant.

"I was up there myself one day and the only way I could get out was with a compass," he declared.

"It's very heavily forested country, rough and mountainous and rocky," added Beecham. "Some places you can only get in on horseback."

Teams of deputies from Yuba and adjoining Butte counties, some 150 miles northeast of San Francisco, have been searching the mountains on horseback, with dogs, in four wheel-drive vehicles and in a helicopter — to no avail.

The men were to attend a basketball game the night of Feb. 25 at Chico, and were to have gone back to their homes. But their car was seen abandoned the next day some 20 miles east, on a Plumas National Forest road closed farther on by snow. The elevation of the site is 4,400 feet.

The missing men, who lived with their families and were part of a program for the mentally handicapped, are Jack A. Madruga, 30, Marysville; William Sterling, 29, Yuba City; Ted Weiher, 32, and Gary Mathias, both from Olivehurst, and Jack Huett, 24, Marysville. Madruga and Mathias had driver's licenses.

The family and friends of the missing men have offered a $4,215 reward for information on where to find them.

The men, Grant and Beecham said, were reported to be able to function very well with their retardation handicap — except if placed in a stressful situation when their behavior tended to "deteriorate."

"We hate to guess what happened to them," said Grant. "They could have stopped to aid somebody, and the people they aided took advantage of them."

Beecham noted that a study of the personality profiles of the missing men shows their disappearance to be totally out of character. The men were to play in a basketball game in the area the night of the day their car was found.

"In fact, as time goes on it looks more and more like foul play," Beecham said.

Grant said that among the tips received by deputies was a telephone call from a woman in Brownsville, 30 miles from where the car was found.

"She said she saw four of them that Sunday," said Grant, adding he thought it was impossible for the men to have walked that distance in the kind of terrain they were in.

"The prevalent theory is it could be anything," said Beecham.

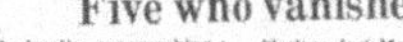

Five who vanished

Yuba and Butte (Calif.) County sheriff's deputies are searching a snowy California wilderness for these five men who disappeared more than a week ago. From left, they are Jack Huett, William Sterling, Sterling, Jack Madruga, Ted Weiher and Gary Mathias. Authorities said the five failed to return to their homes in the Marysville area after attending a basketball game in Chico. (AP Laserphoto)

An article from the Reno Gazette, March 6, 1978, devoted to the case (©Reno Gazette)

From the outset, the disappearance came as a surprise. First of all, the families swore that the five men didn't know anyone in this remote area, and that they weren't the type to organize an unannounced nocturnal *road trip*. What's more, given the moderate temperatures when they left for Chico, they were wearing short-sleeved shirts, light jackets, jeans and tennis shoes—clothing inappropriate for high mountain temperatures.

What's more, when the local police found the vehicle stuck in a snowdrift, they discovered that the *snacks* they had bought at the grocery store had been consumed and the vehicle keys taken away, even though the vehicle had not been locked. On the other hand, explain the authorities, the snowdrift in question is not really an obstacle for five able-bodied men. The fuel tank was still a quarter full, and the engine was still running. The vehicle was therefore abandoned.

A light blue 1969 Mercury Montego, similar to the Five (©Public Domain)

What's even stranger is that the car, found at the end of a tortuous track with no street lighting, shows no signs of mud, as if the driver had manoeuvred with extreme caution through the ruts. All around is a vast, snow-covered pine forest. The following days' search of the area around the vehicle, in extremely rugged terrain, came to nothing.

Madruga's parents say he didn't like the cold and had never been to the mountains. Sterling's father, meanwhile, says he had once taken his son to an area close to where the car was found for a weekend of fishing, but the young man didn't like it and preferred to stay at home when his father returned later. The mystery of the "Yuba Five" (or *Yuba County Five*) takes shape.

Several months later, in June 1978, a young motorcyclist by the name of Roger Koch, 16 at the time, discovered an abandoned forestry service caravan near a campsite, the Daniel Zink campsite.

Roger Koch in 2022 (©The Yuba County Five Podcast)

Ted Weiher's decomposing body lies inside, covered from head to toe in blankets, but without shoes. His feet were covered in frostbite. Two days later, police discover the bodies of Bill Sterling and Jack Madruga, 7 km from Weiher's camp. Madruga still had the keys to his Mercury on him. Both men probably died of exhaustion, forcing Weiher to continue alone. The remains of Jack Huett were also discovered in the area shortly afterwards.

The trailer where Ted Weiher's body was found (©Netflix's 'Files of the Unexplained' trailer [YouTube/@Netflix])

All the police found of Gary Mathias were his sneakers, suggesting that he had taken Ted Weiher's leather shoes and gone on alone, beyond the caravan.

Nothing about this discovery makes sense. The caravan in which Weiher was found is more than 30 km from the Mercury, deep in the forest. Sterling and Madruga died some 18 km from the car. The five men therefore covered this distance on foot, through dense forest, in three feet of snow and in their street clothes, before dying one after the other of cold and exhaustion.

When the police inspect the caravan, the case takes an even more incomprehensible turn. Judging by his beard, Weiher has spent between 8 and 13 weeks in the caravan; he has lost between 35 and 45 kilos from his usual 90 kilos, is wearing the same clothes as the day he disappeared and his feet show signs of gangrene, including several missing toes.

The caravan is filled with canned and dried food, but only some of the cans have been opened. Worse still, the shelter is equipped with a propane burner, sufficient to keep it warm. The appliance was not used. None of the books were torn open to start a fire. Weiher (and probably Mathias) didn't even bother to cover the window they broke to get in.

Police are hunting for Huett, Sterling, Madruga, Weiher and Mathias.

'Bizarre as hell'

How can five fully grown men vanish?

MARYSVILLE, Calif. (UPI) — "It's hard to lose five people, that's for sure," said Yuba County Undersheriff Jack Beecham Saturday.

Especially when they are all 6-foot-plus, 200-pound, slightly retarded men in the prime of life.

The five disappeared in the rugged northern California foothills after attending a basketball game in Chico, 50 miles north of Marysville, more than two weeks ago.

The mother of one of the men believes they are being held captive in a commune and the father of another is positive they are dead. Another parent, totally frustrated by earlier failures to locate the men, called in psychics for assistance.

Officials conducting the extensive search say any help is welcome.

"We are not dealing with the psychics directly at all," said Beecham. "We will not discount any information but will conduct our investigation based on logic. This case is bizarre as hell."

A sheriff's spokesman said detectives would continue working through the weekend on the mysterious case trying to piece together small bits of information and delving further into the backgrounds of the five men.

An air search Friday produced nothing.

In Butte County, deputies resumed their search around Lake Oroville and retraced all routes the five men might have used on their return trip.

"As time goes on foul play becomes a greater probability," Beecham said.

The five, Jack Madruga, 30; Jack Huett, 24; Ted Weiher, 30, Gary Mathias, 25, all of Marysville, and William Lee Sterling, 29, Yuba City, are all over 6-feet and weigh in the neighborhood of 200 pounds.

Their families said the men were "slightly mentally retarded" and unable to care for themselves, but added it was not like them to leave home for any length of time without telling anyone.

Their car was located Feb. 27, three days after they were reported missing, in the snow at the 4,500-foot elevation in the mountains northeast of Marysville, far off the route between Marysville and Chico.

An article from The Billings Gazette, *March 12, 1978 (©newspaper.com)*

Faced with the irrational, all that's left is the possibility of foul play. The police have never ruled out this hypothesis, because on February 24, a witness happened to be on this desolate road, in the middle of the night, just a few hundred metres from the Mercury Montego.

Joseph Schons, from Sacramento, told police that he had spent part of the night of February 24-25 near where the Mercury was found. He had gone there, where he owns a chalet, to check the snow cover before a ski weekend with his family. At 5:30 p.m., about 50 meters from the main road, Schons got stuck in the snow. As he tried to free his car, he realized he was beginning to feel the first symptoms of a heart attack and went back inside, leaving the engine running for heat.

Six hours later, still lying in the car in intense pain, Schons saw light behind him. Looking out, he saw a car parked behind him, headlights on, surrounded by a group of people, one of whom appeared to him to be a woman holding a baby. He called to the group for help, but they stopped talking and turned off their headlights. Later, he saw more lights behind him, this time flashlights, which also went out when he called to them.

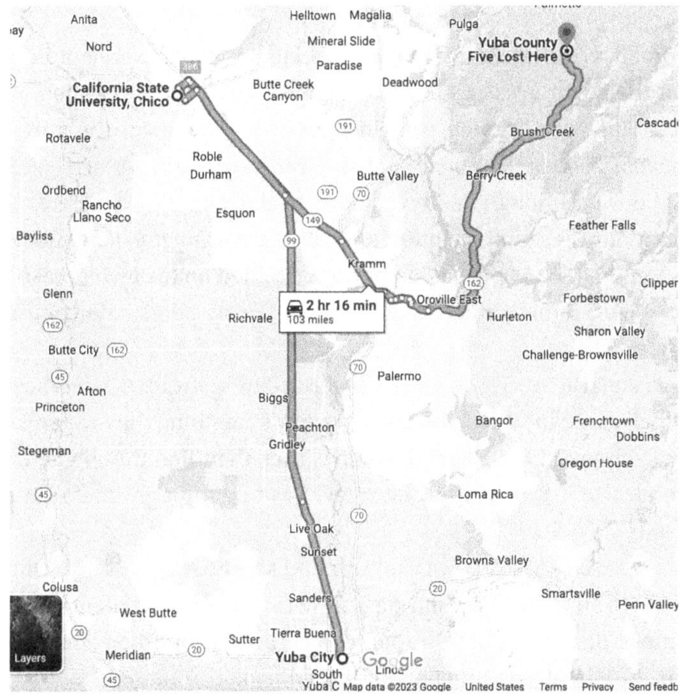

The various locations linked to this case give a good idea of its strangeness (©Google Maps)

The next morning, after Schons' car had run out of gas in the early hours of the morning, his pain had eased sufficiently to allow him to walk the 13 km to a tourist accommodation, where the manager took him home, passing the abandoned Mercury where he had remembered hearing the voices. Doctors later confirmed that he had indeed suffered a mild heart attack.

Weiher's mother said that ignoring cries for help was unlike her son, if he was ever there at all. She recalled how he and Sterling had helped someone they knew get to the hospital after a Valium overdose.

The other notable report came from the employee of a store in the small town of Brownsville, 50 km from where the car had been abandoned, but which the five would have reached had they continued on the road. On March 3, the woman, who had seen flyers distributed with the men's photos and information about the $1,215 reward the families were offering, told authorities that four of them had stopped at the store in a red van the day after the disappearance. The store owner corroborated his story.

The woman said she immediately realized that the men were not from the area because of their "big eyes" and "facial expressions". Two of the men, whom she identified as Huett and Sterling, were in a phone booth outside the store, while the other two went inside. The police said she was "a credible witness" and took her account seriously, although this lead did not lead to anything concrete.

For Jack Madruga's mother, interviewed by the *Washington Post* and *Los Angeles Times*, it's impossible to believe that her son decided on his own to take his cherished car to such a remote and rugged location. "He was persuaded or threatened," she concludes.

In the same articles, Ted Weiher's sister-in-law ventures a hypothesis: during the basketball game in Chico, the five men saw something they weren't supposed to, which precipitated their fateful destiny. They then fled the threat, first by car, then on foot once it was blocked by snow, heading through the forest towards a terrible death.

The fact that Gary Mathias was never found also raises questions. Did he attack his comrades in any way? The man was known to have been violent in the past and to be the most "disturbed" of the group due to his schizophrenia, but if he took his medication, he was able to function in society.

A view of the bunks where Ted Weiher's remains were found (© Center for Sacramento History)

Before joining the army in 1971, he had had a few minor incidents with law enforcement and had been involved in a few burglaries, although this was never proven. Police records showed that he had become violent on occasion and had twice been charged with assault, including battery on a police officer and intent to commit rape. His violent episodes were not related to schizophrenia, as a person with the disease is just as likely to commit acts of violence as a person without it. So it's not impossible that he took it out on his friends.

A final hypothesis suggests possible links with problems associated with Project Gateway, a social reintegration program for the mentally disturbed through which the five had met. The 1970s were a dark and troubled time in the Yuba/Marysville area. Crime was rampant.

And so, on November 12, 1973, Valerie Janice Lane, 12, and Doris Karen Derryberry, 13, who were attending Yuba Gardens Middle School, vanished into thin air. The girls were reported missing after a *shopping* trip to the mall. Their bodies were discovered in a wooded area southeast of Marysville the following day. The case remained unresolved for decades, until 2016 when DNA evidence led to the confounding of the culprits, cousins Larry Don Patterson and William Lloyd Harbour.

Juan V. Corona, 1972 (©Bettmann/Getty Images)

In other news, notorious serial killer Juan V. Corona, was convicted of killing twenty-five migrant workers and burying them on farms near his home in California's Sacramento Valley.

Corona's victims were vagrants who moved from farm to farm, looking for short-term work in the valley's orchards, groves and vineyards. Corona maintained his innocence for years, but then, at a parole hearing on December 5, 2011, he admitted his crimes.

Finally, to return to our case, the Gateway project, in which the Yuba five had participated, was the target of arson attacks on several occasions, and its managing director was murdered. Is there any connection with these stories? Did they see or recognize anyone on their jaunt to the game? Where is Gary Mathias (or, more plausibly, his body)? What madness drove these five men with quiet lives to venture so far from home, on a freezing night, going deeper and deeper into the forest and snow rather than back down the way they came? And why did Ted Weiher apparently starve to death after a slow agony, even though he had food at his disposal? Had the group been kidnapped and the assailant prevented access to food, or was Ted suffering from the effects of gangrene caused by frostbite? And *what about* the testimony of the waitress who thought she saw them in a red van?

The truth has certainly disappeared forever with its protagonists...

The opinion of 1st Commissioner Maillard of the Brussels Judicial Police - Division in charge of crime against property and people.

On February 24, 1978, at around 10 p.m., a Mercury Montego disappeared with five people on board. Jack Madruga, a diagnosed schizophrenic, was at the wheel. All these people had mild mental retardation, which did not prevent them from functioning normally in society. However, they could have malfunctioned in stressful situations.

There must have been a reason for the driver to change direction and head in the opposite direction, despite the fact that only 70 km separated their location from their homes. What's more, they headed into the forest with no real purpose (at least, as far as we know).

Before turning north, they stopped for snacks at *Behr's Market*. For my part, I would have started by checking out this place and hearing from the owners to determine what state of mind the five men were in. Was there any incident or contact with other people at this location?

On the evening of 25/02/1978, the Mercury Montego was found an hour and fifteen minutes down the road from Chico, in the opposite direction to their home. The Mercury was parked in the middle of the road, and appeared to be stuck in a snowdrift that was not large enough to immobilize the vehicle permanently. An analysis of the vehicle and its contents is very important:
- check mileage and tank contents;
- also check for traces of blood or other substances;
- and check the trunk, as well as other places where something might be hidden.

At this stage, it's obvious that fingerprints should be taken, along with any DNA traces, and compared with the profiles of the missing persons to identify any unknown profiles.

According to their families, the behavior of our five missing persons is not in line with their usual way of acting. So something must have triggered a reaction on their part to make them head in the opposite direction to their destination.

All lightly dressed, there was no sign that they were going for a walk in sub-zero temperatures. Yet another element that might suggest an unplanned event.

No traces of mud on the Mercury vehicle: in view of the situation, it would have been interesting to set up a safety perimeter and try to identify any tire tracks from other vehicles. A tow truck could have deposited the vehicle there to confuse the issue.

Some four months later, Ted Weiher's decomposing body was found by a biker named Roger Koch in a forestry trailer near a Daniel Zink campsite. The biker is to be interviewed to find out how often he frequents the site and why he came to this remote area.

Two more bodies were discovered 7 km away. A fourth was also discovered in the area. The discovery of the bodies in very different and distant locations might suggest that they had split up to escape something. Had they simply been lost, they would have stayed together.

The location of Weiher's discovery has been analyzed and several elements are quite strange:

- he has no shoes and his feet are covered in frostbite;

- the propane burner on site was not used, even though the heat would have been very useful to the person concerned;

- the interested party has lost around 40 kilos and sports an 8 to 13-week beard.

It would have been necessary to check whether or not Weiher bore any traces of bonding.

An autopsy should also have been performed to check whether he had been drugged,

A man doesn't let himself die of hunger and cold when he has everything at his disposal to counter this fatal end.

Witness Joseph Schons witnessed strange goings-on near the missing men's car. Yet another valid reason to take note of the tire tracks, which might have revealed the make of the car on the spot near the Mercury. The reason for this witness's presence at the scene is not clear either, and his detailed interview was more than necessary, as well as checking his state of health to confirm his possible heart attack. Did he regularly go skiing there with his family? Did he have a criminal record?

Nowadays, it's obvious that his DNA and fingerprints would be taken. He called for help because he was feeling ill, but no one came to his aid. On the contrary, those present remained silent and covered up their flashlights to conceal their presence. Why was this? What were all these people doing at the same time in this godforsaken hole?

Nowadays, a telephone survey would be de rigueur and would certainly tell us more.

As for the witness who saw them in a red van and whose trail went cold, you have to realize that when there's a $1,215 reward on the line, anything can happen. How were Huett and Sterling recognized? At the time, photos of the missing were presented without further precautions. Today, photos of the missing would be placed in a photographic panel to verify witnesses' claims.

All the indications are that the five disappeared fled a threat and headed in the direction that seemed most beneficial to them.

Naturally, an autopsy had to be carried out on all the members found, in order to determine with certainty the cause of death of each one. *(Geoffrey's note: the autopsies concluded that the men died of hypothermia).*

I imagine this was the case, but in the absence of a plausible lead, we would have had to look at the other acts committed in the area, which were apparently numerous enough to indicate that crime was endemic in this region. It would have been necessary to look at the other perpetrators arrested and, if necessary, question them about their schedule on the date in question. Compare the DNA with the DNA taken from the Mercury vehicle and the various crime scenes.

The presence in the Sacramento Valley of a serial killer named Corona, who confesses in 2011 to the murders of 25 workers, is an interesting point. I don't know if it was done, but an interrogation about the disappearance of the Yuba City five could have been done. At the point this man was at, he could have shed some light on their disappearance.

Finally, the Gateway project, in which the five were involved and which did not meet with unanimous approval to the point of assassinating the general manager, also deserves special attention. Is this why they may have felt threatened?

The Trécesson file

1

The clock struck 3 a.m. on April 13, 1909, when a hellish commotion brought first the innkeeper, then his wife, to the threshold of their room. Someone was pounding furiously on the door of their establishment on the edge of the Paimpont forest, in the heart of Brittany, a land of legends and magic. As for me, I was still dozing in my bed, trying to emerge from that floating state between sleep and wakefulness, when you're not quite asleep but haven't completely left the alley of dreams. I didn't know who was abusing the door so brutally, but I did know that he was there for me, and not for the good innkeepers. Someone must have warned the squire of my arrival.

Burying my face in the fabric of my pillow, I hoped for a moment that the intruder would tire and leave me to finish my night in peace. Just then, I heard the boss and Louise chatting in the corridor.

"Who could that be at such an hour? Do you have any idea, Miss Ribemont?"

"Certainly," replied my daughter's soft, warm voice. "I imagine he's an emissary of Monsieur Prunelé."

"The châtelain de Trécesson? What does he want from you?"

I heard Louise's characteristic little laugh, the one she always emitted when her interlocutor stumbled over the obvious.

"You don't know my father, Monsieur Paul Lambiet?" she asked.

There was a moment's silence, during which I could easily imagine the boss deep in thought, her face flushed with exertion.

"Lambiet. Lambiet… Oh! Of course, of course! I see… It's obvious. You're here about the ghost. I'm off to wake up your father."

You're here for the ghost. How many times had I heard that phrase in the course of my life? I couldn't say. Following my studies in journalism, I had found a small job as an editor at *L'Aurore*, a republican press with socialist leanings. Minimum pay, maximum output. No great luxury, but enough to aspire to be a reporter. I made it after two years, before being noticed by the *Journal de Paris*, which entrusted me with its crime column. I had, in fact, demonstrated a certain talent for covering this kind of event at *L'Aurore*, even helping the police on various occasions. Inspector De Lestre was full of praise for me—or so the rumors went in the editorial offices. My activities required me to visit the capital's most notorious districts and rub shoulders with the most disreputable fringe of its population, which suited me just fine, as the thrill of excitement provided the necessary fuel for the engine of my existence.

After a while, it became clear that it wasn't just out of professional necessity, but out of a taste for adventure that I frequented the taverns of the Ménil'muche[7] every evening, where, among other scoundrels, the guys from the "Loups de la Butte" and the "Apaches" hung out. This propensity for taking risks would soon lead me to incidents that would radically alter my life and make me a famous man, for better or for worse. The worst being, in this case, being bothered at all hours of the day and night.

I jumped out of bed, slipped on my bathrobe, flattened my tousled hair with a gesture, and opened the door just as the boss arrived.

"Mr Lambiet! Good timing!" she exclaimed. "There's a man here to see you."

"A man?"

She nodded in confusion.

"Your daughter says it must have been sent by Monsieur Prunelé."

"I see."

The squire showed a certain impatience in doing so, which aroused my curiosity. I jumped onto the thick carpet of the staircase and descended the steps four by four. Out of the corner of my eye, I saw my daughter joining the boss at the landing balustrade, which offered an unobstructed view of the front door.

The banging at the door resumed, as a male voice, apparently young, shouted my name. The boss stood in the hall, his hand on the latch, confused. It looked as if he was hesitating to let the Devil into his home.

"What could possibly justify such haste?"

I replied with a doubtful raise of my eyebrows. In my opinion, there was no urgency about the White Lady, so the fervor of this nocturnal visitor didn't ring a bell.

Bam! Bam! Bam!

"I demand to see Monsieur Paul Lambiet! It's very urgent! It concerns a matter of the utmost importance!"

Bam! Bam! Bam!

"Here, Lambiet. Who's asking?" I asked through the door.

"My name is Daniel, sir!" Monsieur Prunelé sent me.

---

7. Ménilmontant district, Paris (slang).

A bull's-eye. The boss looked at me and let out a sigh of relief, then opened the heavy wooden door. Outside, silhouetted against the pale moonlight, stood a young man dressed as a servant. He was clearly suffering from lung trouble, as his breathing was labored. A glance over his shoulder told me that he was driving a carriage whose black hood was emblazoned with the Prunelé family crest.

"Please follow me, sir," he said, stepping aside to let me pass.

"Now? But it's three o'clock in the morning! And where shall I follow you?"

"To the Château de Trécesson, Monsieur! It's a matter of life and death!"

"Calm down, young man," I said reassuringly. "Why don't you come in and sit down for a minute, and at least give me time to get dressed? Then you can tell me what's going on."

Understanding that I wouldn't venture out into the night in my pyjamas, he complied without a second thought, despite the impatience that stiffened his features. The boss took him into the kitchen, where he sat him down at the table while his wife poured him a cup of coffee. I returned to my room.

"What do you think it is, Father?"

I turned around quickly. Louise was standing in the doorway, dressed in her usual adventurous outfit, ready to go. My brain wondered for a moment how she'd managed to get dressed so quickly, then decided it had more important information to process.

"It certainly has something to do with our business," I replied.

"Maybe it's time you told me more about that, don't you think?"

"Later, Louise. Right now, I have to take care of our visitor."

She followed me into the kitchen, grumbling. Daniel was still sitting there, a steaming cup of coffee in front of him. Clearly, he had no intention of touching it. So I asked if I could drink it, just to invigorate myself a little, and asked the young man to tell me why he had come at such an hour. To my surprise, he refused, preferring to insist that we lose no more time.

"Every minute counts, sir. Please, can we get underway now?"

"All right, I'll follow you. Louise, you stay here."

"Out of the question!" she raged. "You won't get rid of me that easily!"

"Louise, please... A lady doesn't belong out here in the middle of the night. You'd better..."

But my daughter wasn't listening to me anymore. She grabbed her coat and jumped into the carriage while Daniel took the wheel. I sighed. Louise certainly couldn't do anything like other girls her age, and I had no one to blame but myself for letting her meddle in my investigations from a very early age. Wearily, I trotted after her and dropped onto the dark brown leather bench. I was barely seated when Daniel started the carriage with a crack of the whip, and I clung on as the horses took off across the pavement. I felt my heart skip a beat in my chest. Unfortunately, the bumpiness intensified as we crossed the Paimpont forest and its muddy, potholed paths.

"Aren't you going to be sick, Father?" Louise worried.

"Don't be silly, I've seen it all before."

I was afraid, however, that my stomach wouldn't agree with me.

2

We were heading south-west towards Campénéac and Château de Trécesson, and all the while, I imagined that perhaps something had happened to Monsieur Prunelé. This would undoubtedly have explained Daniel's outburst. I'd only known him for half an hour, of course, but my instinct told me that this was not in his nature. Of course, I could have been told that this hasty judgment was not based on anything rational, but when you spend twenty years tracking down unusual events, you learn to trust your instincts. The young man was sweating despite the cool night air, which was usually a sign of great anxiety. The clatter of hooves and the squeak of wheels forced me to call out to him:

"Is Monsieur Prunelé all right? Where is he now?"

"At the château," he replied, in a tone of obviousness.

Not much of a talker, the kid. I took it upon myself to sit back down without questioning him further.

"Father, perhaps it's time you explained to me why we've come to Brittany?"

I turned to Louise, who was staring at me with her big black eyes. The moonlight brought out the diaphanous whiteness of her skin. If I hadn't been her father, I would have fallen in love with her immediately, and I curse in advance the day when some despicable individual, perhaps interested in my meager fortune, probably in love with her, will steal her affection from me. For this is the lot of all parents, the sword of Damocles for us fathers: to see one's daughter leave for the arm of another man.

Fortunately for me, Louise seemed more interested in the unsolvable riddle of a locked-room murder than in the facts of life.

"You're right, I admit. If you have to come with me tonight, it's probably for the best."

I readjusted my position on the bench and took a deep breath. I hated this moment. Ever since Louise had taken it into her head to accompany me on my investigations, I'd done my best to keep her at a distance, only revealing to her at the last minute what was at stake, naively hoping that ignorance would lead her to give up. This was the terrible mistake of an old man who had forgotten his own adolescent ardor, for, far from keeping Louise away, my secrets only fuelled her curiosity and appetite for mystery.

"Have you ever heard of the White Lady of Trecesson?"

I saw her eyes sparkle with excitement as she nodded her head in reply. I straightened up in my seat, looking serious and grave.

"The story takes place around 1750, on a cold autumn night. The lord of the time, Monsieur de Trécesson, was renowned for his benevolence and respect for the law. That's why he didn't tolerate poaching on his lands, and invariably punished any offenders. In spite of this, hunters abounded in the area. That evening, one of them was lying in ambush in the château grounds, watching for his prey, when he heard a noise. Afraid of being discovered by the squire's men, he hurriedly hid his rifle in a thicket, then took refuge in a tree. From his perch, at the end of the park's long driveway, he spotted a carriage harnessed to black horses, followed by several servants carrying lighted torches."

I paused to observe Louise. She was staring at me without blinking. I'd obviously managed to capture her attention.

"Servants with torches," she repeated. "What next?"

"The crew moved forward slowly and almost soundlessly. No voices interrupted the silence of the night, disturbed only by the measured stride of the horses and the rustle of the wheels on the parched leaves. This strange procession stopped a few yards from the poacher, who soon saw, by the light of the torches, several men with spades and pickaxes advancing in his direction and starting to dig a pit precisely at the foot of the tree in which he was standing. A little later, two masked gentlemen, whose high rank was evident from the elegance of their costume, got out of the carriage and violently pulled down a young woman. She wore a white silk dress, her head was crowned with flowers and a bouquet adorned her bosom. In short, everything pointed to a young bride about to be led to the altar."

"Who could be so cowardly as to attack a bride-to-be?" Louise snarled.

"Terrible men, no doubt about it. Do you want me to stop telling you this story?"

"No, not at all. Please continue."

"Manhandled by her assailants, the bride fell at their feet, kissed their knees and sobbed, begging for her life. But to no avail. Her persecutors remained cold and unyielding in the face of her desperate pleas, and far from appearing moved, one of them brutally pushed her away. "You must resign yourself, Madame. Crying is useless, your time has come. You're going to die." Indeed, the hole was dug. The lords then signaled to their men, who seized the young lady. The unfortunate lady struggled with all her might, trying to escape her executioners, but despite her efforts, despite her pleas and despite her tears, she was thrown alive into the pit, which was hastily covered with earth to muffle her cries. The gentlemen then climbed back into the carriage, and the crew set off at full trot."

Louise, speechless, couldn't hold back a groan.

"And the poacher?" she asked, hopeful.

"According to *Le Lycée armoricain*, which was the first newspaper to report on the case, the poacher, stunned with fear, didn't decide to climb down from his tree until he was sure the carriage had left. However, full of bewilderment and fear, he did not think to remove the earth that was suffocating the unfortunate woman. He hurried home to tell his wife about the crime he had just witnessed. She reproached him vehemently, calling him a coward and a cowardly man. She wanted to take him into the park to open the grave, but a terrible thought occurred to her: if she and her husband were caught near a barely cold corpse, wouldn't they be blamed for this heinous crime? This fear stopped her in her tracks. She decided it would be best to go to the Seigneur de Trécesson and tell him what had happened."

"How did he react?"

"As soon as he understood what was at stake, he hurriedly summoned all his servants and ordered them to go to the place indicated, where he himself soon followed. It was almost dawn when the earth covering the grave was removed. Evidently, the young lady had long since died. Monsieur de Trécesson was deeply saddened by this event. He had the bride's funeral honored in the chapel of his château, where he placed her wedding dress, bouquet and crown of flowers, which remained on the altar for all to see until the French Revolution. Thereafter, he took numerous steps to find the murderers, to no avail. Neither the bride's name nor the cause of her cruel fate was ever discovered. This extraordinary event remains shrouded in impenetrable darkness. Since then, a White Lady has regularly been seen on the outskirts of the castle, her tormented soul waiting for rest. That's why we're here."

"I see."

"For the sake of completeness, it is also said that young girls from Guer, Paimpont, Ploërmel and the surrounding area began to worship the White Lady, gathering once a year to kiss the bride's dress. It seems they hoped to find a husband in the following months."

"What a strange tradition," concludes Louise, her eyes lost in a blur.

Following his gaze, I noticed a gigantic dark mass looming over our horizon: the Château de Trécesson. It was said to be one of the most impressive medieval fortresses in Brittany, and in daylight its imposing reddish schist walls were reflected in the waters of the surrounding pond. I must admit, I was quite looking forward to seeing it.

3

Access to the château was via a drawbridge spanning the pond. Without stopping, Daniel launched our carriage over the thick planking supported by a clever interweaving of rivets and steel beams. The clatter of hooves echoed more loudly on the wood than on the pavement. Strangely enough, the sound gave me a sudden surge of anxiety. I couldn't help thinking that, like the war drums used by Napoleonic troops, these muffled resonances augured no good. At the same time, I was unaware that a very special kind of sacrifice was about to take place in the surrounding forest that very night.

Without slowing down, we passed through the pointed carriage entrance flanked by two narrow corbelled towers, themselves linked by a machicolated gallery. On the right, a long, almost blind facade highlighted a long-sloped slate roof that ended in a hexagonal corner tower. I noticed that a crenellated walkway ran around the loopholed walls. Surrounding the inner courtyard was a more recently-built main building, probably dating from the late 18th century, and to its left, domestic buildings and a small seigniorial chapel.

In front of the latter stood several men dressed in black. From the pale light of the portable lanterns they were carrying, I could see from their white batons and kepi that they belonged to the corps of peacekeepers. But one detail immediately struck me as incongruous: among them was a high-ranking officer. Probably a commissioner, judging by his top hat. After years of investigating on the bangs of the police force, not to mention the experience I'd acquired during my journalistic career, I was well placed to know that this kind of person rarely went out into the field, *let alone* in the middle of the night. This confirmed my suspicions about the seriousness of the matter that had prompted the squire to drag me out of bed.

Daniel stopped the carriage in the middle of the courtyard and stroked the horses' rumps before jumping from his seat to hurriedly open the door for us. Louise and I got out of the carriage, under the cautious gaze of the policemen. The high-ranking officer in particular, whose tired face was spread around the imposing moustache inherent to his profession, regarded us defiantly.

"So, this is the *great* Paul Lambiet," he said with a contempt as heavy as his paunch. "I suppose you think you can fool us again?"

I put a soothing hand on Louise's shoulder, and she glared at the man. I was used to this kind of welcome, but my daughter's flamboyant character still had trouble coping with the sarcasm we were often subjected to.

"Calm down, Louise. It's well known that narrow-mindedness goes hand in hand with being overweight. And the superintendent is certainly not short of it."

Louise smiled, while the policeman's face flushed behind his moustache.

"Gentlemen, please, a little restraint," intervened Daniel. "I would remind you that you are here at Monsieur Prunelé's request, and that this is a serious matter. I would therefore ask you to behave like gentlemen, especially in front of a lady."

He cast a sidelong glance at Louise, who pretended not to notice, but I knew her well enough to know that being called "a lady" was bound to turn her cheeks pink. Despite her tomboyish ways, she was nonetheless a young woman sensitive to compliments.

"That's where it's happening," said Daniel. "Monsieur Prunelé asked that you come straight up."

I headed for the door in the stone wall. A staircase led up to the guard's path.

"Aren't you coming, Superintendent?" snapped Louise.

The moustache twitched as the man turned his head away to light his pipe.

"I saw it earlier," he replied, letting out a cloud of smoke. "That's good enough for me."

I held the superintendent's gaze for a good ten seconds, and I don't think I'm betraying the truth if I say I read fear in it, which didn't help to calm my apprehensions. At my side, Louise trembled with impatience. The ardor of youth and recklessness, no doubt.

I groped my way up the steep steps, and while I was careful not to slip, my detective instincts kicked in. First step: systematic observation, as practised by all the world's policemen, which consisted in observing the facts for oneself and recording one's observations in a notebook. I never deviated from this. It was only later that my methods diverged from those of my fellow investigators. I liked not to limit myself to the usual range of investigative possibilities, which I found too narrow. This included new scientific techniques such as fingerprinting and graphology, as well as those developed by Eugène-François Vidocq, and the psychological profiling of criminals based on their actions, a method successfully tested by the American Laszlo Kreizler in the Manhattan serial killer case. In fact, most police officers considered me a charlatan, a madman or a heretic. For my part, I preferred the term avant-garde.

Louise and I emerged onto the guard path. The crenellated ramparts allowed us to see in all directions: in front of us, the pond that encircled the château and, at our backs, a vast wooded area leading to the forest of Brocéliande. Roughly in the middle of the rampart stood two crouching policemen. Beside them, hands clasped behind their backs, gaze lost on the horizon, a much more dignified figure resisted the assaults of the night wind: Jean-Sébastien Prunelé, the châtelain de Trécesson.

"Monsieur Lambiet," he said without turning around. "I'm sorry to have sent for you at such a late hour. I'd asked you here to investigate the White Lady, who's been making more and more appearances of late, but as it happens, another misfortune has befallen my home."

He turned to face us. Monsieur Prunelé was wearing one of those velvet bathrobes that the rich are particularly fond of. His dark-rimmed eyes seemed too small for his round head, barred by a fine moustache which he absent-mindedly fiddled with with his fingertips. Clearly, something had shaken him.

His annoyance seemed to fade when he saw my daughter.

"My respects, mademoiselle," he said, bowing his head. "What on earth are you doing here? This is no place for young ladies, least of all on such a troubled night."

Despite her nervousness, she managed to retort:

"I'm here as an assistant to my father, Monsieur Prunelé.

"And it's very often useful to me," I added to cut short the growing unease.

The squire let go of his moustache to shake the hand I held out to him.

"Forgive me, Mr Lambiet, I'm a little... disorientated by this whole affair. Have you been informed of the situation?"

"Not yet. Your servant Daniel has sent for us at full speed, but without the shadow of an explanation."

"I can see that. Very well, then. Do you have a strong heart, mademoiselle?"

My daughter didn't answer, merely held his gaze. Finally, the squire stepped aside to let us pass. That's when I saw him. The man of straw. The scarecrow covered in blood. It took a few moments for my brain to decode the images my eyes were sending it. The scene was so incongruous, so surreal...

On the rampart lay a human-sized mannequin, cross-dressed in men's clothes, chic clothes. Outrageous make-up made her canvas face look like a woman of lesser virtue. But what caught the eye, apart from the fact that he'd been smeared with blood, were his hands. In place of the stumps usually found on this type of scarecrow had been planted two human hands, presumably taken from their owner not long before.

"These are those of my son, Charles-Antoine," said the squire. "I recognize his ring and his slightly too-short right middle finger."

For the ten seconds or so it took me to integrate all this information, I massaged my temples, trying to keep my thoughts clear. Louise, for her part, simply looked up at the stars. The sky was clear and cloudless. The moon shone brightly between the twinkling dots of the Milky Way.

"What's up? Has the great Paul Lambiet discovered something we've been missing?"

The superintendent, who had evidently regained a little courage from his pipe, appeared on the guard path. His voice was slightly too thin for a man of his size. He planted himself in front of me, hands in his pockets, and stared at me with a look that contained all the condescension in the world.

The mimicry didn't escape me, but, as usual, I chose to ignore it.

"What can you tell me about our case, Superintendent?"

"*Our* business?"

"Commissaire, please," cut in Prunelé. "We're running out of time."

The man sighed, then drew from his pocket a paper blackened by a series of notes:

"Based on hand temperature and blood clotting, we estimate that they were severed just over two hours ago last night. This means the assailant may not be far away. I've got men canvassing the area. Anything else you want to know?"

"Who discovered this mannequin?" asked Louise, to everyone's surprise.

"It's me," replied the squire.

"What were you doing out at such an hour? Is it your habit to go out at night and walk around the ramparts?"

"Louise, a little tact, please," I interject.

"Leave it, Mr Lambiet. I appreciate this young woman's frankness. This is how we'll find my son. To answer your question, mademoiselle, I don't usually take walks at night. As it happens, I was awakened by laughter. A woman's laugh."

"You didn't tell me," complained the superintendent.

"That's because I doubt it has anything to do with our case. This kind of phenomenon is common in Trécesson. In fact, that's why I initially called in Mr. Lambiet."

"And I thank you for your trust," I said, kneeling down beside the straw man.

Now I understood what had troubled the superintendent. The scarecrow exuded a malignity worthy of the pagan idols of Sumatra. No wonder a small-town policeman was impressed.

Louise joined me a few moments later, imitated by the squire and the superintendent, who were certainly curious to observe my much-discussed working methods at first hand.

"I'm afraid official techniques won't be of any help in this particular case," I said at the outset.

"It's a fact," confirmed Louise. "Bertillon's identification system obviously doesn't apply here."

"Have you studied it, mademoiselle?" said the commissaire, raising an eyebrow.

As Louise nodded in agreement, Monsieur Prunelé confessed his ignorance of Sieur Bertillon's work.

"In a nutshell," I began distractedly, without stopping to examine the mannequin with a magnifying glass, "Alphonse Bertillon, then a simple employee in charge of filing files at the prefecture, discovered that by taking a certain number of measurements on any individual—not only height, but also foot, hand, nose or ears —there was only a very small chance that the same characteristics would be found in another person. The result was a highly effective identification system."

"I'll admit it's been useful on a number of occasions," attested the superintendent. "Problems arise when the suspect has no criminal record. The Bertillon method then becomes ineffective."

"Maybe one day people will be forced to register with the police," suggested Louise.

"God be with you, mademoiselle. It would make our job a lot easier."

"In any case, none of this will help us find my son," cut in Monsieur Prunelé. "What's more, I can assure you that these are indeed his hands."

"Far be it from us to contradict you," I say delicately, "but I think I can speak for the superintendent and my daughter when I say that they were simply hoping to remove the slightest hint of deception."

"Absolutely," admitted the policeman, caught by my turn of phrase.

"I have, however, studied other techniques that could prove useful," I continued.

The superintendent then approached me. I saw his shadow grow over the straw man.

"May I remind you that your... techniques are not recognized by our courts?"

"Yes, they would. They wouldn't help us prove a suspect's guilt. Nevertheless, there's no reason why I shouldn't use them to point us in the right direction, is there? Monsieur Prunelé, are you familiar with fingerprinting?"

"I don't think so," stammered the squire.

"It's more commonly known as fingerprint analysis. It was first used in 1896 by the Isaacson brothers, two New York investigators, and in 1902 even helped to confound a French criminal."

"Actually, that's not quite true," Louise corrected. "Other cases have been solved using this method before, but in remote corners of the world, corners you've probably never heard of."

I raised my head in amusement. My daughter particularly liked to have the last word.

"See, here," I said to Monsieur Prunelé.

I stepped aside and pointed to the base of the scarecrow's skull. The three heads of my colleagues moved closer to examine it. There was an ovoid bloodstain.

"A fingerprint?" Louise asked aloud.

"A fingerprint, I confirmed. More precisely, the index finger of a woman's right hand."

"How can you be so sure?" spat the superintendent.

"Look at the shape of the finger, elongated and slender."

He pulled me aside to bend over and hold out his magnifying glass to check my words.

"This proves nothing. I know men with women's hands."

"A matter of probability. This print is the only clue we have. Unless there's something you're not telling me, Superintendent?"

His jaw dropped in astonishment.

"How dare you, you little impostor!" he growled.

"Gentlemen, temper Louise. Do I need to remind you, once again, that a life is at stake and that Monsieur Prunelé expects us to help him, not engage in pugilistic brawling?"

My daughter was right, as always. In my arrogance, I'd let myself get carried away with poking this obtuse policeman, purely for the pleasure of ridiculing him. A highly unprofessional attitude, I admit. So I immediately apologized to him.

"I accept your apology. However, I would like to remind you that this print has no legal value. It's a clue, nothing more.

"Sure, but it's a starting point. Ask your men to concentrate on finding traces left by women's shoes.

The dubious commissaire looked for approval from Monsieur Prunelé, who reacted in the usual way when confronted with an unfathomable mystery.

"Do as Mr Lambiet says. That's why I called on him.

"Thank you once again for your confidence in me. Louise and I are going to take a tour of the château while the commissioner's men search the surrounding area.

I must confess: I had no doubt at the time that the case would have anything but a happy conclusion. Indeed, whatever reservations the superintendent had about me, the stars seemed to be aligning for Monsieur Prunelé to find his son alive. As luck would have it, I was present on the very evening of Charles-Antoine's disappearance, and fingerprinting, though rejected outright by most of the world's police forces, had provided us with a lead in less time than it takes to say it.

This was to forget that fate likes to play tricks on the over-confident. As Louise and I examined the footprints leading to the chapel, a ghostly howl reminiscent of the wind in the trees was heard in the distance. I remember that it was followed by a brief scream of terror, then that the superintendent ran down the stairs to the guardhouse and skidded in the mud. Before I could react, there was another sound, like glass breaking, and the châtelain de Trécesson toppled over the rampart.

4

With a long swear, the superintendent stood up. His coat and suit were stained with mud. For my part, sensing that we might be dangerously exposed to the sight of those who had abducted the Prunelé son, I forced Louise to take cover in the cart. In the distance, the squire was calling for help from the moat into which he had fallen. I hurried over to give it to him, while the superintendent swore and took off his jacket to examine his wounds. A nasty gash ran down his forearm, but it looked less serious than spectacular. Using his belt, he made a tourniquet which he tightened over the wound before using his jacket to mop up the blood.

"Fichue pour fichue...," he grumbled.

Monsieur Prunelé saw me happily approaching. I noticed from his uncoordinated movements that he obviously didn't know how to swim. Luckily, I could. So I took off my jacket and dived in without hesitation. As I surfaced, I realized that if someone had told me an hour earlier that I'd end up in the icy waters of a moat, I'd have laughed in their face.

"It's all right, Monsieur Prunelé, I'm here," I said in my most detached tone. "Put your arm around my neck, and I'll do the same under your armpits."

Her water-soaked velvet bathrobe weighed a ton. For a moment, I considered asking him to get rid of it, but then changed my mind. A squire was not expected to strip.

Ignoring my cautious advice, Louise came to my assistance and together we hoisted Monsieur Prunelé onto the bank, where he slumped over, out of breath.

"Thank you," he gasped. "Thank you very much. I'll double your pay."

"That's very generous of you, but I'd prefer it if we stuck to what was agreed. Otherwise, I'd feel like I was taking advantage of the situation."

"My father is very principled," confirmed Louise. "You can't change his mind."

"Very well, then. I won't insist, then."

Out of the corner of my eye, I saw Daniel rushing towards us. A blanket for his horses hung from his arm. He wrapped it around his boss, who was shivering all over.

"Follow me, sir. I'll take you back to your room. You need to warm up."

"Thanks, Daniel. But I still have a few things to do before I can enjoy the fire."

"Could you tell us what happened?"

"Certainly. The superintendent and I were looking in this direction (he pointed to the chapel entrance), when the White Lady appeared. She seemed to be watching us. I'm used to this kind of phenomenon myself, but the superintendent was very impressed by the apparition and stumbled backwards. Unfortunately, I was behind him. As a result, I toppled over the rampart and into the pond."

"You've been lucky," Louise remarked.

"Indeed, mademoiselle. For the same price, I could break every bone in my body."

"You said the White Lady was near the chapel," I cut him off.

"Exactly. Do you think it means anything?"

"I don't know, sir. Did you hear the noise when you fell?"

"You know, Mr Lambiet, when you fall twenty meters, you don't pay much attention to the rest..."

"It looked like broken glass," commented Louise. "But all the windows look intact."

"Do you think this has something to do with my son's disappearance?

"I've got a hunch that this could be the case, indeed," I say, gazing up at Château de Trécesson. I need to check something out. Daniel, please come with me. Louise, take care of Monsieur Prunelé.

"But..."

"Don't argue. The troubles we face can be deadly."

"Very well," sighed my daughter. "Where are you off to?"

"Inspect the chapel."

"Are you going to ask the superintendent to accompany you?"

"That's my intention, yes. He may be rude and arrogant, but his expertise could be useful to us. Coming, Daniel?"

It took us less than a minute to cover the fifty meters to the entrance. Around my head, the air seemed to hum. A curious phenomenon, I hoped, linked to the anguish flooding my veins.

I found the superintendent sitting on the floor, leaning against the wall. His clumsy tourniquet was bleeding again. After tightening it, I helped him to his feet.

"Now we're forced to work together," I said in a low voice, as if I feared the White Lady might hear me.

"Very well," grumbled the policeman. "What do you suggest?"

"To begin our investigations in the chapel."

"What do you hope to find? It hasn't been in use for years."

"We'll see. My instincts tell me to follow this trail. And I like to think my instincts are right."

"What a strange way to conduct an investigation!"

"If you wish, I can provide you with more concrete information," I retorted, my pride stung.

"Please enlighten me, Mr Lambiet. I'm all ears."

"With pleasure. Daniel, correct me if I'm wrong, but the château doors were all locked when the Prunelé son disappeared, weren't they?"

"That's right."

"The attacker(s) could therefore only have come from inside. This leaves us with two possibilities: either they were already in the castle, or they entered through a secret passage."

"Can't we imagine that the servants did it?" objected the superintendent.

"I doubt it very much, sir," said Daniel indignantly. "There aren't many of us, and none of us were missing when Monsieur Prunelé raised the alarm."

"What's more, your men searched the castle from top to bottom. If Charles-Antoine was still there, they would have found him. We can therefore assume that someone smuggled him out of the castle. All that remains is to find out how. My dear Daniel, do you know of any hidden passageways?"

"No, Monsieur. And before you ask, I happened to ask Monsieur Prunelé once. He replied that he knew of no secret entrance to his home. However, Charles-Antoine spent more time than anyone else pacing the corridors and halls of the château. It's not impossible that he eventually discovered one."

We were approaching the entrance to the chapel when something cracked under my foot. I took a step backwards and knelt down to examine the floor. Shards of glass glinted in the moonlight. And there was quite a lot of it, enough to form a large pane of glass.

"Curious," said Daniel, head raised. "But there's no window nearby."

I delicately picked up a shard measuring about five centimetres by three centimetres and twirled it between my fingers, taking care not to cut myself. The lunar reflections on its surface immediately told me that something was wrong.

"Gentlemen, this is no ordinary glass," I announced gravely. "Take a look at this piece. A layer of silver salt is clearly visible. Nothing to do with the amalgam of tin and lead usually found on this type of glass."

"Which means?" the superintendent said impatiently. "Speak up, Lambiet! Don't make us languish needlessly!"

"This debris belongs to a one-way mirror."

"What's the point?" asked Daniel, a little embarrassed to show his ignorance.

"This type of mirror is generally used when you want to see without being seen. However, its effect only works if the observers are behind the layer of silver and, above all, in a room darker than the room being observed."

"What is this thing doing here, in the middle of the castle courtyard?"

"That's the whole point, my good fellow," I said, rising to my feet.

A scenario was slowly taking shape in my head, but it was too early to share it with my companions. Too crazy, perhaps. I needed proof to back up my theory.

My eyes fell on the chapel door, which had obviously been opened not long before. I could tell by the handle, which was shinier than the rest, and by the flattened grass in front of the threshold. As luck would have it, a footprint had become imprinted in the damp earth.

"I suppose you're going to tell us it's a woman's foot," the superintendent chuckled.

"That's right. The measurements match."

"In this case, she must be plump."

"Why do you say that?" asked Daniel.

"The superintendent certainly noticed the depth of the print," I replied. "It's true that it's unusually deep. Perhaps we're dealing with an obese woman, but I'd lean more towards a woman supporting a substantial weight."

"Come on, Lambiet, no woman has the strength to carry a man, if that's what you're thinking," challenged the policeman.

"Maybe she wasn't alone. You should consider broadening your horizons, my dear."

I got up quickly, walked over to the door and turned the knob. To the superintendent's great surprise, it opened without a moment's hesitation.

"It was closed not an hour ago!" he exclaimed. "I'd swear to it!"

"Well, it's open now. And if the traces on the ground are anything to go by, my hypothesis is confirmed. Several people have walked here recently. Look at these marks. The dust hasn't had time to cover them yet."

"They seem to lead to the altar."

"Maybe we should call for reinforcements," suggested Daniel. "The assailants may still be in the chapel."

"I doubt it," I replied confidently. "That said, you're not wrong, it's better to be cautious. We don't know who we're dealing with. Women who can cut off a man's hands and stick them on a dummy are certainly not in their right minds."

"Very well, then. I'll get my men," said the commissioner.

"We look forward to seeing you here."

The policeman turned and headed back towards the drawbridge, while Daniel and I remained alone on the chapel threshold. I took the opportunity to ask him about the missing man.

"What kind of man is the squire's son?"

"The kind to get into trouble, if you ask me," the servant replied bluntly.

"What do you mean by that? Don't be embarrassed, anything you tell me will stay between us, I promise."

"Well, it's rumored that the young master is, shall we say, of the flighty type. And not very elegant with his conquests, if you know what I mean."

"Not very well, no. Please be clearer."

"Rumor has it that he can be violent if a woman doesn't give him complete satisfaction."

"Interesting..."

"Do you think so?"

"Don't get me wrong. It's interesting in the sense that all the elements seem to point in the same direction. A female fingerprint and footprints, violent behavior towards the ladies..."

"I probably shouldn't say this, especially about my master's son, but if half the stories are true, maybe he deserved what's happening to him."

"Don't be so definitive. No one deserves to be treated this way. We have a judicial system to judge this kind of criminal. No one has the right to take its place."

"You're absolutely right, sir. But may I remind you that your system sends mostly wretches to the guillotine? The Prunelé son would never have been tried for his crimes, however heinous they might have been. Rumor has it that the police didn't even bother to listen to the testimony of his victims."

Daniel's answer offended me deeply. I wanted to retort that he was wrong, that justice didn't apply double standards, that criminals were judged equally, but Louise chose the right moment to reappear.

"Monsieur Prunelé has been returned to his apartments," she announced. "Did you find anything?"

I pointed to the footprints in the dust.

"What are we waiting for to follow them?"

"The arrival of reinforcements. The commissioner should be here soon."

"Charles-Antoine may be in danger! Every minute counts!"

"I know, but..."

"I'm going!" she cut in with a definitive tone.

"Louise, come on..."

"You can't stop me, Father. You know that very well."

Lassitude made me sigh. Of course I knew. Nothing could change her mind once she'd made up her mind. There was only one thing left for me to do: take the lead.

"Are you coming, Daniel?"

"I'll wait here for the Commissioner's men. They'll need to know which way you went."

"You're right. See you later."

"Take care of yourself."

I nodded in agreement, then indicated to my daughter to follow me closely into the darkness of the chapel.

The footprints led us to the altar, which had been moved and then replaced. The arched scratches disfiguring the tiles left no room for doubt. However, this feat could not have been accomplished by one person alone. At least two people were needed to move the solid granite table. If not three. Louise and I struggled to lift and move it sufficiently to reveal the trapdoor it concealed.

"So that's where they came in," I soliloquized, as my daughter crouched down to run her fingers along the frame.

"I feel a cold draught. There's a cavity just below."

And without waiting for my permission, she pulled on the latch. The wooden panel swung open with a groan. A ladder descended into the darkness beyond.

"When are you going to stop being so reckless?"

My voice echoed off the walls of the well.

"Don't be a killjoy, Father. Doesn't the thrill of adventure excite you?"

"A man's life is at stake, Louise! This is not entertainment!"

But she wasn't listening to me anymore. I saw her put her foot on the first rung of the ladder and disappear into the shadows of the underground. Having no other choice, I followed her lead.

At the very bottom, a corridor stretched for some five hundred metres. The white circle of the exit was clearly visible on the far wall, despite the vegetation that hid it from view. For the secret passage ended in the middle of the woods, just a few metres from a footpath. It had certainly been designed as an emergency exit to evacuate residents in the event of an attack. Its architect certainly hadn't imagined that it could one day be used to cause harm to these same inhabitants.

Louise tripped over a stump as she left the tunnel and fell headfirst into a puddle, from which a series of footsteps formed a makeshift path between the thickets. Here and there, drops of blood had stained the leaves red, and two parallel grooves clearly indicated that a body had been dragged. I helped Louise to her feet, sponged her face with my sleeve, then led her after me, keeping an eye on the Château de Trécesson beyond the wood, so as not to lose my way.

"Aren't you waiting for reinforcements, Father?" asked Louise with a touch of irony.

I didn't answer. My impetuous spirit had taken over, just as it had in the days when I rubbed shoulders with the dregs of Paname's delinquents in the taverns of Ménil'muche.

5

We'd been walking for about ten minutes when an imposing English-style building emerged from between the trees. The gray of the stonework was now a dirty green, covered in moss. Most of the windows were boarded up, and the porch over the entrance had long since disappeared, eaten away by time and humidity. Weeds grew wildly in what had once been a garden, and what remained of the roof threatened to collapse at the first opportunity. The night wind stirred the leaves on the trees. They seemed to be dancing with joy.

I shivered.

The incongruity of this strange dwelling in Breton territory faded before the urgency of the situation: ritual incantations were rising from the bowels of the house. The woods were completely deserted. Apart from the hymns, only the sound of a carriage in the distance disturbed the eerie serenity of the place.

"What do we do, Father?" asked Louise, which startled me. "We can't afford to wait any longer. Charles-Antoine is certainly in a bad way."

She wasn't wrong. Experience had taught me that religion and disappearance generally didn't mix.

"Wait for me here."

"But..."

"Be nice, Louise, don't argue. I need you to cover my back and wait here for the Commissioner's men. (I reached out to stroke her cheek.) Besides, I'll be able to concentrate on my mission better knowing you're safe."

She lowered her head in resignation.

"You'd better come back to me unscathed. Otherwise you'll have to deal with me!"

"Fear not. I have too much left to accomplish to allow myself to die tonight."

I crossed the filthy lawn towards the nearest window. Some of the rusty nails securing the boards had been ripped out, freeing up the bottom right-hand corner. I turned and, despite the distance, Louise and I exchanged a knowing glance. She then shook her head to let me know that if I wanted to change my mind, there was still time. I declined her offer and rushed through the opening with determination, nearly grazing my arm on a shard of glass.

I landed nimbly on the hall floor. A quick glance told me there was nothing in the room but piles of dead leaves, a surprisingly intact staircase, greasy furniture and silence. Too much silence. It was as if I'd entered a parallel dimension forbidden to noise. Then I realized that the hymns had fallen silent.

The next moment, they resumed with more vigour than before. I gave my heart time to calm down, then turned my attention back to the staircase that led both to the cellar and upstairs. A disintegrated carpet covered the steps. My stomach formed knots at the sight of the muddy footprints that had soiled the fabric. They were all heading for the cellar.

"Old Paul, it's time to live up to your reputation," I mumbled aloud, trying to muster up some courage.

Playing the intrepid was usually no problem, but something about this house made the experience singularly unpleasant. Usually, the houses I visited at night were occupied only by so-called ghosts—often the result of the wind's whims— or rats that had found refuge in the walls. There were no piles of decaying leaves, no broken glass on the floor, no icy wind sweeping across the first floor... and no twilight darkness accompanied by shadows. Shadows everywhere. I could see them moving, amusing themselves, mocking me. For a brief moment, one of them took the form of Baron Samedi, the New Orleans death smuggler. I recognized his skeletal form, top hat, cane and tailcoat.

Definitely, my eyes were playing tricks on me.

I took a long breath to clear the image from my mind, then, my senses alert, I started down the stairs. The ritual chants resounded with ever-increasing vigor. I was undeniably getting closer to their source. So I redoubled my caution.

The floor below was composed as follows: a first room, of reduced size, linked by a corridor to a second room, which I imagined to be more imposing. A door closed the entrance, the frame of which let in a ray of red light that cut out a scarlet rectangle on the wall.

I hesitated for a moment before continuing. After all, what could I do alone against a group of criminals? Yes, the evidence in my possession had convinced me that several women had acted in concert to orchestrate the kidnapping of the Prunelé son.

There was nothing pleasant about the smell in the basement, but even today it's hard for me to define why. But that didn't stop me from stepping up to the door and pushing it open with my fingertips. Luckily, it was unlocked. It opened slightly, allowing me to observe the strangest ritual I've seen to date.

Several columns of light fell from the ceiling, through the perforated floor of the first floor, illuminating a quite singular spectacle. A simulacrum of an altar occupied the far wall. To her right stood a lady dressed in white, whom I at first mistook for a priestess, before realizing that it was merely a mannequin similar to the one the squire had discovered on the ramparts. This time, it was dressed in a wedding gown.

In front of the altar, on which Charles-Antoine Prunelé was tied, lined a score of women, also dressed in white. They were chanting in chorus a pagan song to the glory of the White Lady, a song I couldn't possibly transcribe here. Nevertheless, I understood from the chorus that they were part of the cult formed by the young women of the region, who gathered once a year to kiss the dress of the accursed bride. I also understood that the Prunelé son had undoubtedly mistreated a number of them, and that they had joined forces to pay him back. With interest.

A noise echoed behind my back. I gasped and held my breath as several people burst into the cellar. A glint of light sparkled off the Lebel rifle held by the leading man. I closed my eyes, fearing the detonation. Then I realized it was the superintendent.

"What took you so long," I growled.

"Your daughter told us where to find you," replied the policeman, ignoring my remark. "What's the status of the situation?"

"The Prunelé son is on the other side of this door, tied to a table. I can't say for sure if he's still alive. I counted about twenty women in the room."

"Are you sure?"

"Just about."

The superintendent grumbled into his moustache.

"Very well, then. I'll settle for that. Gentlemen, with me!"

He kicked in the door, which burst open; the hymns ceased; red light filled the room; the women howled. As if in response, the Lebel spat fire three times.

PAN! PAN! PAN!

Two impacts perforated their targets, who collapsed with a groan, while the last bullet disintegrated the bride's straw head. The pungent smell of gunpowder stung my nostrils.

"Everybody back!" shouted the superintendent over the din. "Against the wall!"

For a few moments, several women, probably the ringleaders, opened their mouths to shout insanities, but they were quickly subdued. Calm returned. It was all over.

I too rushed into the room, towards the altar, where Charles-Antoine lay on his back. His dead eyes stared uselessly at the ceiling. His shirt had been cut away with a knife, and a gaping wound pierced his chest at heart level, which had been ruthlessly extracted and laid at the feet of the faceless bride. We were too late.

6

"When did you understand, Father?"

I tore myself away from the spectacle of nature awakening at dawn to turn my head towards Louise, seated opposite me on the other seat of the carriage that was taking us back to the inn. It occurred to me that none of the policemen, probably overcome with emotion, had thought to ask me.

"When did you get to the bottom of it?" she insisted. "I bet it was the print on the mannequin that tipped you off."

"Not only that. I became suspicious when Daniel claimed that Charles-Antoine had spent more time walking the castle corridors than anyone else. I wondered, if he had indeed discovered a secret passage, what he would have done with it and who he would have told. Given what we were told afterwards about the character, his idleness and his propensity to multiply his conquests, the answer seemed obvious to me: he had used it to introduce women, discreetly."

"Why only women? Why not friends or casual acquaintances?"

"Because a man in his position likes to impress his guests, and the grandeur of his home can only be fully admired via the main entrance. He would never let his friends through the underground. The only people he had any interest in letting in there were his one-night stands, titillated by the thrill of danger and the forbidden."

"I see. So that's where the female laughter Monsieur Prunelé said he regularly heard at night came from."

"That's what I concluded."

"You impress me, Father."

"You're welcome, Louise. I just happen to have a great deal of experience of human behavior," I replied wistfully, letting my gaze slide back to the horizon.

I thought back to Monsieur Prunelé and the way this strict-looking man had burst into tears when told of his son's death. Would I have behaved in the same way in similar circumstances? I doubted it, but could you really anticipate his reaction to the death of someone close to you?

"And what about the appearance of the White Lady? How did you find out about it?

"Remember the shattered two-way mirror? The White Lady's worshippers simply used candles and a clever play of reflections to make it appear as if her ghost had appeared, before escaping via the chapel basement. However, in their haste, they broke the mirror, which explains the clatter of glass we heard.

"I see (she paused). What do you think will happen to these women?"

I waited a few seconds before answering. In the distance, a hawk watched the world with a superior air, a haughty attitude that reminded me of my friend Edmond De Lestre, inspector with the Paris police. A man of great kindness, which he was careful to conceal beneath his execrable demeanor—in his profession, philanthropy was rather frowned upon.

I smile sadly.

"I'm guessing the cheerleaders are ready for the guillotine. Kidnapping, torture and premeditated murder are guaranteed capital punishment."

"The death penalty should already have been abolished," Louise said imperiously.

I sighed as I realized that the subject, which had deeply divided French society the previous year—the Keeper of the Seals in the Clemenceau government had seen his bill to abolish the death penalty postponed in December 1908—was about to come up again.

"You know what I think, Louise. We'll never agree on this. Prison is meant to give criminals a chance to atone for their sins before reintegrating into society. Unfortunately, not everyone is recoverable or excusable. They deserve to die."

"What you're defending, Father, is the law of retaliation, nothing more, nothing less: an eye for an eye, a tooth for a tooth! There's nothing civilized about that. If the greatness of a nation is measured by the way it treats its criminals, then ours is in a sorry state!"

"This way of doing things is there to protect you! How would you like to live in the bosom of a man who has murdered children in the past? Or slaughtered women in cold blood? I don't think I would.

"Maybe, but what about miscarriages of justice? Unjustly accused innocents?"

"Our justice system isn't perfect, I'm the first to witness it, but I believe it's the price we have to pay to live in safety. And you'll never convince me otherwise."

"I don't understand how you, who are so progressive when it comes to scientific techniques, can be so retrograde on this issue."

Here we go again. Like every time we broached the subject, we both stuck to our guns, knowing that we had no chance of changing each other's minds. However, I didn't blame Louise for being idealistic. She hadn't witnessed, as I had, the horrors of which human beings are capable. Some men were advancing like masked demons within our society, and those had to be eliminated. At least, that was my opinion, motivated by years of experience and the fear of losing what was dearest to me, Louise in particular. In a way, I envied her innocence. I realized that my various adventures had perverted my optimism. From then on, it was up to me to ensure that our future investigations did not do the same to my daughter.

The facts

Le Lycée armoricain, 1824 edition (©Bibliothèque nationale de France)

The first version of the story of La Mariée de Trécesson was published in 1824, in the Nantes-based Romantic magazine *Le Lycée Armoricain*. Its author, who signed the story under the pseudonym A., claims to have collected it from the château's janitor. The text is presented as a historical fact that took place a few years before the French Revolution.

Nous avons de M. Ogée :

1.° Une carte du comté Nantais , levée en 1768 et dédiée au duc d'Aiguillon ;

2.° Une carte géographique de la Bretagne , levée par ordre des États de cette province , avec approbation du conseil du roi : cette carte , en quatre feuilles , grand papier , a été contrefaite par les Anglais ; on en trouva plusieurs exemplaires à Quiberon , lorsqu'ils y firent une descente , en 1795 ;

3.° Une carte de la même province , réduite en une feuille ;

4.° Une carte itinéraire ;

5.° Un atlas itinéraire de Bretagne , contenant les cartes particulières de tous les grands chemins de cette province , avec tous les objets remarquables , qui se trouvent à une demi-lieue , à droite et à gauche , dédié à nos seigneurs des États de Bretagne : Paris, Merlin, 1769 ; in-4.° oblong ;

6.° Dictionnaire historique et géographique de la province de Bretagne , dédié à la nation bretonne , Nantes , chez Vatar. — 1778 , 1780 ; 4 vol. in-4.°

J. LE BOYER.

TRÉCESSON.

Le château de Trécesson , situé dans la commune de Compeneac , à deux lieues de Ploërmel , est digne de fixer les regards et l'attention des antiquaires. Ses tours , son pont-levis et ses fossés , ses vieilles murailles couronnées de créneaux et de machicoulis , reportent l'imagination aux siècles de la féodalité et de la chevalerie. Cependant , cet antique manoir est moins célèbre aujourd'hui par les tournois et les faits d'armes dont, sans doute , il a été le théâtre , que par le souvenir d'un événement extraordinaire dont la tradition subsiste encore parmi les habitans du pays. Le voici tel qu'un vieux concierge me l'a raconté.

« Ce château , il y a soixante ou quatre-vingts ans , était habité par M. de Trécesson , si connu par son attachement pour sa nourrice , et dont vous avez vu

Page 5 of the Lycée armoricain, *1824 edition, including the beginning of the story*
(©Bibliothèque nationale de France)

According to this anonymous account, the lord of Trécesson was a benevolent man. There was, however, one exception to his kindness when it came to hunting, for which he was harsh and inflexible. One night, a poacher ambushed in the château grounds heard a noise that put him on his guard. He hurriedly threw down his rifle and climbed a tree. Just then, he spotted a carriage with two black horses, followed by several servants carrying torches. The procession stopped and some men began digging a grave. Two gentlemen got out of the carriage, then violently pulled down a young woman dressed in a white silk dress, her head crowned with flowers and carrying a bouquet on her bosom. Her eyes full of tears and fear, she pleaded with them, calling them "brothers".

"What do you want from me," she said, "and why have you brought me here?"

"You'll know, Madame."

"The loneliness and darkness of these places frighten me."

"We're there with you."

"Why this gloomy device? My brothers, my friends, do me no harm."

"Your brothers, no. Madame, we are no longer brothers; you have ceased to belong to a family you dishonor."

"In God's name, don't kill me. Must I die so young! At the moment of reaching happiness, ah! How awful death is!"

"But you've got to make up your mind, Madame; crying is useless, your time has come: all that's left for you to do is die."

"Stop, please stop; one moment, just one moment to prepare myself!"

"There's no time: stop complaining, we don't have the time to listen to it."

Anonymous (1824) op. cit. p. 7

After this last exchange, she was thrown into the pit and covered with earth. The carriage and its servants drove off, and silence returned to the château grounds. The poacher, still frightened by the scene he had just witnessed, didn't dare rescue the young woman. He hurried home and told his wife of his terrible adventure, who reproached him for his cowardice. The couple then decided to alert the lord of Trécesson, who rushed to the scene to rescue the young woman. The castle staff dug her up and, for a brief moment, the hope of saving her ran through the audience. But she heaved a long sigh and died instantly.

"Moved by her misfortune and her beauty, Monsieur de Trécesson brought tears to this young stranger's eyes, and, unable to show any other interest in her fate, he had her honored with a pomp worthy of the rank she seemed to have occupied in the world. Having discharged this first duty, he did his utmost to fulfill a second, which seemed to him just as sacred, and spared neither care nor steps to discover the murderers, in order to avenge the victim; but all his researches were useless, neither the name of this young lady who had disappeared in such a strange manner nor the cause of the cruel fate she had been made to suffer could be known, and, to this day, this extraordinary event has remained shrouded in impenetrable darkness."

Anonymous (1824) op. cit. p. 9

Subsequently, Monsieur de Trécesson decorated the château chapel with the bride's wedding dress, bouquet and crown of flowers. They remained on display until the French Revolution. However, on page 12 of his memoirs *Archives de la famille Maufras du Chatellier,* Armand du Chatellier attests to the presence of the dress in 1881.

Château de Trécesson, before 1914 (postcard)

Since then, the White Lady has been said to appear on the roofs of Trécesson castle on the evenings of the full moon.

More generally, the name "White Lady" is given to myths or apparitions of various kinds. They may be supernatural entities playing the roles of fairies, witches, night washerwomen or harbingers of impending death, or the ghosts of deceased women haunting castles or ghostly hitchhikers.

Whatever their form, white lady legends can be found all over Europe and North America.

The Josh Maddux file

Mike, in his forties, with greying temples, was reading his newspaper without really paying attention. The words flashed before his eyes, but their meaning stubbornly remained obscure. War in the Middle East, bombings, robberies—he didn't care. Not that he was insensitive to the world's misfortunes, only that another subject monopolized his attention. As proof, his gaze, unable to remain riveted on the articles in the *Pikes Peak Courier* for more than three seconds, shifted from the newspaper to the antique clock hanging on the wall with increasing nervousness as the hands progressed across the dial.

4:48pm, already...

His wife—or rather ex-wife, but he'd never been able to think of her as such—was just as stressed as he was, constantly moving from one room to another in the cottage, dusting and moving the same objects over and over again without even realizing it. Exasperated by this back-and-forth, Mike would have liked to shout at her to stop, to calm down, but he knew perfectly well that this would upset her even more, and the last thing he wanted right now was to provoke yet another argument. Gathering his strength and all the *self-control* he was capable of, he plunged back into his reading.

Fortunately for his nerves, a few minutes later, tired of fussing in vain, Megan came and sat down on the sofa opposite him.

"I can't wait for tonight," she says. "I'm exhausted."

"Cheer up, Meg. Soon we'll have plenty of time to rest."

His eyes drifted to the wall where a yellowed photo of them stood proudly, all smiles, surrounding their daughters Kate and Ruth, as well as their sons Josh and Zachary, aged eight and ten respectively at the time of the snapshot. A picture in your mind. The perfect representation of a close-knit family. But this photograph was all that remained of that blessed time, because in the last five years, their lives had turned into a living hell.

"What time is he due?" asked Mike.

"I don't think he'll be long," said Megan. "Andy's mom said she had an appointment around 5:30 p.m. and would drop him off on the way."

She hesitated a moment before adding:

"Mike?"

"Yes?"

"Don't you think…"

The end of his sentence faded into a sigh. Mike noticed his fingers tightening in his lap.

"Megan," he said softly, folding up his newspaper. "We've talked about this. You know it's the right thing to do. It can't go on like this. You know what he's done. Because of him…"

His ex-wife nodded, her head down. A heavy silence fell between them, a silence that only the diffuse ticking of the wall clock dared to disturb.

At 5:03 p.m., an engine sounded in the driveway. Megan rushed to the window.

"It's them!" she shouted feverishly. "It's them! It's them!"

Mike rose to join her and laid a reassuring hand on her shoulder.

"Calm down, act as if nothing's happened and everything will be fine. I promise you everything will be fine."

A series of knocks against the wooden door sounded in the cottage and Megan moved towards it to open it, forcing herself to remain calm. A smiling lady stood on the stoop. In her wake followed limply a young man of eighteen, dragging his backpack as if it were the heaviest object in the world. He was exaggeratedly unkempt, his long hair cascading to his shoulders, while the guitar protruding from his back gleamed in the sunlight. Moreover, his dirty, mismatched clothes gave him the air of an alcoholic tramp. The teenager stared at his feet, not deigning to glance at anyone.

"Hello Caitlin, how are you?" asked Megan in a cheerful tone that betrayed nothing of her inner turmoil.

"Very well, thank you. And yourself?"

"Very well too. Come in for a moment," she added, stepping aside to clear the way.

"No thanks, we're in a bit of a hurry," replied the lady, pointing to the car where her son Andy was waiting. "We'll take advantage of his father's late return to spend some time together. I'd like to introduce him to cooking, and we've got our first workshop in less than half an hour."

"What a great idea!" exclaimed Megan, clearly sincere.

"Yes, I'm very lucky to get along so well with my son. Like you, you're lucky to get along so well with Mike."

"It's true. So many divorced couples end up hating each other. I'm not saying it's been easy these past few years, but we've managed pretty well, especially after…"

Again, the words choked in his throat. An angel passed. To put an end to the turmoil clouding the atmosphere, Caitlin glanced at the teenager waiting nonchalantly, staring at the ground.

"Well, Josh, aren't you coming in?"

Without a word, the young man made his way between the two women and slipped inside the house without bothering to greet his mother. He unceremoniously unloaded his backpack behind the front door, then made his way to the armchair by the fireplace, which hadn't been used in years, where he dropped down before plunging into the contemplation of his telephone screen, ignoring his father who had risen to greet him.

"What a strange place," said Andy's mother, scanning the outside of the house with her eyes. "Is this yours?"

"No, this cottage belongs to Chuck. Chuck Murphy," Megan clarified. "His brother lived there for a few years before moving out, but since Chuck doesn't use it, we've converted it into a second home. We spend weekends there from time to time, to recharge our batteries as a family, in the middle of the woods."

"Well, it's pretty *cosy*," admitted Caitlin, consulting her watch. "I'd almost be jealous. Unfortunately, I have to go. The kitchen won't wait, you know how it is."

The two women burst out laughing, and Caitlin promptly returned to her car, having made Megan promise to attend a girls' night out in the next few weeks. The latter accepted willingly, then waited until the sound of the Chevrolet Malibu's engine had died down before closing the door.

Mike put his hand on his shoulder again.

"You've done very well. You're going to be fine."

The end of his sentence was covered by the suave notes of *There Is A Light That Never Goes Out*, a song by The Smiths that Mike had listened to a lot in his youth and whose volume Josh had just turned up while flipping on MTV. *Ironic*, Mike thought. *Yours is about to fade.*

He returned to his armchair and picked up his newspaper, which he apparently still had no intention of reading. In the meantime, Josh had abandoned his sneakers in the middle of the living room and settled into an awkward position on the sofa. He reached for the remote control and switched on the antediluvian CRT TV that sat on a pedestal table in the corner of the room, then zapped from one channel to another without taking the time to watch the programs he was hovering over.

"How did it go at Andy's?" asked Mike.

In response, the teenager turned the volume up a notch.

"Your mother made *spare ribs*. For you to enjoy."

He stuck two fingers in his mouth and let out a loud "beuuuaark" before bursting into a sonorous laugh. Then he got up, left the living room and climbed the stairs four at a time to his bedroom upstairs.

"Good riddance," muttered Mike. "At least, as long as he's in front of his computer, he'll leave us alone."

Sighing in exasperation, he folded up his copy of the *Pikes Peak Courier*, then retrieved the remote control his son had so thoughtlessly dropped on the floor. He scrolled through the channels until he found CBS and settled down, hoping to relax for a minute.

Again, heavy footsteps were heard on the stairs, heralding Josh's arrival in the living room. Fury was written all over his face.

"Who gave you permission to change the channel? Didn't you notice I was watching?"

"I thought you were in your room," her father retorted limply.

"Well, you made a mistake! You're such an idiot!"

Mike sighed, placed the remote control on the armchair cushion and headed for the kitchen where his wife was busy. As he passed his son, he refrained from giving him the slap of the century: the little bastard mustn't suspect a thing, otherwise his plan would fall apart. So he simply took his usual place at the nicely laid table.

The loud sound of a music channel exploded once again in the garden shed. Megan, who was about to put the dish in the oven, interrupted herself to violently slam the door separating the *living room* from the kitchen. Josh was quick to react.

"Oh! A little less noise, dammit! I can't hear a thing!"

Megan paid no attention to her son's ranting and sat down opposite her ex-husband.

"And what about you? You still let yourself be insulted without reacting?"

"As if I care," Mike retorted, a grim expression on his face. "You know better than to rush him before tonight. Everything would fall apart if he decided to run away again."

"He'll have driven me mad by then," lamented Megan, on the verge of a nervous breakdown.

"Patience, my dear, patience..."

The man gently grasped his former wife's hand and touched it lovingly. She returned the caress as their eyes met. True, they were divorced, but love had never been the problem between them.

"Five years. It's been five years! I can't take it anymore... Suppose our plan fails."

"Don't worry, everything's going to be fine. There's no reason for it to fail."

"I know, I know, I know. I know," sighed Megan. It's just..."

Mike stood up to nibble her ear. This always amused him, and this time was no exception. Megan smiled broadly at him, a smile immediately interrupted by Josh's sudden burst into the kitchen.

"I see we're having fun around here. And the food isn't ready yet?! Move your asses, damn it!"

Then he turned on his heels, muttering bird names. Mike watched him angrily walk away.

"I'm going to check one last time that everything's ready," he announced coldly to his wife.

"All right, then. Don't be too long."

He responded with an affectionate smile and left the kitchen.

Josh hadn't always been like this. When he was younger, he was an adorable child who made his parents proud. But by his thirteenth year, something had gone wrong and the charming young man had spiraled out of control. Ignoring the values and rules his parents were trying to instill in him, he gradually imposed his will on the whole household, turning their glittering family life into an abominable ordeal.

He had been expelled from three successive schools before taking up drinking, smoking and drugs. To top it all off, he was also guilty of several thefts. His parents also suspected him of occasional *drug dealing*, but no concrete evidence had ever been found to support this theory. They couldn't understand how it had come to this. Josh had never lacked for anything, especially affection. The psychologists kept telling them, like a mantra: "Be patient with him, it's just adolescence. He doesn't feel good about himself and is probably suffering as much as you are."

But no matter how many times the specialists told them, five years was a long time. An awfully long time. Zachary, the eldest of the siblings, was fed up with his little brother's harassment and took his own life. And now Mike and Megan feared the same thing might happen to their daughter Kate.

"So, they're coming, the damn *ribs*?" shouted Josh from the living room. "Are you trying to starve me or something?"

"Just a minute, darling, I'm about to take the dish out of the oven."

The teenager's reply was inaudible, but Megan guessed it must not have been very pleasant to hear. This was the moment Mike chose to reappear, after almost thirty minutes' absence.

"What took you so long?" whispered Megan, trying not to be overheard by her son.

"Sorry, I really double-checked every detail. It's all ready to go."

He handed her a bottle.

"It's the most powerful I could find."

Megan took the bottle and examined it for a long time, looking vaguely hesitant. A shout came from the *living room.*

"Damn it, Mom, it's been five minutes!"

"Coming, coming! It's very hot, you know!"

She hastily removed the hash from the oven and placed it on the table.

"Will you eat with us?"

"What's next? Take my plate to my room! I've got porn to finish."

With that, Josh stood up. Hearing him stomp back up the stairs, his mother hurriedly filled a plate and poured in the vial of sleeping powder. After spreading it evenly over the ribs, she handed it to her husband.

"Here, carry it for her. I can't."

Without seeking to reply, or even to argue, Mike complied. He knew what state his ex-wife was in, so he didn't blame her: it was hard enough for him. Before leaving the kitchen, he gave her one last look; she nodded briefly with her chin.

Arriving in front of Josh's room, Mike gazed longingly at the door covered with various stickers. He felt he had to hurry or risk his courage melting like snow in the sun.

He jerked the door open.

"Couldn't you knock before coming in?" his son belched.

"Your plate," he retorted nonchalantly, avoiding eye contact.

Josh grabbed the *ribs* and returned to his computer screen, where a woman was clearly enjoying herself with three men.

"I'll put it in front of the door when I'm done. I don't want you setting foot in here again. This is MY room."

"As you wish."

Mike closed the door and joined Megan, who was pacing back and forth.

They ate in silence, waiting an hour for the product to take effect.

When the clock struck 8 p.m., the couple made their way to the sticker-covered door, hand in hand. Megan, tense, unintentionally dug her nails into her ex-husband's knuckles, but he was far too focused to notice. At the sight of the empty plate on the floor, they froze.

"It's still possible to stop everything," said Mike.

"No, we're going all the way. It's him or us."

Megan stepped forward and opened the bedroom door wide. Josh was asleep, his head resting on his arm in front of his computer screen, which was still on. A slight trickle of drool dripped from his half-open mouth. Megan approached silently and stroked his hair, a sad smile tugging at the corner of her lips. Asleep, he looked like an angel.

This outburst of affection was stopped short by the memory of everything he had put them through.

"It worked," she said, turning to her husband, her gaze once again cold and determined.

"Let's not dawdle. We've got to get him up to the attic before he wakes up."

He took his son under the arms while Megan took care of his feet, then they set about getting him out into the hallway. Josh's head hung pitifully backwards, his mouth wide open.

The climb up the stairs to the attic proved more arduous than they had imagined. As they neared the top, Megan missed a step and kept her balance as best she could. One of Josh's legs slipped out of his hand and hit the banister hard. He groaned in his sleep, which made Mike blanch.

"Be more careful," he said nervously to his wife. "The sleeping pill is powerful, but still..."

Megan stammered a few words of apology and then, as best she could, resumed her walk backwards. In her pocket, a flashlight compressed her left buttock.

The attic was littered with empty crates, miscellaneous objects and dead leaves that had accumulated over the years due to a gap in the window. At the other end of the room, a gaping hole cut into the chimney wall.

The duo deposited Josh on a musty mattress, where Mike hurriedly tied him up. He wrapped adhesive tape around his hands, feet and legs, not skimping on quantity. His son now looked like a parcel post. Megan sighed.

"Do you realize what we're doing?"

"I know, but we've discussed it dozens of times and you agreed it was our only option."

"I still am, but if we get caught…"

"I'm telling you for the hundredth time, it won't happen. In three or four days, I'll report him missing, on the pretext that he used to disappear for several days at a time, which didn't worry us. Given his background and previous runaways, the case will eventually be closed."

"But the police will be snooping! They'll see that part of the chimney has been redone!"

"Come on, come on. They already know us. The last few times, they didn't even bother to come, remember? They knew it was pointless since Josh came back every time anyway. Besides, I'm sure no one will think of coming here to look. And even if they did get up to the attic and noticed that the bricks had recently been repointed, do you really think they'd break the wall to see what's behind it? All I'll have to do is claim water infiltration and I'll be good to go. If you behave as usual, everything will be fine."

Concluding his tirade, he took his ex-wife in his arms and kissed her tenderly on the forehead as he had done so many times before.

"Well, I don't want to rush you, but we've got a job to finish."

He took a sock rolled into a ball and stuffed it into his son's mouth, covering it with adhesive tape before hoisting him onto his shoulder and leading him to the hole he'd patiently dug in the chimney wall. A noise was heard as he swung him headfirst into the opening. Megan then turned on the flashlight she'd brought with her to illuminate the interior of the fireplace. Josh was lying in a gray, pasty liquid.

"I hope your concrete is really fast-setting."

"It'll only take about thirty minutes," says Mike. "Hand me the bricks and I'll fill in the damn hole."

*

When Josh came to his senses, he was surprised at first not to be able to open his mouth, then to find that his right eye remained hopelessly blind. His jaw ached. He tried to scream, but only a hoarse sound emerged from his throat. Then it dawned on him: half his body had been fused with concrete, which covered his entire right leg, his counterpart arm and much of his face. Breathing had become difficult, and it got even worse as panic took hold of him. A trickle of snot began to flow, clogging his nostrils. At the same time, his one good eye widened in terror as he saw his father place a brick on top of the hole that connected this enclosed space to the rest of the attic. The hole was now the size of a shoebox, and not a size 44, more like a 36. The only thing he could still see intermittently was his father's face against the light.

The teenager's underpants became soaked with urine. He ached all over, would have liked to scream, to shout tons of apologies, to promise he'd go back to being the good boy they'd loved so much, but the action of the concrete combined with the sock prevented him from doing so.

Lord, don't let them lock me in there! I beg you, please! Daddy! Daddy! Mommy! Mommy! I love you guys!

The rectangle of light gradually narrowed. The minced meat stirred in Josh's belly, began to flow back down his esophagus, but stalled at his Adam's apple. His cheeks and throat began to swell, distending until they reached an intolerable threshold of pain. Tears streamed down her cheek, blurring her vision and irritating her eye.

Then darkness descended upon him. And in silence, choking, whimpering, begging for mercy, he began his slow agony…

The facts

Before moving on to the true story, I must confess to having taken a great many liberties for the purposes of this horrific short story, to the point of changing Josh Maddux's personality completely, since this young man was never described by those closest to him as a troubled teenager. It's also worth exonerating his parents, who were never even remotely suspected in this sad affair. There is no evidence to suggest that they were, and their criminal involvement in my story is a complete fabrication.

Forget what you've just read, because here are the facts.

In 2008, Joshua Vernon Maddux, aka "Josh", lives in Woodland Park, a small town of around 7,900 people[8], nestled amidst the natural beauty of the Pike National Forest in Teller County, Colorado. Josh is 1.80 m tall, weighs 70 kg and apparently possesses a mind as free as it is creative. He has a carefree attitude to life, wears his hair long, loves music and spends much of his free time writing. At school, he is a bright, well-liked and well-known pupil. His mother and father are divorced; Josh lives with his father Mike and his two sisters, Kate and Ruth.

On May 8, 2008, he left the house, telling his sister Kate that he was going out for a walk. He enjoys the outdoors and often goes hiking alone, so no one worries when he doesn't come back, even if later that evening his family is surprised when he doesn't return. Josh has always been a free spirit, so there's no need to worry.

However, as the days passed and Josh didn't return, his father decided on May 13 to call the police to report the disappearance: "I got up one morning," he declared, "and Josh was there, and then he never came home. The next day, he still hadn't come home. I called his friends, but nobody had seen him. Nobody knows where he is.

---

8. In 2020.

Mystery of chimney death deepens
Coroner acknowledges troubling questions remain

By Bill Vogrin
billvogrin@yourpeaknews.com

Troubling questions still surround the shocking death of 18-year-old Josh Maddux, whose mummified corpse was discovered Aug. 7 deep in the chimney of a vacant cabin being demolished by workers.

Maddux had walked away from his Woodland Park home on May 8, 2008, and vanished.

On Monday, Sept. 28, Teller County Coroner Al Born ruled Maddux's death an accident, saying the 6-foot-tall, 150-pound teen had slid down the chimney "Santa Claus-style."

Four days later, Born reopened his investigation after the cabin owner, Colorado Springs builder Chuck Murphy, came forward with details about the chimney that he says makes the accidental death theory impossible.

Born's re-examination also followed calls to his office from tipsters offering the names of people who allegedly had bragged about killing Maddux in the cabin.

After a two-hour meeting on Friday, Born and Murphy emerged with vastly different opinions of the case, agreeing only that no one will probably ever know exactly why Maddux died or how he ended up in the chimney.

Murphy remains convinced Maddux was murdered, either forced up the chimney alive, trapped there and left to die or he was killed in the cabin and his remains forced through the damper and into the smoke chamber just above the firebox.

Murphy hasn't wavered from his immediate opinion after his workers made the chilling discovery Aug. 7 as they used an excavator to peel open the chimney, one of two in the century-old cabin.

Murphy, 80, said it was impossible for anyone to slide down the chimney because a "heavy steel mesh grate" was installed near the top of the chimney when it was built 25 years ago as part of addition to the original cabin, which was part of "Big Bert" Bergstrom's notorious Thunderhead dining, drinking and gambling casino that operated from the 1930s-50s along Rampart Range Road on Woodland Park's north side.

"It was a heavy wire grate, a wire mesh, installed across the chimney about one row of bricks from the top," Murphy said. "We didn't want trouble with raccoons and things getting in the chimney."

Murphy is convinced the mesh remained intact and prevented anyone from sliding down the chimney. But investigators didn't see it when they responded to the call of the body because his crew had already tossed it in a truck.

"They were just gathering up all the steel, angle iron and things as part of the demolition," Murphy said. "They had no idea the mesh had any significance."

But there are even more disturbing questions, Murphy said, that debunk the chimney theory.

The mystery deepened further when investigators found most of Maddux's clothing next to the hearth.

"He was mostly naked inside the chimney," Murphy said. "He was only wearing his thermal shirt. No pants. No shoes or socks."

Murphy said it's ridiculous to think the teen stripped down to just his shirt, climbed up on the roof, up on the chimney and slid down, knowing he'd be trapped.

He said Maddux knew he'd be trapped because there was a steel "Heatilator" insert in the fireplace. And a large, heavy wooden breakfast bar had been ripped from a wall and dragged from the kitchen and placed across the front of the fireplace, blocking it.

"It's a real conundrum," Murphy said. "A

See "Maddux" on page 14

Iconic American Eagle | GMF delinquent

Pikes Peak Courier article, October 7, 2015 (©Pikes Peak Newspapers, Inc.)

The search spreads through the neighborhood, then into the national park, as days turn into weeks and weeks into months, with no clues to his disappearance ever being discovered. Hopes of finding Josh begin to fade, and his sister Kate says she hopes he's simply left town to play music or start a new, different life, and remains optimistic.

In an online article, she writes about her brother's disappearance:

"I expect Josh to be home at any moment with a wife and young children so they can meet their grandparents and two aunts. Josh has always been known for his musical and literary talent, so perhaps we'll find him playing music with a touring band, or we'll catch him writing best-selling novels under a pseudonym so he can maintain his favorite hermit lifestyle in the woods."

MISSING SINCE:	May 08, 2008		
LAST SEEN:	Woodland Park, Colorado		
HEIGHT:	72.0 in	**SEX:**	Male
WEIGHT:	150.0 lbs	**EYES:**	Brown
		HAIR:	Blond/Strawberry
SCARS/MARKS:	SC L FARM;SC R FARM; SC L WRST; MOLE CHIN; MOLE BACK		
AMPUTATIONS:	MISS FGR		

Wanted by Josh (©NamUs)

They have no reason to believe that Josh was involved in any trouble, and he had not expressed any concerns about his mental health to them, although two years before his disappearance, on June 1, 2006, a week before his high school graduation, Josh's older brother Zachary committed suicide.

Photos by Josh (©Handout, via dailymail.co.uk)

His father later spoke about his son's tragic death and how it affected Josh:

"I buried my eldest son two years ago, and it was very difficult for Josh. His brother's death pushed him over the edge. It was a big shock for the family and a big shock for Josh. He thought the world of his brother."

Despite this difficult period, the family claims that Josh was well and happy at the time of his disappearance. The police have no reason to suspect any criminal activity, and have placed him on the missing persons list. The search continues, while the case remains open. The family moves, but his father, Mike, retains ownership of the family home, in case Josh ever returns.

The story stays that way until 2015, when a local builder named Chuck Murphy makes a dark discovery.

Chuck Murphy, a contractor in nearby Colorado Springs, decides to demolish an old wooden shack. The cabin is located on a plot of land surrounded by tall pine trees and, having been unused for over ten years, has fallen into disrepair over the years. Chuck decided to demolish it to start another real estate project.

Originally purchased in the 1950s, the cabin was once the property of Thunderhead Ranch, an infamous drinking and gambling complex owned by "Big Bert" Bergstroms, a criminal who came from Sweden in 1912 and was involved in both prostitution and alcohol smuggling.

The famous hut (©Rob Carrigan/Pikes Peak Courier)

Chuck Murphy's brother had lived here until 2005, but since his departure, the cabin had become an unattractive, animal-infested storeroom.

While dismantling the fireplace, Chuck makes the gruesome discovery of a young man's body in the fetal position, legs over his head. He calls the police, who arrive with the county coroner, who, with the help of a forensic odontologist, uses dental impressions to positively identify the corpse of Joshua Maddux, less than a mile from his home.

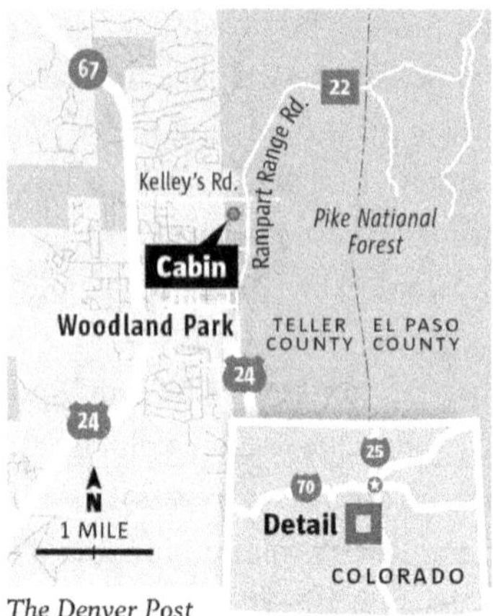

Location map (©The Denver Post)

The Maddux family is stunned when the news of Josh's body is announced. His sister Kate declares:

"This situation makes no sense. We really expected him to be somewhere else in the world, when in fact he was very close to us. The only thing we can imagine is that he was an 18-year-old kid, exploring a cabin—it had already been abandoned for a long time—and a horrible accident happened."

Teller County Coroner Al Born performs an autopsy and finds no evidence of drugs in Josh's system. Speaking to the press, he states:

"The hard tissue showed no signs of trauma. There were no broken bones, no knife marks. There were no bullet holes. So far, there are no answers to a number of things. It's very confusing."

The cabin is on Meadowlark Lane, just two blocks from the Maddux family home, but the search had overlooked this building. There was no sign of life in the vicinity, and it hadn't attracted much attention due to its banality. Chuck Murphy, the shack's owner, rarely visited, but hadn't noticed anything unusual. The police suggested that, in the absence of adjacent houses, if Josh had called for help, no one would have been able to hear him anyway.

"It was not an instant death. How Josh died remains shrouded in speculation, but we know he didn't starve to death, as that takes several weeks. Then we have dehydration, which can take just a few days, and the final possibility would be hypothermia, which can take a day or two. But we have no evidence to determine which came first."

Finally, on September 28, 2015, after failing to find a rational cause, Al Born announces an "accidental death". He suggests that Josh descended the chimney and became trapped in the masonry. He concludes that the most likely cause of death is hypothermia, as the temperature at the time of Josh's disappearance reached -6 degrees Celsius at its coldest level in that period.

Joshua Vernon Maddux with his sister Ruth Maddux (©The Denver Post)

Chuck Murphy, however, finds this conclusion far from satisfactory.

Immediately after the announcement, he questioned the coroner's conclusion that it was an accidental death. Born stated that Josh's position in the chimney "appeared to have been a deliberate act to gain access", but Chuck believes that this would, in fact, have been impossible. The chimney was built twenty years earlier and fitted with a steel frame, a large wire mesh suspended from hooks to prevent animals and debris from lodging inside the chimney or entering the cabin itself.

This statement to the contrary was the starting point of a public back-and-forth between the builder and the coroner, with Born replying that the grille could have been rusted or corroded, before adding: "Nobody has seen this wire mesh, we haven't seen it on any of our photos. It may have disappeared."

However, Born admits that during the demolition, all the metal parts were collected and piled into the back of a truck to be sent for scrap, which would explain why the grill was not clearly identified by the coroner, as it was not in the vicinity of the chimney.

Taking Murphy's allegations into account, Born reopened the case three days after his initial conclusion. It's not just the rebar that raises doubts, as there are several other pieces of information that make no sense to Murphy and lead him to doubt the coroner's report. These include the mysterious movement of a large wooden plank that was ripped from a kitchen wall and dragged to block the chimney from inside the cabin. Who took it down, and why?

Josh's body was also found in the fetal position, with his legs above his head. To be in such a position, he would have had to enter the chimney head first, which is quite an unusual way and Born has already stated that he thinks it would have taken two people to position him in this way.

A final mystery remains: when Josh's body was found, he was wearing only a thermal *T-shirt*. His other clothes were found inside the cabin, folded next to the fireplace.

"This question really challenged our brains," admits Al Born. "We found his clothes just outside the fireplace. Josh was wearing only a thermal *T-shirt*. We don't know why he undressed, took off his shoes and socks, and why he went outside, climbed onto the roof and came down the chimney."

Nevertheless, Born concludes: "We have found the most plausible explanation and it will remain an accident. Josh went down the chimney, that's our conclusion".

Murphy, however, remains convinced that Joshua Maddux's death was no accident, especially as several calls were made to both the police and the coroner's office, suggesting leads and naming suspects who bragged about killing Josh, including an unnamed man who had previously spent time in Seattle and Portland prisons for violent criminal behavior.

Nevertheless, modernity and the Internet were to come.

In 2015, on the famous Reddit forum, a message most likely from one of the people who contacted the coroner and suspected the aforementioned man, whose name he reveals, leads to new facts.

An abridged version of the message tells this side of the story:

"I went to high school with a skinny, goofy hippie named Andy, who played guitar in a band. I was never friends with him or anything, but about a year after I graduated, a good friend of mine, Josh, started hanging out with him, then disappeared.

Later, Andy traveled to New Mexico, where he befriended the caregiver of a disabled man and was invited into their apartment. At one point, the caregiver left to take a shower, and when he emerged, his patient had been stabbed to death and Andy was gone. When he was finally arrested, he claimed to have killed a woman in Taos and put her body in a barrel.

The cops had indeed found a woman locked in a barrel in Taos, but already had someone in custody for it and decided to stick with the guy. Years later, I found out that the caregiver had died in a bar fight and that without him, the cops didn't have much evidence, so the case against Andy was also dropped.

Several of us went to the cops and said, "Yo, Josh was last seen with Andy, maybe you should check this out?" Despite our pestering, nothing ever came of it, and by nothing I mean the police didn't even return our calls.

Someone ripped a heavy board off the kitchen wall and leaned it against the chimney. And Josh's belongings were already inside the cabin, which means (a) he'd already broken in and would have had to lock himself out to seek entry through the chimney, and (b) he might have noticed that either the wire mesh or the large plank would have prevented him from entering through the chimney. Or the fact that when he was found, Josh's knees were above his head, whereas it seems to me he should have gone in head first. Or perhaps the fact that Josh was barefoot and naked from the waist down.

This is just my opinion, but it doesn't matter: you don't try to dive headfirst into a chimney through a rusty hole in a metal grate with your dick hanging out.

As far as I know, nobody even bothered to call Andy to ask if he knew anything".

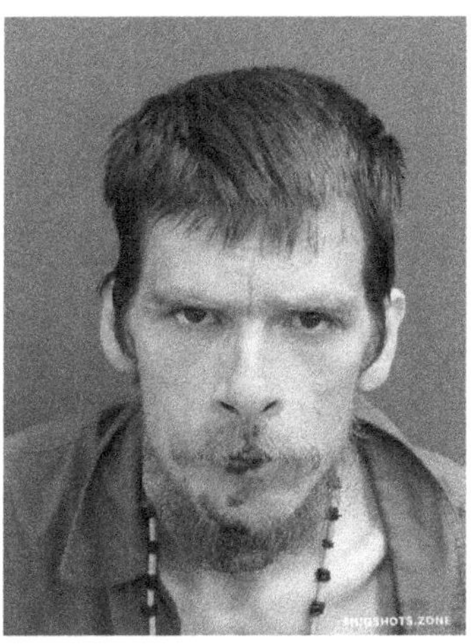

Mugshot of Andrew Richard Newman, dated 2023. (©mugshots.zone)

As it turns out, "Andy" does exist. His full name is Andrew Richard Newman, and he was indeed arrested on suspicion of fatally stabbing a man in New Mexico.

Mugshot of Andrew Richard Newman, dating from 2009.
(©Colorado Springs Police Department)

In high school, he played guitar in a band called The Baumers and was also rather well-known and well-liked. In an article about his arrest for stabbing, there are several comments from users who went to school with him and describe him as "smart". Although he seems to have left the state and traveled nomadically around the country after graduating from high school, he has kept in touch with many of his old friends. It's not hard to believe that Andy and Josh knew each other. They shared common interests and had a fairly similar outlook on life. But in the absence of any official investigation, all this remains conjecture.

Joshua Maddux's case is puzzling for several reasons. It seems safe enough to assume that Chuck Murphy is telling the truth about the metal framework of the chimney. After all, why would he lie about its existence? However, when you start to consider other factors such as the clothes near the chimney and the plank dragged to cover the chimney, the mysteries pile up. It remains to be seen whether the case will ever be reopened, or whether the coroner's findings will remain definitive.

The opinion of 1st Commissioner Maillard of the Brussels Judicial Police - Division in charge of crime against property and people.

Several thoughts come to mind. Of course, once again, I don't have the file documents, and in any case it's always easier to point the finger at what might have gone wrong after the investigation.

What's more, we don't know how much manpower the police had to investigate, or whether Geoffrey's evidence is totally complete, since it would be very surprising if all of it had leaked online.

However, here are a few points to ponder:

1/ Family survey

- It takes a father 5 days to realize that there is a problem with his son. This delay should automatically lead to an inquiry with the family.

- A divorced father whose son committed suicide! At the very least, you need to read the file on the brother's suicide to get an idea. The reason for Joshua's disappearance may be hidden there. Are there any similarities between the two events?

- Why did the first son commit suicide? Is the father responsible, or is he the cause?

- Was Joshua followed by a doctor after his brother's death? If so, please contact this practitioner.

- Did Joshua take any personal belongings with him, and was his room visited? Who are the victim's friends? We need to interview all his contacts, and certainly those who were in contact with him before his disappearance.

- Did Joshua own a mobile phone? If so, a boundary marker is imperative in order to know his last location.

- You need to analyze all the contacts listed on your cell phone and record the last contacts before it disappears.

- A tracking dog should have been called in, especially in places like the one where the missing man lived. In all likelihood, the dog would have led them directly to the cabin where the body was found.

2/ Neighborhood survey

- The search is said to have been carried out in the neighborhood, but the body is found two blocks from the family home. In the event of a disappearance, it is imperative to carry out a thorough neighborhood investigation, check any cameras and contact all nearby residents, whether present or not.

- Direct contact with all these people can be very useful in furthering investigations.

- In 2015, the body was discovered in a house that had been abandoned for 10 years, since 2005. As a reminder, the disappearance dates back to 2008, and no one thought to go and look in this dwelling that had been abandoned for 3 years!

3/ Autopsy

- I think a second autopsy should have been performed, as the situation offers no logical explanation.

- The forensic lab should have raided the site for clues, and I can't believe they didn't.

4/ Cabin owner

- The owner's brother, who lived there until 2005, should have been investigated. Did he still visit the cabin sporadically? Did he have a history? Why does the owner feel that an accidental death is far from satisfactory? His words are not open to question, because he has no interest in lying.

- Does he still come to this cabin, and when was his last visit? Is he aware that a plank has been placed on the mantelpiece?

5/ Body of the deceased

- The position of the body suggests entry through the chimney, but was it ever checked to see if the body passed through?

- The fact that he's naked, apart from a thermal T-shirt, is a real eye-opener. Who's going to venture practically naked down a chimney flue at the risk of serious injury, and headfirst to boot?

- Logic would dictate that we enter the feet first, not the head.

- Assuming this is the case, because the victim is under the influence of drugs or no longer in his right mind, it doesn't explain his outfit and the fact that a board is placed inside to block the chimney from the inside.

- If Joshua got stuck in the chimney flue, he must have tried to free himself. Are there any marks on the walls inside the chimney? Are the bones in his hands damaged from trying to free himself? Surely he didn't die without trying to free himself, or he was already dead when he was placed there?

- What's more, his clothes were found folded inside the cabin next to the fireplace.

- Was any thought given to questioning known sex offenders in the area during the investigation? The young man was found naked for no apparent reason.

All these factors suggest that an accident is unlikely.

6/ Telephone calls to the coroner and the police

- These leads should have been explored further. It is sometimes possible to trace a call to determine who the caller is.

- Why were the suspects targeted by these calls not heard? Did they have an alibi for the day of the disappearance and the days that followed?

- The lead about a man who had been incarcerated in both Seattle and Portland prisons for violent criminal behavior was not pursued. A single inmate who had been in both prisons should be identifiable through some cross-referencing.

- Unfortunately, we had to wait until 2015 to identify it.

7/ Miscellaneous

- Why wasn't Andy Newman's trail followed? His interview is essential to find out whether he knew the victim and where he was in the days following the disappearance.

- The interested party has a serious history that should have been taken into account.

In short, there are many troubling elements in this case, and it's not easy to think on the basis of the fragmentary clues we have. However, it seems that the accident theory is not very plausible.

The Sarah Platts file

1

On a Tuesday in February 1880, shortly before 9:30 a.m., at the bottom of a grave recently opened by a grave robber, Marshal Frank Russel's gloved fingers brushed a human bone. Relief washed over him; he hadn't waded into this pit, drowned in fifty centimeters of water, for nothing: the corpse was still there, amidst the debris of its shovel-broken coffin. Through the piece of cloth pressed over his nose and mouth, he heaved a sigh of relief, immediately followed by another, this time of dismay. Who would have wanted to desecrate this unfortunate woman's grave? What morbid impulse could drive someone to indulge in such an atrocity?

Carefully, Russel stepped over the body to stand on top of it. His fingers were the only instrument at his disposal; he was going to have to be patient, a quality he had fortunately developed through his work. As he bent over, the barrel of the Colt clipped to his belt grazed the muddy surface.

"Marshal?"

The voice of his deputy Earl Reeves, tinged with a hint of southern accent—an uncommon feature in this Midwestern state—bursts from the top of the hole.

"Marshal, be careful, your firecracker's about to take on water."

Russel straightened up and looked down at his hip. A drop beaded on the tip of his gun. Without a word, he undid the buckle on his belt and handed it to his deputy.

"Is everything going the way you want it?" asked the latter, reaching for the leather belt.

"It's okay, Earl. I found it. Just making sure everything's here. Damn rain."

Earlier that morning, a witness had reported a gaping grave in the cemetery of South Bend, Indiana, which had left Russell puzzled. He knew the town well, having been a marshal there for several years, and, like all its residents, he was well aware that no grave robbing had been reported there for decades. The Indian tribes that had been pushed back to the shores of Lake Michigan were quiet, and the Ku Klux Klan, whose influence was still very strong throughout the state, would never have attacked a white woman's grave. What's more, the victim, a young woman by the name of Sarah Platts, had recently died of consumption[9],

---

9. Former name for tuberculosis.

all the more reason to stay as far away as possible. The torrential rains had washed away any footprints and filled the pit with water, so the marshal was now wading through a pool of mud.

"Fucking business," he grumbled, dipping his hand in to begin his digital examination.

He found Sarah Platts' arm, felt it gently, eyes closed, found it surprisingly soft, then moved up to her shoulder before letting his hand slide down to her torso. The body was lying on its back. And it was a woman, judging by the double swelling of her breasts. Unceremoniously, Russel let his fingers move up to the base of the neck and shivered as his racing mind tried to put together the pieces of the puzzle to give him a complete picture of the situation.

Ugly. The corpse had been decapitated. The cervical vertebrae protruded from the flesh at the point of separation, apparently caused by a 360-degree rotation of the head. Further examination would be required to determine the exact process of decapitation, but initial findings seemed to indicate that the head had been torn off by force of the arms. "*That's unusual,*" thought Frank Russel.

"Marshal? How does it look?"

"It's a woman, probably Sarah Platts. She's in a bad way."

"What do you mean by that?"

"She was decapitated."

"Stripping..."

Earl winced. He'd known Sarah Platts when she was alive, a good girl, a little crazy and moody, but always smiling. Despite her lack of education, she volunteered at the Lakeville school. She loved children, and they loved her for it.

"God's holy shit," he muttered. Who could blame him?"

"I've no idea. As someone who knew her a little, do you know if she had any enemies, someone who would have wanted to kill her, but wouldn't have had the chance because of her illness? A lover, perhaps?"

"Not as far as I know. Someone cut off his head, you say?"

"Not exactly... But Dr. Kirk will no doubt enlighten us on the subject."

Russel straightened up with a sigh, pretended to mechanically put his Stetson back on, but changed his mind when he saw his hand covered in mud. His deputy held out his arm to help him extricate himself from the hole, then, after getting to his feet, the marshal cracked his effort-tested knuckles and took one last look at the submerged body.

"Well, I'll have Kirk's boys come and pack it all up. A skull thief, that's all I needed..." he grumbled, taking off his dirty boots."

In truth, South Bend was a rather quiet town. Crime was confined to cattle rustling and public defacement, often the work of transient, mostly alcoholic thieves; murder was as rare as a tattoo on a preacher's buttocks. Occasionally, of course, a marital dispute ended badly—for the wife—or a duel left a body in the middle of Main Street, or a drunken brawl degenerated in the saloon, but real murders, premeditated or motivated by a morbid impulse, South Bend hadn't seen in a long time. In fact, Frank Russell, despite his passion for hunting and firearms, was unaccustomed to stalking human prey—quite the opposite of his deputy Earl Reeves, who had spent several years enforcing the law in New Orleans before requesting a transfer to a quieter posting. The marshal was approaching sixty. His curly white hair was cut very short, and his skin was prone to sunburn, despite years spent riding horses across the plains of the Midwest. He'd started his career as a deputy, then moved up to marshal when his predecessor was shot; sometimes he regretted that turn of events. He didn't like being in charge. That morning, he'd rather have lead shot a wild beast than been at the helm of the biggest case the city had seen in years.

"Quite a mess we've got here," he grumbled as his horse trotted slightly behind Earl's. "I don't have to point it out, but it's going to make a lot of noise around here. I don't have to say this, but it's going to cause a stir around here. I bet the whole town already knows. We'll have to keep a cool head. Focus. There's a lot to cover here. Let's recap."

With his free hand—the other holding the reins—he traced a list of points on an imaginary board in front of him.

"In a nutshell: Sarah Platts, a pretty, friendly young woman who was much loved by the students at her school. Died of consumption. A large circle of acquaintances—no known lover. Her head was torn off. Why was this?"

He nodded, gazing into the distance.

"That's THE question: why steal just his skull?"

"I spoke to her mother before coming," Earl pointed out. "When we found out it was Sarah's grave, I wanted to let her know myself."

"Did she teach you anything interesting?"

"No. But it reminded me of a case I once worked on."

"In Louisiana?"

"The mother of a young woman had desecrated her daughter's grave because the pain of her loss was too much to bear. She had brought the corpse to a table opposite dolls and 'brought her back to life'. Cups of tea had been placed in front of her. It looked like a painting. It was… rather strange."

"Do you think Mrs Platts had anything to do with it?"

"No, I don't think she did. She seemed affected by Sarah's disappearance, of course, but not to the extent of desecrating her grave. Besides, the mother I'm talking about had only one daughter, which is not the case with Mrs Platts. She has three other children to look after. I can't see her taking Sarah's skull home and putting it on the mantelpiece, you know what I mean?"

Russell let out a grating chuckle.

"I think I understand, yes."

"To be honest, the whole thing reminds me of voodoo."

"To… what?"

"Voodoo," smiles Earl. "To cut a long story short, it's a type of religion practiced by 'witch doctors' in Louisiana. Its use is forbidden, punishable by death or imprisonment."

"Do they steal heads off corpses over there?"

"Let me tell you an anecdote. As part of an investigation, I interviewed Dr. S.M. Lambert of the Rockefeller Foundation's Western Pacific Health Service. In only one case had the healing been striking. At the Mona Mona mission in North Queensland, there were many indigenous converts, but in the vicinity of the mission there was also a group of non-converts, including a certain Nebo, a famous healer. The missionary's assistant was a native named Rob, who had himself been converted. When Dr. Lambert arrived at the mission, he learned that Rob was in trouble and that the missionary wanted him examined. Dr. Lambert proceeded with the examination, but found no fever, no pain, no signs or symptoms of illness. He was, however, impressed to see that, despite this, Rob was very ill and very weak. He then learned from the missionary that a bone had been pointed in Rob's direction by Nebo, and that he was convinced he was going to die as a result. Dr. Lambert and the missionary went to Nebo and threatened him that his food supplies would be taken away if anything happened to Rob, and that he and his people would be forced to leave the mission. Immediately, Nebo agreed to go and see Rob. He leaned over his bed and told him it had all been a mistake, a simple misunderstanding, and that he hadn't pointed any bones in his direction. The relief, as Dr. Lambert attests, was almost immediate. That evening, Rob regained his strength and returned to work. He seemed perfectly recovered."

"The use of bones is therefore quite widespread in voodoo," observes Russel.

"That's right. The sorcerer, healer or chief tacitly possesses the power to kill by pointing a bone at his victim. It's a form of black magic. I also know that monkey skulls have a strong symbolic power, but I'm not aware of any use of human skulls."

"To be honest, it all seems a bit far-fetched," confessed the marshal thoughtfully. "This is Indiana, not Louisiana. Back home, we solve problems like men, with firecrackers."

"I'll grant you that, Marshal, but for the moment I can't think of any other explanation for this beheading."

"There's certainly another, less... extravagant one. Perhaps someone opened the grave to remove the jewels, and a coyote took Sarah's head to devour it. That sounds more plausible than your magician stories."

"Mmmh."

"Don't make that face, Earl."

"So do me a favor: I'd like to involve the local residents in the research."

"In what way?"

"Well, in the usual way: by offering a reward. Let me print some posters."

"For a head?" exclaimed the marshal."

"Or for one of its parts. Any information would be good, don't you think?"

Russell sighed. An APB for a skull was unheard of, but since he'd bruised his assistant's ego, the least he could do now was accede to his request. Besides, as Earl said, in this case, any information was good information.

2

The day after the grave violation was discovered, Wyatt Kern's saloon, The Black Bear Tavern, located on the edge of Lakeville about four hours' walk from South Bend, opened its doors at the crack of dawn, as it did every day. Only the regulars were already up, sipping their morning whisky and chatting about anything and everything, their eyes fixed on old Fred Auer hoeing his field in the distance. Discussions usually revolved around the Civil War, which had profoundly transformed Indiana society, politics and economics, causing a population shift from the center to the north, and contributing to the decline of the southern part of the state. The growth of industry and manufacturing in the *Hoosier* towns[10] had ushered in a new era of economic prosperity. In fact, by the end of the war, Indiana had become a less rural state than before, much to the chagrin of modest farmers who were repelled by the urban lifestyle. However, this revival had yet to infect towns like Lakeville and South Bend, whose position on the Michigan border made them difficult to reach. And then there was the growing metropolis of Chicago to the west, which was sucking up much of the resources and capturing all the attention.

On this day, however, it was a far less trivial subject that occupied the regulars at Wyatt Kern's saloon. The beheading of Sarah Platts' corpse in nearby South Bend was on everyone's lips. And who said skull in the region said Gordon Truesdale, that broad-shouldered fellow who smoked infamous hand-rolled cigarettes. He lived in a small farmhouse behind the trees with his wife Maggie and their four daughters. Truesdale had received some education, but he was renowned for his laziness and apathy, and for devoting most of his spare time to his great passion: phrenology, a theory that the bumps on the human skull reflected the character of its owner. His love of phrenology was well known to the people of Lakeville, as he gave lectures on the subject in the surrounding schools.

"And I'll tell you what," said Wyatt Kern, leaning over his counter as if about to confide a secret. "I'm sure he did it. But we're not going to find that unfortunate girl's head. He's too smart for that."

Teddy Rivers took a swig of alcohol before taking a risk: contradicting Kern in his saloon—in other words, in his kingdom.

"I don't think he's guilty. Why would he do that? If he was so smart, he'd have picked a cemetery farther away than South Bend."

"Well, I know people who don't agree with you," replied Kern, scowling as he picked up a whisky-stained coaster from the counter. "They say he sometimes loses it a bit, and even hits his kids."

"They say, they say... I remind you that you were suspected of smuggling and supplying weapons to the South during the war."

"Never!"

---

10. *Hoosier* is the term used to describe the natives and inhabitants of the state of Indiana. It means "earthy ass".

"That's what I'm saying. They say, they say... it doesn't mean a thing."

The sun was beginning to peek over the horizon, but the countryside was still shrouded in darkness. This didn't stop Teddy Rivers from spotting Fred Auer gesticulating his arms out from under the branches of a tree. He was clearly crying out for help.

Both rushed out. Fred was yelling at them to hurry up. Rivers, in better physical shape than the saloon keeper, was the first to reach the foot of the tree. Immediately, his nostrils picked up the smell of death.

"Holy shit!" exclaimed Kern, arriving in turn.

He had almost screamed. His face was livid, almost as white as the jawbone lying between the roots.

"What do we do?" asked Rivers.

An angel passed over the dusty plain. In the distance, a raven cried out in amusement.

"Well," sighed Fred Auer after a long moment of silence. "What's the name of the marshal who asked to be notified if we found anything suspicious?"

"How much is the reward?" replied Kern.

"Shut up, I'm the one who discovered this thing," replied the old farmer.

3

Fred Auer and Wyatt Kern were still arguing about the reward when Frank Russel and Earl Reeves arrived on horseback an hour later. The two men, accompanied by Teddy Rivers, were waiting for the marshals at the edge of the field, stoic in the face of the dust kicked up by the wind that had begun to blow. A *tumbleweed*[11] passed them without stopping.

"I'm the one who found the bone," attacked Fred Auer as Russell stepped to the ground. "I'm entitled to the reward."

"We'll see about that," said the marshal. "First tell me what happened."

"Well, I was hoeing my field not far from the trees over there (he accompanied his words with a wave of his arm) and I came across this thing."

---

11. A well-known wandering plant ball in western landscapes.

He held out the jawbone, still clinging to bits of moldy flesh, wrapped in a cloth. Earl seized it with a grimace of disgust.

"I can confirm it's a human remnant," he says.

"We think it's Gordon Truesdale's fault, the guy who lives on the other side of the trees," said Teddy Rivers.

"Why?"

"He's a weird guy. He likes skulls. The other day, he even said he'd like to collect them. So he decided to start with this poor girl."

Russel and his deputy exchanged puzzled glances.

"Do you know if this guy practices voodoo?" asked Earl.

"The... what?"

"Nothing, forget it."

"Very well," concludes the marshal. "We'll go and check it out. Gentlemen, thank you for your cooperation."

"And the reward?" Fred Auer protested.

"At the moment, all we have is a piece of jaw," replied Earl Reeves. "And there's no guarantee that it came from Sarah Platts' skull. But I promise you'll get what's coming to you... if we catch the culprit."

"So get off your butts," muttered the old farmer.

"It's planned, Mr. Auer, it's planned..."

The two policemen turned onto the road winding along the field, then walked for nearly a kilometer before coming upon a sign that hung pitifully askew. "TRUESDALE FAMILY RESIDENCE", it read, etched into the metal. Once green, the rusty sign was now suspended only by a chain, the other having long since resigned. Beneath the first sign, a second, made up of red letters hand-painted on a wooden board, announced: "PROPRIÉTÉ PRIVÉE" (PRIVATE PROPERTY). In a nutshell, Truesdale Farm looked like any of those places where visitors were greeted at gunpoint, which is why Russell and Reeves set out on the trail with a mixed feeling of apprehension and resolution.

A hedge of honor made up of peonies led directly to the porch of the house, which was reached by means of a small staircase. Earl knocked on the door while Russel peered around the side of the farmhouse. Silence stretched for a few seconds before someone came to open the door. Gordon Truesdale didn't at all match the image Russel and Reeves had formed of him. Anyone would have described him as a tall, handsome man, not forty years old. The only flaw: his left eye was screwed up, perhaps as a result of an accident or youthful fight. As Russel stuck his marshal's badge under his nose, he saw, or thought he saw, a glint of anger in his eyes. He looked as if he'd been interrupted in the middle of an activity, sweat dripping from his brow.

"Marshal Russel," said Truesdale in a monotone voice. "How can I help you?"

"May we come in, Mr. Truesdale?"

The man reluctantly stepped aside after a moment's hesitation. He was clearly not pleased to see them, but that didn't prove anything; marshals were rarely welcomed with open arms.

When Truesdale closed the door after letting them in, Reeves had the distinct impression that he was trying to hide something. What was it? Impossible to say. He thought he caught a whiff, perhaps a very vaguely familiar scent, of meat and moisture. The policemen followed him down the corridor, taking care to memorize each door they passed.

"You can call me Gordon," declared Truesdale, as he preceded them into his living room.

Then he went over to the anatomy books stacked on the table and put them away in his bookcase, without a glance at the agents. It was as if he didn't care or had nothing to hide.

Russel placed a hand on the back of a chair.

"May we sit down? We'd like to chat with you for a few minutes, if we could. You're not in too much of a hurry?"

In front of the library, Gordon hesitated. Reeves thought he saw his gaze drift to the kitchen door and again had the sensation of interrupted activity. But it didn't last.

"Of course, of course," he says, turning around. "Won't you sit down? Sorry, we're not used to entertaining. Can I get you something to drink? Coffee, perhaps?"

"That'll do, thanks," declined Russell.

He prepared his notebook and a pencil to collect the words of the suspect—who didn't yet know he was one.

"Do you know why we're here?" inquired the marshal.

"Not really, no. I don't get out much."

"A corpse was decapitated in the South Bend cemetery and..."

"Oh, I see," cut in Gordon. "So, you thought: let's go and interview this guy who's into skulls, right?"

"Well," stammered Russell, unsettled. "In a way..."

"What do you expect me to do? For me to hold out my arms and say, 'Go ahead, it's me. I snuck into a cemetery in the middle of the night, dug around and took a head'? I'm a scientist, gentlemen. I study anatomy with a predilection for the skull, as you've no doubt read on the cover of my books, but that's just theory. I'm not a doctor."

Russel let a few seconds pass before answering. He looked deep into Gordon's eyes, a classic interrogation technique. His left pupil was gray and cataracted.

"You know, you see everything in this business. What's more, my assistant here spent several years in New Orleans, so he's no stranger to cases that defy the norm.

"Why would I do what you accuse me of?"

"What do I know? In Europe, there were grave robbers who sold the bodies to medical students so they could get their hands on real people. I don't care why people do what they do, all I care about is stopping them. We've heard about a skull collection you'd like to start. Where were you last night?"

Gordon took his time. He quietly let himself sink into the back of his chair, crossed his legs and, when his right leg was resting on his left, put his hands on his thighs.

"I was here," he said, huffing and puffing, as if the question provoked nothing but boredom in him.

"Was anyone with you?"

"No, no one."

"Your wife and daughters aren't here?" said Reeves.

"No, they went to visit their grandmother. They'll be back in three days."

"All right, then. Without... an alibi...," mumbled Russell, writing the words in his notebook.

"Did you know Sarah Platts?" asked Reeves.

"Sarah? Is she the victim?"

"Just answer the question, Mr. Truesdale."

"Well... Yes. She volunteered at one of the schools where I lectured. Poor woman. To die so young. I was at her funeral, you know."

"Did you know of any enemies?"

"To Sarah? Oh, no! She was goodness incarnate, benevolence made woman. I so wish I'd had the opportunity to study her skull... Gee, that wasn't anything to say," he added, vaguely amused by his own impertinence.

"I'm afraid not, Mr. Truesdale. May we visit the house?"

"You mean, search her?"

"No, let's say, let's just have a look. I'm not hiding the fact that you're our only suspect and that your behavior... well... let's just say your passion is unusual. Make it easy for us and I assure you it will work in your favor. I'm thinking of your future, Gordon. I'm thinking about your future and that of your children. You know what it's like to be falsely accused. I assure you, I wouldn't wish it on anyone. The gossip, the looks on the street..."

He left his last sentence hanging to increase its impact.

"It won't just affect you, but your loved ones too," he continues. "I think of them and I see a terrible life, an unhappy life."

He saw that Gordon was thinking.

"Very well," he said. "You go around, I'll wait here."

"Thank you, Mr. Truesdale. My deputy will stay with you for..."

"To keep an eye on me, I understand. Don't worry, I have no intention of running away."

"Just a precautionary measure, I assure you."

A search of the farmhouse turned up nothing, and although Gordon Truesdale was suspected by the police, Sarah Platts' family and the people of South Bend, no one dared, in the absence of proof, to formally accuse him of having desecrated the young woman's grave, so the case remained at a standstill for several months.

4

The first buildings of what was to become South Bend were erected along the St. Joseph River in the 1820s by two *American Fur Company* merchants, Pierre Navarre and Alexis Coquillard. Initially intended for trade only, the prosperity of their little town prompted the duo to add additional structures to accommodate homes, schools and stores—more and more stores—notably at the intersection of what is today Michigan Street and LaSalle Avenue, thus initiating the development of downtown South Bend.

As a result, the city's population grew rapidly in the 1830s. The first general store had opened in 1837, followed by a doctor's surgery wedged between the *General*

Store and the imposing plot of land that would, three decades later, house the luxurious Oliver Hotel, named after the inventor of the "quiet" plough, James Oliver.

The doctor's surgery was relatively small compared to its imposing neighbors. A porch greeted patients and also served as a waiting room, surmounted by a trough for patients' horses—the wait could sometimes be long. Dr. Kirk, thirty-seven years old, his face chiselled by the sun, was nervously smoking a cigarette, leaning against one of the porch's wooden pillars. He kept his eyes on Russel and Reeves as they dismounted and tied the horse's harness around the bar. Then he crushed his cigarette under his heel and shook the policemen's outstretched hand before inviting them in.

In the vestibule, a few medical posters set the mood. Some touted the merits of fake pharmacists and other snake-oil remedy salesmen, circulating on modest carts, or promoted *Medicine Shows* very much in vogue in the hinterland. *They also advertised "WHITE EAGLE INDIAN OIL, the real Indian treatment for rheumatism, inflammation and hay fever".*

"Please, it's this way," said Kirk.

Russel and Reeves followed him into his office, where he welcomed his patients.

"A pick-me-up?"

Russel looked at the empty glass the doctor was showing him. Even though it was a little too hot for his taste, he thought it best not to be rude. After all, it was the doctor who had asked to see them, so it was best not to give him anything to brag about.

"With pleasure."

"What about you?"

Reeves agreed too. They pulled a chair from under the desk and sat down. The young doctor placed two glasses in front of them.

"Doctor, you asked us to come. We understand you have information about Sarah Platts."

"That's right."

He grabbed the bottle of whisky from the cupboard and filled himself a glass, swallowing it dry before serving his guests. Clearly, this head-stealing business was troubling him.

"About ten days ago, Mr. Truesdale went to see my colleague in Lakeville to ask him whether it was possible to poison oneself by handling a corpse. He replied in the affirmative to this curious question and, according to him, although he made no comment, Mr. Truesdale seemed quite disturbed. The next morning, he began to complain, telling his wife that his nose hurt terribly and that he probably had erysipelas, a bacterial skin infection. She tried to apply bread-and-milk poultices, but to no avail. Over the next few hours, her face began to swell and, in less than three days, her head had doubled in size. Horrified, Mrs. Truesdale called on me, much to the annoyance of her husband, who didn't want to hear about it."

Russel readjusted his position on the chair; he was clearly uncomfortable. Reeves, on the other hand, leaned forward, very interested.

"Did you go to his place or did he come here?"

"I moved. Mrs. Truesdale felt her husband was in no condition to make the journey. And she was right."

Dr. Kirk took a second drink of whisky.

"Would you like a refill?" he asked, grabbing the bottle."

"No, thank you."

"As you wish. I need it. So I arrived at the Truesdale farm in the middle of the afternoon. There I found a man in abominable pain. His eyelids were horribly drawn, his gums were receding over his teeth, and the skin of his nose was so tight that it looked as if it might tear at any moment, guaranteeing the flow of the purulent substance that could be seen just below. As for her eyes... her eyes..."

Kirk inhaled deeply before continuing, more scientifically:

"His eyeballs were frightfully swollen, and as they had turned over in pain, only the white was visible."

"What can cause these symptoms?"

The doctor shook his head as if this question remained a mystery to him.

"Multiple causes could have explained the symptoms separately, but taken all together, I concluded that a terrible poison was slowly but surely permeating his entire nervous system."

"Poison? Do you think his wife was trying to kill him?"

"No, I didn't suspect it for a second. Let alone after what followed. I made the decision to operate on Mr. Truesdale without delay, to relieve his pain. His wife and daughters helped me lay him down on the kitchen table, then I used my scalpel to incise his skin from the center of his nose to his hairline. I did the same to his forehead from temple to temple (he mimed a line running across his brow bones). A disgusting mass oozed out. The smell was so terrible that his daughters ran out of the house."

"Could a disease have caused this?" ventured Reeves.

"I don't think so. I'm not saying it's impossible, but I don't know of any that cause this kind of effect."

"What did you do next, Doctor?" urged Russell.

"With a steady hand, I lacerated Mr. Truesdale's scalp, which had previously been shaved by his wife, and the same foul substance began to flow uninterruptedly. I waited until his whole face had 'drained', and he was approximately back to his usual self, before attempting to clean the wounds by injecting water, but..."

He ran a hand over his cheeks, then over his nose and eyes, as if trying to cleanse himself of an invisible grime. Russel and Reeves listened in silence, disgusted, fascinated.

"When I tried to fill the large incision I'd made in the forehead, the water immediately came out through the other holes in the scalp. It was as if all the flesh between the skin and the bone had been corrupted and disintegrated. It was... awful, I have no other word for it."

"Forgive me, Doctor," intervened Reeves, "but why are you telling us all this?"

"Because Gordon Truesdale died this morning. His body is in the morgue at the back of the building. And his widow has asked me to tell you that she wishes to speak to you."

5

Standing in front of her kitchen window, Maggie Truesdale smoked pensively —a nasty habit she'd never been able to kick despite her four daughters' incessant protests: "Cigarettes are for men, Mum, real ladies don't smoke!" Basically, she didn't disagree with this point of view, but she didn't care, since she never saw anyone. The few times she left the four walls of her house, it was to visit her mother or to pick up groceries at the grocery store. The rest of the time, she never left the farm.

Of course, she would have liked to participate in the activities of the small Lakeville community, but her husband's curious passion had made their family an object of curiosity. Whenever they showed up in town, they were stared at like freaks, so much so that the girls decided they'd rather not leave the farm.

"Please? We're sorry to disturb you."

She glanced over her shoulder. Marshal Russell and his deputy had just appeared in the doorway. Earl found her rather elegant with her well-coiffed hair and earrings that made her look like a woman of the world. She was dressed in a black dress, a sign that her mourning had begun.

"Marshal. Deputy Reeves. Won't you come in?"

"Dr. Kirk said you wanted to talk to us."

Mrs. Truesdale crossed her arms, shivering, even though it wasn't that cold in the room, at least not to the point of shivering.

"That's right," she says, nervously stubbing out her cigarette. "Thank you for taking my call. Would you like something to drink?"

"No, it's kind of you."

"I've asked you here to give you some clarification."

"About your husband's death?"

"Well, sort of, but... Let's go into the living room, shall we?"

She preceded them into the corridor, then invited them to sit on the sofa. All the while, Earl kept watching her. Her face was drawn, and he could tell from the reddening of her eyelids that she'd been crying a lot.

"Are you all right, Mrs. Truesdale?" he inquired.

"Given the circumstances, I guess you could say yes."

"Let's get to the point, shall we," Russel grew impatient.

She stared at him warily. Her washed-out eyes showed an astonishing power of penetration.

"If you like..." she said, wearily.

Russel opened his notebook and grabbed his pencil.

"Let's hear it."

Silence settled in. All that could be heard were the cries of the four girls playing on the plain outside.

"They're just taking their minds off things," Mrs. Truesdale justified. Don't think they're happy about their father's death.

"Isn't that the case?"

Her hand tightened on her knee and, after an infinite time, she began to unpack her story.

"I imagine Kirk explained to you that my husband was unwell?"

"Yes, ma'am."

"For the past week, he had been putting him up in his surgery to 'keep him under observation,' as he put it, but he only got worse. When he learned that he wasn't going to make it, my husband asked to see me. He had something important to confess."

"Something like what?"

Madame Truesdale sniffed disdainfully.

"He confessed to me that he had desecrated the grave of young Sarah Platts."

Russel jotted down a few words in his notebook, more to hide his satisfied pout than out of any real concern to preserve in writing this information that would not fade from his memory anyway.

"Can you give us more details?"

"I'll give it a try, but I warn you it's not very pleasant to think about. Do you mind if I smoke?"

Russel shook his head. Mrs. Truesdale lit herself another cigarette, taking a long puff before continuing.

"It happened in the middle of the night, while the girls and I were asleep. Gordon slipped out of the house and rode his horse to South Bend Cemetery, where Sarah had been buried the week before. There, he dug the grave, then broke open the coffin with a shovel and, using his knife, cut away the flesh around the neck, right down to the bone. Having done this, he placed one of his feet on her chest and, taking her head in his hands, pulled and twisted it with all his might, until it gave way."

Russel mentally reconstructed the scene: a man with a shovel in a moonlit cemetery; the hoot of an owl; across the street, the sleepy town of South Bend. The ground is soft, because it's been raining for days; the shovel hits the wood; Gordon Truesdale's heart races. Next, he rips off Sarah's head; bodily fluids from the decomposing body stain his pants; he doesn't care, he's achieved his goal. He climbs back on his horse and heads for home, without bothering to recork the grave. That's not important; what's important is the bag bouncing off the nag's hindquarters.

Unlike Earl, Russel had never worked on this kind of case, and he hoped with all his heart that this would be his last.

"Why did he do it?" he asked, taken aback by such an attitude.

"He said Sarah was goodness incarnate. He hoped he could unlock the secret of people's character by studying their skulls. Gordon wasn't a bad person, his intentions were noble, only..."

"The desecration of corpses is a crime. Worse than that, it's insanity. Your husband had lost his mind."

"That's precisely what I told him. It made him angry. But I was angry too! Because of his behavior, he'd fallen ill and I was going to be alone with the girls, thrown into public disgrace."

"Why did he get rid of the lower jaw of the skull?" asked Earl.

"It came loose in transit. Since he didn't need it, he simply threw it away where Fred Auer found it. He hadn't envisaged that this would draw suspicion on him. As if his passion wasn't blatant enough..."

She shook her head. Her disapproval of the whole thing was obvious.

"One last question, if you don't mind," added Marshal Russell. "Do you know where Sarah Platts' skull is?"

"Gordon concluded his confession by telling me that the skull could be found under the straw of the manger in the stable. I didn't have the nerve to check. He wanted it returned to Sarah's family and put back in its place in the coffin, out of respect for her."

"Did you get the impression that your husband was feeling remorse?"

Maggie Truesdale gave a grin.

"Mostly, I got the impression that he regretted having fallen ill and not having been able to study that skull as much as he would have liked. You know, his last days were terrible. His appearance had become terribly shocking, and the heat and smell of his breath were so unpleasant that no one could stay near him for very long, not even our daughters. Dr. Kirk was obliged to wear gloves, as it was impossible for those who approached him unprotected to remove the smell from their hands afterwards."

"It would seem that the Lord has taken it upon himself to make him atone for his faults," commented Earl.

"I don't know if it's the Lord's work, but by the time of his death, his eyes had putrefied to the point of blindness, and the corruption had cut so deeply into his flesh that it detached from his bones at the slightest movement. I have no idea of the extent of his crimes—Dr. Kirk seems to believe that the desecration of Sarah's grave was neither the first nor the last—but what I do know is that he suffered beyond reason. May his tormented soul now rest in peace.

6

The funeral service was held at the South Bend church. Barely thirty years old, the building cast a shadow over the few people who had come to pay their last respects to Gordon Truesdale. It was a hot day, with the smell of ozone permeating the atmosphere, a sign of an impending storm.

As Maggie Truesdale's family filed out of the church following the casket, two men watched from afar. Frank Russel and Earl Reeves. Two marshals. Two diametrically opposed characters united in the same incomprehension, bound together by a kind of incredulous stupor at the succession of events that had led them there. The dust rose all around them, carried by the autumn wind, but they didn't bother to turn their heads to contemplate its voluptuous arabesques.

"The remains of Sarah Platts have been returned to her family," announced Earl. "I personally made sure of that."

"Very good," replied Russell. "Very good, indeed."

They fell silent again, their eyes riveted on the coffin. After Gordon's death, Dr. Kirk had given the order to place the body in it and bury it without delay, but none of his assistants had had the temerity to touch it for fear of being poisoned in turn. After a brief consultation, they carefully grasped the corners of the sheet with their gloved hands, lifted it and carried it to the open box. The coffin was quickly sealed, but before the wagon could take it away, the corpse began to swell, causing the lid to burst. The two parts of the coffin therefore had to be reattached so that the brief service could take place in the church, as requested by the family. Sturdy ropes had been passed around the box, giving it the appearance of an unlikely gift-wrapped package.

Despite this precaution, the lid popped off again on the way to the cemetery, revealing the disproportionately swollen body of the deceased. Such was the fetid stench of the decomposing mass that no one could get near it, and the corpse continued to swell before the horrified audience.

"Somebody do something!" pleaded Maggie Truesdale, in tears, desperately trying to spare her four tetanized daughters from this disgusting spectacle.

Earl, who was following the procession at a respectable distance, hurriedly looked around. His eyes caught sight of an abandoned blanket on the back of a wagon. He rushed to grab it, then hurriedly threw the makeshift tarpaulin over the coffin, bringing to an end the sad climax of Gordon Truesdale's life.

The family farmhouse, which had retained the smell of the owner's slow putrefaction, remained unoccupied for many years, and all attempts to fumigate it proved ineffective. Inexplicably, its doors and windows were left open day and night, and the smell remained as strong as ever. Marshal Russel wrote in one of his reports: "It always seems that you could cut the air out of this house with a knife.

No one ever knew what Gordon Truesdale had died of. Some assumed he had contracted some mysterious illness while indulging in his dark nocturnal activities, others that he had fallen victim to the vengeance of those whose repose he had disturbed. But all agreed on one thing: whatever the reason why fate had set its sights on this poor man, his punishment was richly deserved.

The facts

The incredible story of Gordon Truesdale was brought to us by the *Andersonville Intelligencer* newspaper, dated April 22, 1880. Except for the characters invented for the story, namely Marshal Russel and his deputy, and the people in the saloon, the facts are accurate—at least, that's how they were reported in the newspaper.

Illustration: Grave robber flees from a corpse that has come to life,
by Jacques Winslow (1746)

In February 1880, in South Bend, the grave of Sarah Platts, who had recently died of tuberculosis, is found open, and an examination reveals that only the corpse's head is missing, which directs suspicion to Gordon Truesdale, a big fellow with a reputation for laziness and apathy, who devotes all his spare time to his great passion, phrenology, a theory that the bumps on the human skull reflect the character of its owner. He lectures on the subject at local schools, and often talks about his ultimate ambition: to own a large collection of skulls.

The cemetery where Sarah Platts was buried is close to his home, and while he is obviously under suspicion, no one dares formally accuse him of desecrating the young woman's grave.

Shortly afterwards, Gordon falls ill and dies in agony, without the doctors being able to do anything to help him.

The disease progression described in the article is most likely gas gangrene, an extremely virulent flesh-eating disease caused by the *Clostridium perfringens* bacterium. It can be contracted through contact with a body already infected with the bacteria—for example, by handling the body of a deceased person. It's actually more likely that Gordon Truesdale contracted it in the soil he had to dig up to desecrate Mrs. Platts' grave, because that's where the bacteria usually lodge so they can feed on the various bits of organic matter found there.

Unfortunately for Gordon, the treatment for gas gangrene consisted of massive doses of antibiotics, combined with wound debridement and/or amputation. As amputating a person's head is rather complicated, he probably couldn't have been saved, even with the help of modern medicine.

The opinion of 1st Commissioner Maillard of the Brussels Judicial Police - Division in charge of crime against property and people.

Gordon Truesdale Track:

- the cemetery is close to his home;

- He is passionate about phrenology and his ambition is to collect skulls;

- he died shortly afterwards of an unusual disease that can be caught by contact with corpses or the soil in which they are found.

Research that could have been done :

- it's obvious that digging up a corpse leaves its mark, even in 1880;

- the footprints around the grave could have been plastered over and compared with Gordon Truesdale's shoes;

- we could also have stopped by his house to see if he had a collection of skulls on his mantelpiece!

- Here, a neighborhood survey could have been carried out.

At present :

- down the laboratory to record the various clues;

- photograph of footprints for comparison with Gordon Truesdale's shoes;

- Gordon Truesdale's hearing to see what he has to say about the case;

- search of his home on the basis of presumptions ;

- analysis of the soil in which the body was found for Clostridium perfringens bacteria and comparison with the bacteria that caused Gordon Truesdale's death;

- check the tools of the person concerned for soil residues to compare with cemetery soil.

The Roanoke file

July 2, 1584

My beloved daughter,

How nice to hear from you, Eleanor! What a joy it was, when I entered the tiny cabin granted to me by Captain Barlowe, my loins broken by the interminable boat trip, my skin eaten by the cold, to find on the pillow of my bunk a letter sublimated by your inimitable handwriting. Believe me, I began reading it as soon as my frozen fingers could grasp it.

I'm delighted and relieved to hear that you've recovered from that terrible fever that's been bedridden for weeks. I have no hesitation in awarding your mother the title of healer. I remember the science she deployed when she used simple remedies, ointments and poultices to treat me. I'm delighted to see how sharp your mind is, as evidenced by the quality of your beautifully crafted sentences. However, I beg you to continue taking great care of yourself and, until your body is fully healed, not to risk a premature return to your mundanities. What's the point of my exploring the New World if I can't help you discover it afterwards?

We've been sailing for eight weeks, and as I write these lines, we're skirting the eastern coast of the Americas. After descending to the Canary Islands, we stopped off in the Caribbean to stock up on food and water, then headed north. Captain Amadas leads the way aboard the *Bark Raleigh*, the flagship of the fleet. If only you could admire this two-hundred-ton behemoth splitting the waves... It's an incredible sight, as if Man had finally succeeded in taming nature's most tumultuous elements. In comparison, our own vessel, the *Dorothy*, looks like a walnut shell. I've tried unsuccessfully to depict her in charcoal, but my poor scribbles have yet to do justice to her grandeur, so I've thrown them all overboard, without exception.

This morning, we awoke to the sweet smell of a delicate garden, indicating beyond doubt that there was land nearby. If all goes according to plan, we could be landing in three days' time in the heart of the area discovered by Juan Ponce de León half a century ago. As you know, Sir Walter Raleigh is financing this expedition and hopes to add to the title of Her Majesty Elizabeth, already Queen of England and Ireland. We hope to take possession of this virgin territory in the name of the Queen and Sir Raleigh, and build a permanent outpost.

Excitement aboard the *Dorothy* begins to reach a fever pitch! The men speak of rivers of gold and opulent harvests. I don't have the heart to dash their hopes. After all, the Spanish have been looking for El Dorado for ages. Who knows? Perhaps we'll be the first to unearth the remains of this ancient city. If so, I'll be sure to bring you and your mother plenty of jewels to make your friends jealous—not a very Christian or charitable thing to do, I admit, but their insufferable, smug husbands deserve to be put in their place.

Yes, this country is as beautiful and vast as the reports of previous expeditions had led us to believe. These reports, however, failed to mention the sinister nature of these lands. The native tribes differ in every way from the civilized peoples of the old continent. Their impious rites seem dedicated to unknown gods. I hope we can save the souls of these poor strays, and will write to the bishops of the House of Lords as soon as I return to London, insisting on the necessity of sending missions there.

It's been a gloomy day, punctuated by showers. The landscape, as it appears to me at this moment, evokes an infinite melancholy: the sky, gray and tired, overhangs the ocean, which hurls itself relentlessly against the hull of the *Dorothy* with a crash that seems to me more like a vibration than a sound; the echo of each wave propagates through the fibers of the wood, even as I write. The sensation is not as unpleasant as you might think.

I know, my dear Eleanor, that you disapprove of this expedition, which I accepted out of friendship for Sir Raleigh, but I assure you that this makes me feel happy. Your mother made no difficulty whatsoever when I told her of my departure; she didn't say a word. I'm sure she knew that deep down I was longing to explore the flora and fauna of these unexplored regions. I promise not to let you down and to be careful in all circumstances. By the time you receive this letter, I'll probably have been ashore for several weeks and already witnessed a number of astonishing sights. I promise to write to you regularly to report on my undertakings.

Please convey to your mother the affectionate feelings you both inspire in me, and my best wishes to your husband.

Your devoted father,
John White

July 20, 1584

My dear, sweet Eleanor,

What an incredible place! It never ceases to amaze me, day after day, but the savages who inhabit it are even stranger.

As expected, we entered the land once scouted by Juan Ponce de León. These are particularly rich lands. Several encounters with natives taught us that this land is called *Wingandacoa* in the local language, and that it is ruled by a "king" called Wingina. In homage to Her Majesty Elizabeth [1], the "Virgin Queen", and by the grace of an amusing aural proximity, Amadas and Barlowe agreed to christen it, in sobriquet, "Virginia".

Construction of the outpost is well underway, but we had underestimated the amount of equipment we would need, so we're forced to lodge aboard the ships. I can't deny that we're starting to feel a little cramped.

Not far from the shore are several islands, which we have named after the local tribes. Roanoke Island, estimated by Captain Barlowe to be thirty-three thousand yards wide and six thousand five hundred yards long, is home to two races of Indians, the Roanokes and the Powhatans. A little further south is the island of the Croatoans, home to the Secotans and, of course, the Croatoans. Relations have been established with the latter, and Captain Amadas has ordered weekly provisions from them. He has also arranged for these natives, in exchange for a fair fee, to supply us with the timber we need to build our fort. The Roanokes and Powhatans, on the other hand, are far more suspicious of us, not to say downright hostile. Their animosity is perhaps due to our altercation with a fifth tribe, the natives of Aquascogocs.

At this point in my story, I feel it's important to define the context in which the events to come took place.

During our initial exploration of the archipelago, savages broke aboard the *Bark Raleigh* and stole several items, including a silver cup of considerable commercial value, but above all of irreplaceable sentimental value to Captain Amadas. It had been given to him by his own father, who in turn had inherited it from his grandfather. If I explain this to you, it's in the hope that you won't judge the captain's actions too harshly. Life out here is a far cry from the London comforts we're used to, and the barbaric practices of the natives demand a response that's just as harsh as their actions.

Following the incident, Captain Amadas went to the village of the Aquascogocs to parley with their chief and negotiate the recovery of the silver cup. He returned in a gloomy mood, and when we asked him why, he replied glumly:

"Gentlemen, they think we're demons."

I suggested to him that perhaps our skin tone was to blame, a color—or rather absence of color—which, as I'd already witnessed, sometimes inspired crazy reactions. You may not know it, but Indian skin is reddish.

Captain Amadas replied that this had nothing to do with it.

"What I've been told, Mr. White, is that anyone who comes from the ocean is either already dead or destined to become so. So, in their eyes, there's nothing wrong with skinning the dead. In fact, in a way, it's a necessity."

This surprising revelation left me, as you can easily guess, rather perplexed. I asked him from whom he got this assessment.

"From an Indian who calls himself Wanchese. He seems less sullen and moronic than his fellows."

We discovered, however, that the opinion expressed by Wanchese was quite shared across the island, for when Captain Amadas spoke with other tribal chiefs, it came back to him in roundabout ways. Clearly, we weren't welcome on Roanoke, and Amadas had no desire to linger any longer than necessary. But giving up his silver cup was out of the question. So, in retaliation, he ordered and led the sacking of the Aquascogoc village, which he then burned to the ground. I know this may sound excessive—and it undoubtedly is—but you have to understand that our spirits are put to the test in this hostile and foreign environment. So please don't judge us too harshly. There were no casualties on either side.

Write to me without delay, my dear Eleanor. Tell me about your health, give me news of your mother and our friends. Has Ananias finally won his coveted scholarship? Has William finally succeeded in perfecting his curious knitting machine? Are the troubles with Spain continuing to grow? I look forward to reading more.

Please accept my warmest regards.

Your loving father,
John White

September 7, 1584

Dear Father,

London is buzzing with the news of your expedition. It's all the talk of the town, from the seedy pubs of Clerkenwell to the refined taverns of Southwark.

But that's just the tip of the iceberg. Beyond our capital, the whole country is eagerly awaiting your return. I doubt, however, that anyone in this world is as impatient as I am. I've thought of you often since you left Lincolnshire, dreading to receive a letter announcing your doom. Fortunately, it has not arrived so far. May God grant that it may continue to do so!

At home, all is well, at least as far as our family is concerned. The conflict with Spain is escalating. The signing of the Treaty of Joinville between Philip II of Spain and the so-called Holy League has deeply angered Her Majesty Elizabeth I. I fear that trouble is brewing. I fear that trouble is brewing. I shall not fail to provide you with a detailed account as soon as certain personal events allow me to do so. Our move, Ananias and I, to our home in East Kirkby is indeed going more chaotically than expected. Nothing to worry about, rest assured! Mere trifles. A broken vase here, a damaged piece of furniture there... My husband sometimes goes into rages that take him a long time to get out of, but I don't hold it against him. He's also quite charming; but I don't need to tell you that, as you know better than anyone, having worked with him for many years in the parish of St. Martin Ludgate.

My body has regained all its vitality, and the fever seems to be a thing of the past. Mother is also doing just fine, even if—just between us—she longs for your presence. I sometimes catch her dusting the same knick-knack for the third time in a row.

"Everything has to be perfect for your father's return," she replies when I ask her about it.

I confess I'm amused by her behavior. You know how cold and distant she can be, so this kind of facetiousness reminds me that a loving heart beats behind her icy façade. I hope that on your side, tensions with the natives have eased. Strange rumors have reached us. It seems that on their return, expected later this month, Captains Amadas and Barlowe will bring back with them two Indians charged with informing Sir Raleigh of the political and geographical situation in the region, and with learning English to serve as translators on future missions. Is this true? If so, I can't wait to meet these primitives from another world!

I may have to tell you this, but Her Majesty Queen Elizabeth has officially decreed the name "Virginia" for the land you've discovered. Don't hesitate to notify Captains Barlowe and Amadas, as they'll be delighted. They are now considered among the greatest explorers of our century. I'm sure Sir Raleigh deeply regrets not having led this expedition himself. It is said that he is already thinking of organizing a second expedition to colonize the region for good. I'd love to be part of it! Ananias wouldn't mind. The scholarship he coveted has been awarded to someone else; he's been so bruised by it that he's thinking of building a new life for us, far from London where he feels his career opportunities are blocked; the New World would be perfect for that. What do you think, Father? How would you like to explore these new territories with us?

I look forward to seeing you again, and wish you all the best.

Your loving daughter,
Eleanor White, wife Dare

October 3, 1584

My dear, sweet Eleanor,

This missive will be succinct, as circumstances urge me to be concise—there are many tasks demanding my attention. In the absence of Captains Barlowe and Amadas, I have, as it were, been promoted to head of the expedition. The scientist Thomas Harriot assists me in my duties, and is working hard to learn the Algonquin language so as to communicate more easily with the natives.

Thank you for your letter. Reading your words always inspires me with inexhaustible joy. I'm more than delighted to hear that the fever has finally left your body. If I understand your words correctly, you are asking my permission to join Sir Raleigh's possible colonization mission. Who am I to dissuade you, who has crossed the ocean to be the first to draw unknown landscapes, plants and animals? I'll be delighted to welcome you if that's your intention.

It's true that Barlowe and Amadas are bringing aboard two natives, a Croatoan named Manteo and a Roanoke. I'm surprised this information reached you so quickly, especially as it was a secret. We hope that contact with our civilization will facilitate future exchanges, as we continue to encounter problems with the natives. That said, tensions are slowly easing. We're still at the stage of taming each other, but I'm sure we'll end up getting on well together and becoming, if not friendly peoples, at least reliable trading partners.

Construction of the outpost is now complete. It wasn't all plain sailing, and the comfort of the camp still leaves something to be desired. However, we're pleased with it, despite some nights that could be described as "complicated". Howling rips through the night, depriving us of sleep time and again until daybreak. We suspect the Aquascogocs want to avenge the destruction of their village by frightening us. But we're determined not to be impressed by these primitives.

On rereading this letter, I realize that I've been even more succinct than I'd intended, for which I'm truly sorry. I promise you a fuller explanation in my next letter.

Once again, convey to your mother the deep feelings you both inspire in me.

Your loving father,
John White

December 11, 1584

My dear, sweet Eleanor,

So much has happened since I sent you my last missive! I have a story to tell you. It struck Thomas Harris and me as a little strange, not to say disturbing. I'm curious to know what you think. If nothing else, maybe it will distract you in your new home —I know how uncomfortable moving can be.

Three days after my previous letter, two young women arrived under the authority of Nathorod, a closed-faced warrior. They had been commissioned to chase away the evil spirits from our outpost—Thomas had in fact informed Wanchese of our nocturnal problems; Wanchese had then reported our grievances to King Wingina, who decided to come to our aid to prove his good disposition towards us. To say the least, our three guests didn't look very comfortable. In fact, one of the ladies, elegantly dressed in animal skins, couldn't help but squeal when she spotted my prints strewn across a table.

As I asked Nathorod why (with the help of Thomas Harris, who used his experience of the Algonquin language to interpret for me), the warrior faced me and said with a hard face:

"She doesn't like it here, sir, and neither do I, because this has always been a bad place. For her, your drawings are a means of expressing the demons that inhabit this place."

(Of course, I'm reporting his words in my own words, for ease of understanding. The actual communication was long and arduous).

I was speechless as Nathorod softened and clarified:

"My people consider these lands to be cursed. It is said that people from the sky once dwelt here, only to be driven out to sea by our ancestors. That's why some of us believe you are the descendants of these beings and treat you with suspicion."

"What about you? What do you believe?"

"Personally, I don't think so. You're a lot like us, if we strip you of those curious clothes and deprive you of your science. Our ancestors' tales show that beings from the sky were foreign to us in every way."

There are people with common sense on this Earth, don't you think, Eleanor? Nathorod continued:

"This land has been stricken with the seal of misfortune ever since the beings from the sky were pushed out to sea. Blood has reddened the soil, there have been disappearances and accidents. You've spent many hours here, Mr. White, and you're not deaf or blind. You've heard the noises—the screams that wake you at night. It made your blood run cold, otherwise you wouldn't have told Wanchese. This is a cursed place. That's why we emigrated to the archipelago. Please don't think that we're happy to submit to this hostile habitat. In fact, the inlet protects us from what's here."

He left it at that, aware that he had perhaps said too much about the beliefs of his people. As for me, I didn't know what to make of it. On the one hand, I felt offended that a primitive man would tell me such nonsense, which was little more than bedtime stories in my eyes; on the other hand, I couldn't deny the reality of the howling that kept us awake night after night. Yet no investigation had yet succeeded in demonstrating the Aquascogocs' involvement in this phenomenon.

"And what do you think it is, Nathorod? Ghosts?"

He looked at me, unable to grasp the meaning of my words. Clearly, the concept of ghosts was beyond his comprehension.

"Demons, then? What do they want from us?"

His face alternated between terror, resentment and, I'd bet, religious superstition.

"Demons want nothing. Demons are. That's all there is to it. The only way to calm them is to satiate them."

I learned no more, although I continued to question him for several minutes, but he frowned and refused to loosen his jaws to say anything more. Perhaps he feared I was mocking him, or perhaps his beliefs compelled him to keep quiet about what he knew of these "demons". In any case, fearing to alienate this unexpected ally, I gave up questioning him further.

The story could have ended there, but a second incident marked the end of the afternoon.

I'd settled down in front of the fireplace whose cozy flames warmed my shed, dozing over an expedition report while listening to the wind make the treetops sing, when Thomas knocked on the door, visibly excited and nervous.

"Are you asleep, John?" he asked through the door.

"Almost," I replied in a pasty voice. "What's the matter?"

"You should come and see," he said with the same air of contained anguish.

I got up and followed him outside. As we hurried between the hovels, he said to me:

"I was lying on my bed, reading a book—a curious one, indeed, *L'histoire entière des poissons*, by G. Rondelet—when I heard noises under my window."

"The usual howling, I suppose."

He stopped, urging me to listen. The wind made a brief complaint before dying down with a growl. Then, to my surprise, I heard the muffled rhythm of a tom-tom combined with sounds reminiscent of the sacred hymns of certain primitive North African tribes. A glow emanating from the center of the camp cast ominous shadows on the walls and facades of the houses, which the darkness transformed into faces from Hell.

Thomas then guided me to the point of origin of these mysteries and I discovered, my eyes wide with amazement, a scene I could never have imagined, even in my most fevered nightmares. The two Indian girls had embarked on a tribal dance in the middle of a circle of poles carved in our image. I'm sure of it, because I recognized my own features on one of them—albeit magnified by the chisel. I counted a dozen of these poles—a dozen of these *totems*, as Nathorod would later call them when I asked him for further explanations.

The two young women, whom I'll call "the priestesses" for want of a better term, seemed to be plunged into a kind of trance, twisting themselves lasciviously around the sculptures, which the changing light of the fire brought horribly to life. You can imagine my amazement, Eleanor. We'd crossed the Atlantic in search of a new world, and now the dissimilarities of that new world were slapping me in the face. A certain nervousness came over me. I had lost the sense of calm that had so enchanted my evening.

The two priestesses moved tirelessly towards the fire with their fluid movements, while Nathorod beat time with a beast-skin drum. Suddenly, they slashed their palms together and joined them over the flames. Streams of blood dripped from their clasped hands, making the fire hiss in a most ghastly fashion. Thomas and I stood dumbfounded, as did the other colonists who had joined us, attracted by the noise.

The ritual lasted as long as a dozen "Our Fathers", after which Nathorod assured us that the demons would no longer trouble our nights. I must confess to a certain circumspection at the time. I pride myself on a certain open-mindedness, but I fear that what I had witnessed was beyond the reasonable boundaries of my intellectual field.

Despite this, I have to admit the following: we haven't been confronted with the nocturnal phenomenon for two weeks now, since the evening of the ritual. I must therefore admit that Nathorod has not lied to me. Unless, of course, he instigated the manifestations in the first place and was merely deceiving us in order to gain our trust, but however seductive this rational explanation may be, I can't bring myself to believe it. His fear on arriving at the fort was unfeigned, as was that of the priestesses. That's why, in the absence of sufficient proof, we'll admit for the moment that there are things beyond our comprehension.

I must now leave you, my dear Eleanor. Winter is coming, and it's going to be harsh. We need to build up a sufficient stock of wood and victuals to last until March. So don't expect to hear from me before then.

Give my love to your mother and accept the expression of my most tender feelings.

Your loving father,
John White

April 13, 1585

Dear Father,

I hope with all my soul that your winter went off without a hitch. On this side of the Atlantic, even far from this profusion of exoticism, life proved eventful. First, Captains Amadas and Barlowe returned to report to Her Majesty. On his arrival, Captain Barlowe described Virginia as "a heavenly place, conducive to all sorts of cultures" and the Amerindians as "hospitable and peaceful", deliberately forgetting to mention the altercation you told me about. This information strengthened Sir Raleigh's resolve to organize a second expedition with the mission of establishing a colony in the region. He entrusted the command of the expedition to Sir Richard Grenville, who set sail from Plymouth harbor on April 9 at the head of six hundred men and five ships: the *Tiger*, the *Roebuck*, the *Red Lion*, the *Elizabeth* and, of course, the *Dorothy*.

Although Ananias agreed, I decided not to take part in this campaign, for one unfortunate reason: Mother is unwell. She fell ill during the first months of winter. A nasty flu. Her life is not threatened, I assure you. However, her condition requires constant monitoring. You'll understand that this is the least I can do. My daughter's duty is to look after her. This time, it will be me and not you who will be taking care of her. So I had to give up accompanying Sir Grenville, but I assure you it's only a temporary reprieve. As soon as Mother's condition improves, I promise to join you, unless you decide to make the reverse crossing in the meantime.

Here's some news from the country, I know you like to be kept up to date. In response to the signing of the Treaty of Joinville, which I mentioned in a previous letter, Her Majesty has signed the Treaty of Sans-Pareil with the Republic of the United Provinces. This agreement supports the deployment of an expeditionary force of several thousand men, whose mission will be to retake the citadel of Antwerp from Spanish hands.

What's more, the privateer Francis Drake is currently cruising south of your position in the Caribbean, intent on sacking Santo Domingo, Cartagena and St. Augustine, three Spanish strongholds. Beware if you venture into this area.

I love you, Father. Please let me hear from you. I miss you terribly.

Your grateful daughter,
Eleanor White, wife Dare

July 2, 1585

My dear, sweet Eleanor,

A million letters wouldn't excuse my long silence. Can you forgive me? So much has demanded my attention these past few months! Only now do I have the respite to sit down at my table and put pen to paper.

I'm sorry to hear that my beloved Tomasyn is unwell. Please wish her a speedy recovery on my behalf, and inform her that I shall be addressing my next letter directly to her—an action I should have taken long ago. I have no doubt, however, that you have reported my previous letters to her in detail, and expressed my affection for her. I am fully aware of the sacrifice my absence represents.

I'm happy to report that the winter passed pleasantly. Our relations with the natives improved considerably after Nathorod performed his ritual in November. There was a new rumor in the archipelago: we were not terrible demons and our camp had been "purified". The natives still dreaded venturing in, but at least they no longer greeted us with arrows, with the exception of the Aquascogocs, who didn't seem to forgive us for sacking their village—and we couldn't hold that against them. We'll still have to be patient to heal this wound.

Sir Richard Grenville finally docked at Virginia after a series of ups and downs. A violent storm separated the *Tiger* from the rest of the fleet off the Azores, in the middle of the North Atlantic. The captains had agreed to meet up in Puerto Rico if such a situation arose, so the *Tiger* entered Mosquito Bay on May 11, in accordance with their arrangement. While waiting for the other ships, Sir Grenville took the opportunity to establish relations with the Spanish. Shortly afterwards, the *Elizabeth* arrived in Puerto Rico. However, there was no sign of the other ships.

Tired of waiting, Sir Grenville set off for Roanoke on June 7. In reality—and this is a secret—Grenville was under pressure from the new colony's governor, Irishman Ralph Lane. The stopover in Puerto Rico was bound to provoke conflict between these two men of strong character. Lane felt that the prolonged stopover in Puerto Rico had cost the colonists valuable time to prepare for winter. In addition to the hostilities between Grenville and Lane, the *Tiger* was significantly too large to penetrate the reefs around Roanoke. She was therefore forced to remain off the Atlantic coast, exposing herself to the bravado of the climate and the most unstable seas. It was on this occasion that the *Red* Lion caught up with the *Tiger* and *Elizabeth*.

Still in Lane's hurry, Sir Grenville attempted to bypass the reefs via the Ocracoke grau, where he hit a shoal, ruining most of his provisions. His men nevertheless managed to repair the ship in less than two weeks, and with no access to Virginia's camp, Sir Grenville decided to land the one hundred and seven colonists at the northern end of Roanoke Island to build an outpost, promising to return in April with new volunteers and food. Having been through a similar ordeal, I sincerely pity these men. I wish they'd come through it unscathed.

The colonization missions are just beginning. The future will hold many opportunities for you to join me on this fantastic journey. I must warn you, however, that the harshness of the environment is matched only by the sobriety of our comforts. When the time comes to make a final decision, be aware that life here has nothing in common with your peaceful London existence. My role as a father obliges me to make you aware of this.

My love to you and Tomasyn.

Your father,
John White

July 22, 1585

My beloved Tomasyn,

In your absence, time stretches as if never to dry up again. I long to see you again. Our Eleanor has informed me of your condition, and I hope it has improved over the last few weeks. If so, please don't hesitate to write back and let me know what's on your mind. At present, I am only aware of them through Eleanor's skilful words, but I know that they certainly embellish and detract from the real expression of your feelings.

On this side of the world, happy events are to be reported: the *Roebuck* and *Dorothy* finally made their reappearance at the beginning of the month. Their crews were bloodless, but mostly alive. The perilous storm had not spared them, and Spanish ships had boarded them on several occasions. Stripped of their food and precious cargo, they were forced to stop off on small islands to gather food for survival. As a result, scurvy, the vile disease that eats away at our crews from within, spread like wildfire among the sailors on the lower decks. We were able to treat them on arrival, however, and most of them are back on their feet.

On Roanoke, the one hundred and seven settlers quickly built a small fort. They also began to exploit the surrounding land and precious metal deposits. But things are taking a worrying turn. The disastrous weather conditions of recent days have wiped out their first seedlings, while they remain under constant threat from the Aquascogocs. Although our initial belief was in subsistence, thanks to agricultural ingenuity, it has become clear to us that, to survive, they will have to rely on the help of the native tribes. This dependence is likely to lead to increasing paranoia on the part of Governor Lane. He now exercises strict control over the settlers, going so far as to build a prison to maintain order and discipline. I must confess to fearing for their lives, although I have every confidence in Lane to protect his men.

For my part, the return of Captain Barlowe has freed me from the burden of command. I can now concentrate again on my illustrations. I'll send you a few with my next letter.

Until then, my beloved, take good care of yourself.

Your obligation,
John White

The following are excerpts from the register of Ralph Lane, governor of the Roanoke outpost.

October 20, 1585

Outpost construction almost complete. Took the liberty of enlarging the prison. More conspirators came to light, bringing the total to six.

Hear cries at night. Seem to come from the open sea.

Mr. Booth has taken it into his head to coax the Roanokes into helping us counter the Aquascogocs if necessary. Let's hope his new-found health can withstand these negotiations.

November 12, 1585

Disastrous weather conditions. Crops reduced to nothing. Starvation looms if nothing is done.

More and more conspirators in our ranks.

Let's sleep during the day to escape the night cries. Suspect the Aquascogocs are trying to scare us.

January 11, 1586

Aquascogocs seek quarrel. Our increased dependence on Roanoke natives for food intensifies the tension, as does the tribes' exposure to our diseases. Smallpox and other ailments begin to decimate the native population, fueling the Aquascogoc belief that we are demonic creatures bent on harm.

Our ally Wingina, chief of the roanoke tribe, happily rejected this argument on the grounds that we can't control drought or food shortages any better than the aquascogoc deities. He did, however, suggest that we should withdraw from the region, for our safety and theirs.

January 21, 1586

Natives have exhausted their reserves. Unable to continue exchanging food with us. Wingina is looking to join forces with other tribes to attack us and drive us off the island.

Night cries always present. Seem to emerge from the sea. Aquascogocs out of the question.

February 8, 1586

Thought it wise to imprison Wingina, then release him. Held his son hostage.

March 22, 1586

Wingina is now called Pemisapan. Change indicates new hostile stance towards the Crown. Will try to cut off our food supply routes to force us to split up in search of food. Detachments are easy targets. Could easily be overwhelmed by a larger Roanoke force. Can't let Wingina/Pemisapan do as they please.

June 11, 1586

Decided to attack the Roanoke village. Wingina/Pemisapan perished in the fighting. Recovered a large stock of food and materials.

June 14, 1586

Outpost assaulted by Roanokes.

June 17, 1586

We managed to repel the natives. Large fleet spotted off the coast. We fear it may be Spanish.

June 18, 1586

Relief that it's an English fleet. Commander Sir Francis Drake. Returns from a glorious expedition against the Spanish in the Caribbean. Sir Drake brought food and water. Asked him to help us find a more suitable settlement.

June 27, 1586

Violent hurricane sweeps the island. Sir Drake offered to take those who wished back to England. All men decided to leave. Can't stay on Roanoke alone. Forced to abandon outpost to leave with Drake.

July 3, 1586

Sir Grenville has left a detachment of fifteen men on Roanoke to protect the island from the Spanish and maintain an English presence, in accordance with Sir Raleigh's orders. Let's stop off at Virginia to repatriate other settlers to England. Among them are John White, an artist and friend of Sir Raleigh who brought back many illustrations, and scientist Thomas Harriot, who has learned the Algonquin language and spent the last ten months collecting samples of minerals and pharmaceutical plants.

Arrival in Portsmouth in three weeks.

February 16, 1587

Dear Mr. White,

Dear John, my old friend,

Before introducing the subject of this missive proper, I'd like to congratulate you on the sumptuous illustrations you've brought back from the New World. These astonishing drawings, I'm sure you know, have caused quite a stir among the members of the Academy. I'm thinking in particular of the "ritual dance", which is terrifyingly realistic—if I may say so myself. However, they were very useful in helping us to understand what awaits us on this unknown continent.

Learning from our previous failure, we have decided that the future colony should be established a little further north, inland. Our intention is to send three new ships to the New World as early as July, carrying farmers and craftsmen who will each receive two hundred hectares of land in Chesapeake Bay. We will not suffer further exposure to famine: you and the men stationed at Roanoke have paid the price, and the tribute was too heavy to pay.

However, to these new settlers must be added a handful of individuals with invaluable experience of the primitive harshness of these lands. That's why I've thought of you, my dear John. I'm appointing you leader of the expedition and governor of the future colony, should you accept my offer.

I hear that Lady Eleanor Dare, your daughter, is expecting her first child. Congratulations to the parents-to-be. They are most welcome to accompany you on your journey. I know what an ordeal it was for you to be separated from your family for two years, so I don't ask you to repeat the sacrifice, especially since, if my memory serves me right—and it does, I can assure you—Eleanor asked me for a place aboard Sir Grenville's *Tiger*.

By the way, I hope your wife Tomasyn's health has improved. If not, I solemnly promise you that she will receive the best treatment during your absence.

I look forward to hearing from you. Please accept, my dear friend, the assurances of my highest esteem.

Sir Walter Raleigh

February 20, 1587

Sir Walter,

You do me too much honor! It would be impudent of me to refuse such a wonderful offer, which can only bring glory to my name for centuries and centuries to come. So I accept with the greatest of joys and the most modest of humblenesses.

My daughter and son-in-law approved this choice and agreed to join me on this expedition. They are particularly moved by the prospect of giving birth to the first Englishman born across the Atlantic. We can only hope that this newborn settler will lead the way for whole generations of heirs to the Crown.

A shadow, however, hangs over this idyllic picture. My beloved Tomasyn's health remains stable, but she can hardly embark on such a perilous undertaking. That's why I'm asking for the help you've offered me, and imploring you to hand her over to the care of your trusted doctor friends.

Your devoted friend,
John White

July 24, 1587

My beloved Tomasyn,

God knows I can't bear to be separated from you. I miss you every hour of the day and night. I dare to hope that the doctors recommended by Sir Raleigh are taking good care of you and doing all they can to counteract this devilish sweat you've been diagnosed with.

You'll be happy to know that our dear Eleanor's long-awaited child is doing just fine. You should see your daughter, she's as round as a sail stretched by the wind (please forgive this quaint and discourteous literary outburst, I'm afraid I'm overjoyed). Together with Ananias, they're looking forward to their new role as parents. As for me, I'm sure I'll fit in just fine as a grandfather.

I must confess that things aren't going as smoothly on board the *Lion* as I'd hoped. Captain Simão Fernandez, in charge of commanding the fleet, is a complicated man with whom it's not easy to communicate. He refuses to acknowledge my status as expedition leader and governor of the colony as long as we're at sea, and therefore deems my every remark null and void. As a result, our collaboration is proving to be very delicate, all the more so as he makes decisions that are devoid of all common sense, with which, as you will have gathered, I profoundly disagree.

The latest example: our stopover in Roanoke.

It had been agreed that, before continuing on to Chesapeake Bay, we would make a detour to pick up the fifteen men left on the island by Sir Grenville. We docked there two days ago, on July 22. To our astonishment, we found that the outpost had been completely emptied of its occupants, with the exception of a curious skeleton that we were unable to identify. It did not correspond in age or size to any of Sir Grenville's men. What's more, certain anatomical features suggest that he suffered from significant physical deformities. For example, we found only four fingers on each of his hands, and his feet were longer than average.

Apart from these singular remains, we found nothing significant, nothing and no one. We have, of course, considered the hypothesis of a native attack, but there is no sign that the fifteen men were massacred or forced to leave the island. To this day, their disappearance remains a mystery. This is where Captain Fernandez's clouded judgment comes into play. For some unfathomable reason, he opposed my desire to set sail again for Chesapeake Bay as soon as possible. Worse still, claiming to need to set sail quickly to avoid the next hurricane season, which would make the return journey dangerous, he refused to let the farmers back on board the *Lion*, advising us to found a new colony on Roanoke.

He left for England this morning, after his men had unloaded our equipment. I find it hard to fathom the behavior of this individual. Was he frightened by the emptying of the fort, or did his tired mind weave artificial links between the misshapen skeleton and the extravagant Indian legends about creatures rising from the sea? I knew he was impressionable, especially as I'd had the opportunity to observe him during the storms we weathered on our crossing, but he didn't strike me as a coward. So, once again, the old adage that adversity reveals a person's true nature has been borne out.

Perhaps he just couldn't wait to get back out to sea and indulge in his usual acts of piracy.

In any case, here I am, faced with a situation that is, to say the least, unexpected. A return trip is out of the question. The next vessel won't reach Roanoke for several weeks, which, given Eleanor's advanced pregnancy, would expose us to the risk of giving birth at sea. I can't take that risk. My choices are therefore severely limited. I have to rehabilitate the derelict fort, and I don't have the luxury of considering any other option.

Pray that we may be spared what happened to its previous inhabitants.

I wish you a speedy recovery.

Your beloved,
John White

August 18, 1587

My beloved Tomasyn—or should I call you Grandma from now on?

Roanoke is radiating happiness. Just this morning, our dear Eleanor gave birth to a beautiful little girl named... Virginia. This is the first English child born in the New World. How glorious for our family! Both mother and child are doing wonderfully well. As for Ananias, he drinks with whoever wants to join him. I don't think I've ever seen him so dissolute. Far be it from me to hold this somewhat unseemly behavior against him, for God knows we need rapture in these troubled times.

The situation on the island remains unstable. Thanks to Manteo, one of the two natives brought back to England three years ago by Captain Barlowe, I've managed to re-establish our friendly relationship with the Croatoans. However, the tribes we fought against in the past refuse to meet me.

I've been investigating the matter of the fifteen missing men, questioning the Croatoans for days—but in a completely courteous and benevolent manner, I assure you, there's no question of repeating Ralph Lane's mistakes. The natives told me that Sir Grenville's men had probably been decimated by an enemy tribe. I suspect the Roanokes did this in retaliation for the assassination of their chief Wingina.

But enough painful news, it's time to rejoice. Order the bishop to ring the bells of St. Paul's Cathedral: we're grandparents!

Your beloved,
John White

August 29, 1587

My dear Tomasyn,

New torments beset the island and spirits are at loggerheads. Just two days after my previous letter, a settler by the name of George Howe was murdered by a native while gathering crabs on the shore. The motives for this savagery escape us: we have no witnesses. All we know is that he was unarmed—apart from the tools needed to catch the crustaceans, which cannot decently be mistaken for an arsenal designed to cause harm. There was therefore no reason to attack him, unless the assailant's intention was to send us a message.

As governor of the colony, I immediately called my council together and we agreed that this crime had to be punished. Our credibility and security were at stake—no one had forgotten the disappearance of Sir Grenville's fifteen men. I had hoped to build courteous relations with our neighbors; I realized to my horror that, in the same way you would train a wild beast, only fear could induce them to show us the respect we deserve.

With hindsight, I can see that we should have reacted differently, but at the time, I saw no alternative but to take reprisals to punish the perpetrators of this terrible crime. The evidence pointed to the Roanoke as the culprits, who had been harassing us ever since our return with their quarrelsome and quarrelsome ways, with the aim of getting us to leave the island. We therefore decided to launch a night raid on their village to force them to leave us in peace.

What a fiasco!

It was dark that night, so dark... My troops were operating in hostile and notoriously unfamiliar territory, as we'd hardly had a chance to explore this part of the island. I'm ashamed of the words I'm about to put down on paper, for they're bound to come back to haunt me for the rest of my life. The men I sent on a punitive expedition made a mistake in attacking the village of our Croatian allies. It was dark, I repeat, and it's difficult to distinguish one native village from another.

Since this abominable misunderstanding, the Croatoans have refused to trade with us—which goes without saying that I understand—but the fort is no longer supplied with food and famine is looming. Our farmers' ploughing will not yield a harvest for several months, making us heavily dependent on our trade relations, which have obviously deteriorated with the other tribes as a result of the dramatic events I've just mentioned.

Some colonists begin to fear for their lives and beg me to return to England to plead our cause. They pin their hopes on my persuasive skills to get Sir Raleigh to grant us reinforcements. For my part, I fear that the battle is lost in advance. I'm not telling you anything new when I say that the conflict with the Spanish is currently monopolizing all available resources. Since Francis Drake set fire to thirty-seven Hispanic ships in the port of Cadiz, Philip II's planned invasion of England may have taken a major blow, but his Invincible Armada remains a threat of the utmost importance.

In spite of all this, I decided to let myself be persuaded to undertake the Atlantic crossing, out of duty and love for our little Virginia—Ananias and Eleanor are indeed among those who fear a painful turn of events. However, neither our daughter nor our granddaughter is physically fit to face the torments of such a journey. As for Ananias, he vigorously refuses to abandon his family to accompany me. I expected no less of him. I must admit to a certain pleasure in hearing him state loud and clear that he will never leave Eleanor and Virginia alone in the face of peril.

By the time you receive this letter, I shall myself be on my way to England. I leave behind me eighty men, seventeen women and eleven children, whose fate will not cease to torment me until my return to Roanoke, which I hope will be as expeditious as possible.

The settlers and I have agreed on a sign. If, for any reason, they are forced to leave the island, they must write their destination in the bark of a tree, so that I can find them. In case of danger, this inscription will be accompanied by the engraving of a Maltese cross. I pray with all my soul that they will never have the opportunity to use this coded language.

There's nothing else worth telling you, so I'll end here, remaining as ever your humble servant.

Your beloved,
John White

The following are excerpts from John White's diary following his departure from Roanoke.

September 13, 1587
Bad luck is striking us even though we haven't yet left the New World. Is this a sign that the Devil is at work against us? The anchor on our Vlie boat refused to lift. Several crew members were seriously injured during the failed maneuver.

September 20, 1587

Rare and variable winds have blown us off course. Our return journey will be that much longer. We pray that God will keep them out of our way.

September 29, 1587

A storm to the northeast pushed us back towards the Caribbean. Many pirate ships cruise these waters.

October 7, 1587

Our supplies are dwindling. The first case of scurvy has been reported.

October 12, 1587

Several crew members have died. Fatigue and despair are our only companions.

October 16, 1587

We've finally made landfall in Smerwick, in the west of Ireland. I'll be able to get back to Southampton as soon as possible.

November 7, 1587

More bad news awaited me on my return to England. Her Majesty the Queen had decreed a general "stop of navigation", preventing any ship from leaving the English coast. The reason was that the invincible fleets of the King of Spain, combined with the forces of the Pope, were preparing an invasion. Sir Raleigh nevertheless requested —and was granted—an audience to plead my case and provide me with ships to aid the colony of Roanoke. His request was rejected by the Queen.

March 23, 1588

I've managed to acquire a pair of small ships, the Brave *and the* Roe, *which weren't suitable for military service. The voyage aboard them promises to be perilous, as they are hardly suited to an Atlantic crossing. The conflict with the King of Spain looks set to drag on. I haven't received a letter from Roanoke since my return to England. The lines of communication have been interrupted.*

April 12, 1588

Le Brave *and Le* Roe *were intercepted by French pirates. They let us live, but robbed us of all our victuals, powder, weapons and provisions. Our voyage must be abandoned. I'm beginning to realize that I was born under an unlucky star. The damage to my two ships will take months to repair. I can hardly afford to finance such a costly project.*

February 3, 1589

Because of the war, available ships are sorely lacking. However, the words "despair" and "abandonment" have been banished from my vocabulary.

May 13, 1590

John Watts, the country's richest shipowner, was about to send three ships to the West Indies when he was told they could not leave port. Sir Raleigh, who still retains a certain influence at court, intervened and obtained permission for Watts to sail, which he handed over in return for the promise of a stopover on Roanoke to unload supplies and equipment. The Hopewell *and* Moonlight *sail in three days. I can't wait to set sail on them.*

August 18, 1590

My beloved Tomasyn,

Today is our little Virginia's third birthday. By an extraordinary coincidence, I happened to set foot in Roanoke this very morning. However, fate couldn't have played a crueler trick on me.

I apologize in advance for the possible length of this missive; I feel the need to recount, in detail and in writing, the sequence of events that led me to take up my pen this evening, in order to anchor the cruel reality in my mind.

We approached the island's eastern coast under a lull in the weather, but the sky remained singularly low and dark. Roanoke's atmosphere was heavy and peculiar, and we found it unsettling. Not a bird sang, not a single animal scampered across our path as we trudged along. The path through the forest to the south-west is usually maintained on a daily basis to ensure easy access to the beach, but it seemed like ages since this work had been done. Only the sound of our footsteps and the relentless surf of the Atlantic reached our ears. The smell of the ocean, particularly dense,

---

wafted through the undergrowth, covering all other scents. I remember finding it curious, though I didn't attach too much importance to it.

We spoke little. The air, heavy with threats, forbade any quietude to our minds.

The path forked to the right. There, through the undergrowth, the fort loomed like an apparition. It was here that the story took a most peculiar turn. Weeds had grown up between the two open leaves of the front door, which had clearly not been closed for some time.

We advanced between the huts under a leaden sky. They were falling into disrepair: shutters torn off, roofs ruined by the harshness of successive winters, wall planks worm-eaten by humidity... The place was abandoned.

I rushed towards Eleanor and Ananias' dwelling. The door swung on its single hinge with a loud bang, and darkness engulfed me as soon as I crossed the threshold. A heady whiff of rot and mildew hung in the air. And in its wake, always that ocean smell, haunting, revolting.

The interior was intact. Dusty and warped by the sudden temperature changes Roanoke is accustomed to, but otherwise in perfect condition. Four chairs sat on a wooden cradle. I imagined the four of us there, surrounding the child, Ananias, Eleanor, you, my beloved, and me. A child had grown up here, but not enough to play his nails on the walls or carve clumsy drawings on them. Only blind nature had done its outrages to the house, as well as to all the buildings in the fort.

I opened the bedroom door: the bed was made and, at its foot, a pewter pitcher was overturned. Leaving aside the accumulated dust and the awful stench of dampness, one could not help but be struck by the orderliness of the dwelling. Which worried me even more. A native attack would have left its mark, an indescribable chaos. What kind of war went on in good order, without material destruction of any kind?

"What do you think, John?" asked the *Moonlight*'s captain.

"I don't think it's any good, Mr Watts," I replied honestly.

A shadow had crept into my heart. I had never felt such fear, not even in the darkest hours of the night when the screams kept me awake. Having come so close to death on so many occasions, it had seemed to me that nothing so terrifying could be experienced. Clearly, I was wrong.

As we headed for the chapel in the center of the fort, we glanced at the other dwellings and the warehouse, where leather bags still hanging from rusty hooks were gradually decaying, spilling their moldy contents onto the floor. We didn't come across a living soul, not an insect, not a bird, not even a spider's web woven into the corner of a window. Nothing but dust, accompanied by a terrible feeling of abandonment. I had become the governor of a ghost town. But worst of all, I had failed my daughter and granddaughter.

And always that ocean smell, heady, unforgiving.

We finally reached the chapel. I contemplated it from top to bottom and was astonished: it had never seemed so large to me. It stood withered before us, as sinister as it was inhospitable. It was undeniable that all religious sentiment and sanctity had long since deserted it. I shivered as I placed my hand on the handle. When was the last time this door had been touched? A greasy film covered the wood, so oily that I was forced to wipe my palm on the back of my pants.

The rust-ridden hinges groaned as I pushed the door open.

We paced up and down the consecrated space, the damp dust retaining the imprint of our many passages, finding nothing but an open Bible on the lectern, the thirteenth chapter of the Book of Revelation. I looked down and read:

"And he stood on the sand of the sea. Then I saw a beast rise from the sea, with ten horns and seven heads, and on his horns ten diadems, and on his heads names of blasphemy. The beast I saw was like a leopard; its feet were like the feet of a bear, and its mouth like the mouth of a lion".

I winced as I deciphered a sentence that an obviously childish and inexperienced hand had added in the margin: *Slay the demons and the soil will be fertile again, ordered those who came from the water. Croatoan! Croatoan!*

I frantically flipped through the Bible, the rustle of the pages breaking the silence of the chapel. Some of the verses had been torn out and reassembled, obviously to form new chapters. All had the sea as their subject. Occasionally, a so-called sea people was mentioned, which brought back memories of certain local legends.

I didn't have time to ponder the meaning of these words as I was being called outside. One of the sailors had spotted the word *Croatoan* engraved on a post within the enclosure, as well as the letters *CRO* carved into the bark of a nearby tree. I was relieved to see that no Maltese crosses accompanied these engravings. This meant that the settlers were safe and sound, and had retreated to nearby Croatoan Island.

We'll be on our way tomorrow to let them know that their ordeal ends with our return.

My thoughts are with you.

Your beloved,
John White

October 17, 1590

My beloved Tomasyn,

I regret to inform you that the search was unsuccessful. No trace of the colonists has been found on the island of Croatoan or on the other islets of the archipelago. The natives don't seem to know what happened to them. Some say the colony was wiped out by the Spanish.

Our only clue lies in a series of parallel grooves that run from the east coast beach to Roanoke Fort. Some experienced men believe that heavy objects were moved over this distance, perhaps to be loaded onto ships. I can't think of any other explanation for these tracks leading to the ocean. If the purpose of the manoeuvre was to make the settlers disappear, why throw them into the sea? There are more rational and definitive ways.

Please be assured that I will keep you informed of the progress of our investigation.

Don't lose hope, my beloved, I'll find our Eleanor, as well as our little Virginia, so that you can finally make her charming acquaintance.

Your beloved,
John White

The following is taken from Sir Walter Raleigh's memoirs, *Commentaries on the Exploration of the New World*, Chapter 7, *The Failure of a Colony*.

[...] Jamestown outpost led by Captain John Smith; their encounter with the Powhatan Indians; and the loss he suffered. Despite many years of research, I regret to admit that the lost colony of Roanoke has never been found, and that it probably never will be.

John White himself, former governor of the colony and close friend, seems to accept this terrible fact with difficulty. So many setbacks have finally embittered his naturally chagrined mood. It seems," says Moreau, "that he wanted to take revenge on everyone for his suffering. His judgments are harsher, his features rougher, his accusations more violent. Frustrated on both sides, barely relying on the meagre income from his illustrations, powerless to bring in his debts, he had to alienate his annuity contracts and resell his Irish property.

I welcomed him to my property after his wife died of grief—need I remind you that the poor lady, weakened by illness, lost her only daughter in the affair, as well as her granddaughter?

John White draws sea charts on my behalf, and when he's not holed up in his studio, I sometimes catch him strolling through the gardens, reflecting on the unfortunate events that have ruined his expectations in the New World. Yet, I know, he continues to nurture the hope that Eleanor and Virginia are still alive, somewhere in the islands across the Atlantic. [...]

Sunday Register, Beckley, W. Va., Sunday Morning, August 24, 1952—7

The Strange Case of Virginia Dare

What Happened to First American Girl Still Top Mystery of History

By H. D. CRAWFORD
Central Press Correspondent

WASHINGTON — American history has no more intriguing mystery than what happened to the Lost Colony that disappeared between 1587 and 1591 from Roanoke Island off the coast of North Carolina.

Among the 150 men, women and children of this Lost Colony was a baby girl named Virginia Dare. She was the first child of English parentage born in America.

The happy event of her birth took place 365 years ago, on Aug. 18, 1587. This was less than a month after Sir Walter Raleigh's second colony arrived on Roanoke Island.

Virginia Dare was granddaughter of the colony's governor, John White. Her father was Ananias Dare, one of White's 12 assistants in the "Citie of Raleigh in Virginia."

Shortly after Virginia Dare was born her grandfather left for England with two small ships to get supplies. War with Spain delayed White's return, and when he did get back to Roanoke island in August, 1591, the colony had disappeared. No one has ever found out what happened to the Lost Colony.

Look at your map of North Carolina today and you'll see that the easternmost county is named Dare. Between the mainland and Roanoke Island is Croatan sound.

On Roanoke Island are two towns and, at the northern tip, the Fort Raleigh National Historic Site. Manteo is the seat of Dare county. Wanchese is a town near the island's southern tip.

Behind these names is an intriguing story. The county is named after Virginia Dare. Manteo and Wanchese are named after two Indians whom leaders of Raleigh's first expedition in 1584 took back to England, where they were showered with honors before being returned to their native Roanoke island laden with gifts.

Manteo remained friendly to the white men; Wanchese became their enemy. Croatan sound was named after one word, "CROATAN," which the Lost Colony left on a tree to indicate their destination.

Two theories about the Lost Colony's fate have given rise to legends in the folk lore of North Carolina. One theory is that all members of the Lost Colony were murdered. The other is that they went to live among the Croatan Indians, who since have claimed that they have white blood in their veins from the Lost Colony of Roanoke Island.

Among the oldest legends of America are those surrounding the mysterious disappearance and fate of Virginia Dare. One legend is that when she grew to maidenhood a rejected lover, an Indian, changed her by sorcery into a white doe. She lived a charmed life, until one day a cruel chief's love overcame magic and he shot her with a silver arrow.

Superstition spread throughout the south that it was bad luck to see a white doe, and that you could kill one only with a silver arrow.

A related legend is that when Scupperong vines were discovered in 1581 in the Carolinas they bore white grapes with white skins, and their juice made white wine. After the Indian chief killed Virginia Dare with the silver arrow, however, her blood the Scupperong so its grapes were dark purple, yielding reddish juice that produced red wine.

While most people today, naturally, do not believe such legends, the fact remains that no one knows what happened to Virginia Dare and the men and women of the Lost Colony.

Fort Raleigh Historic Site today

Site of the Lost Colony—after National Park Service took it over. Monument before block house tells of the story of Virginia Dare.

An article from The Raleigh Register, *August 24, 1952 (©newspapers.com)*

The disappearance of the so-called "Lost Colony" of Roanoke is one of the most fascinating mysteries in American history.

After several years of exploration of the east coast of North America, under the supervision of Sir Walter Raleigh, the decision was taken in 1587 to establish the very first English colony. A hundred civilians set sail. Among them was John White, an artist who had brought back numerous illustrations of fauna, flora and Indian life from a previous expedition. The fleet, bound for Chesapeake Bay, has to make a detour to Roanoke Island to pick up men left behind in garrison a year earlier. Once there, they find nothing and no one, except for a skeleton they can't identify. There's no sign that they've been massacred or forced to leave the island.

Due to a conflict between John White, governor of the future colony, and Simão Fernandez, commander of the fleet, the colonists had no choice but to settle on Roanoke, despite a tumultuous history between English soldiers and local tribes.

At first, all went well. The little colony prospered and welcomed the very first English baby born on American soil, Virginia Dare, granddaughter of John White. Forced to leave Roanoke towards the end of 1587 in order to bring back more settlers and supplies, White didn't return until 1590, stranded in England by the naval war with Spain.

When they landed on the island on August 18, 1590, he and his men could find no trace of the colony. Men, women and children had vanished. However, there were no signs of violence, no buried bodies and the buildings had been carefully dismantled, a sign that the move had not been rushed. A word is engraved

Title page of a book published in 1589 containing descriptions of Europeans exploring the North American continent, including descriptions by John White.

on one of the fence posts surrounding the village: Croatoan. It's the name of a nearby island, where there's no one either. The letters CRO have also been carved into a tree. Despite numerous searches, White was unable to find the hundred or so settlers.

Illustration of John White discovering the word CROATOAN (©Classic Vision/age fotostock)

Little is known of his life after the failure of the Roanoke colony. He seems to have resided in Ireland, living on the estates of Sir Walter Raleigh, for whom he continued to draw land maps. The last document formally linked to White is a letter he wrote from Ireland in 1593 to the publisher of his Roanoke prints.

Twelve years pass before Sir Raleigh decides to investigate the disappearance of the colonists. In 1602, an expedition set sail for Roanoke. Unfortunately, shortly before reaching their destination, the weather became so bad that they were forced to turn back. On his return, Sir Raleigh was arrested for treason, which prevented him from financing further research missions.

After the establishment of the Jamestown colony in 1607, efforts were made by the English to obtain information from the Powhatan Indian tribe. The famous Captain John Smith learned from the chief that he had ordered his tribe's warriors to murder the Roanoke settlers. This information was brought back to England in the spring of 1609, and King James and the Royal Council were convinced that the Powhatan Indians were really responsible for the disappearance of the lost colony.

A few years later, William Strachey, secretary of the Jamestown colony, obtained the same information from the Powhatan chief, who nevertheless added further details to his story. According to him, the settlers had been living peacefully among the Chesapeake tribe for over twenty years when he ordered their massacre. He claimed to have done so because his priests had predicted that he would be overthrown by the locals. However, no physical evidence ever supported his claim, and no bodies were ever found.

Secoton, a Powhatan Village, *watercolor drawing by John White, circa 1587 (©The Trustees of the British Museum)*

When French Huguenots settled in the area a century later, they noticed that several members of the Tuscorora tribe, friendly natives who lived west of Roanoke, possessed blond hair and blue eyes, rather unusual characteristics for Indians. As Jamestown was the nearest settlement and no marriages between the Tuscaroras and the British had been recorded, they concluded that some of the Roanoke settlers were their ancestors.

The story of the lost colony became part of legend and popular culture. From a scientific point of view, however, the story remained quiet until 2012, when researchers noticed a curious detail on a map of eastern North Carolina drawn by John White: a patch of paper obscured the image of a fort on the tip of Albemarle Sound. The fort in question is located eighty kilometers west of Roanoke. The top of the patch also shows the faded features of a "fort drawn with invisible ink", according to analysts.

According to specialists, White wanted to hide the existence of this fort from the Spanish, who already perceived the Roanoke colony as a threat to their territorial domination of North America. This link rekindles scientific interest in the lost colony.

An article from the Daily Advance, *1939 (©The Daily Advance)*

Several teams of archaeologists set out to establish the truth. One theory quickly emerged: assimilation. The settlers, thinking themselves abandoned by the metropolis, probably sought refuge with the local tribes in order to survive. At least, that's what several excavations suggest, including those carried out in January 2020 on a cliff overlooking Albermarle Bay, where White's map indicated the fort. A team from the First Colony Foundation unearthed a treasure trove of English, German, French and Spanish pottery.

"The number and diversity of artifacts recovered clearly show that the site was inhabited by several members of Sir Walter Raleigh's colony, which disappeared in 1587," says archaeologist and team leader Nick Liccketti.

At the same time, another group led by Bristol University archaeologist Mark Horton is excavating an ancient Amerindian village on present-day Hatteras Island (historically Croatoan, sometimes referred to as Hatorask). With the help of volunteers, the archaeologists discovered European artifacts, including a 16th-century rapier and part of a rifle.

If both discoveries are confirmed, they will support the theory that the settlers split into two or more groups of survivors, no doubt aided by the Amerindians with whom they had forged close ties. We may also receive confirmation that the group established with the Chesapeakes was massacred by the Powhatans.

To be continued...

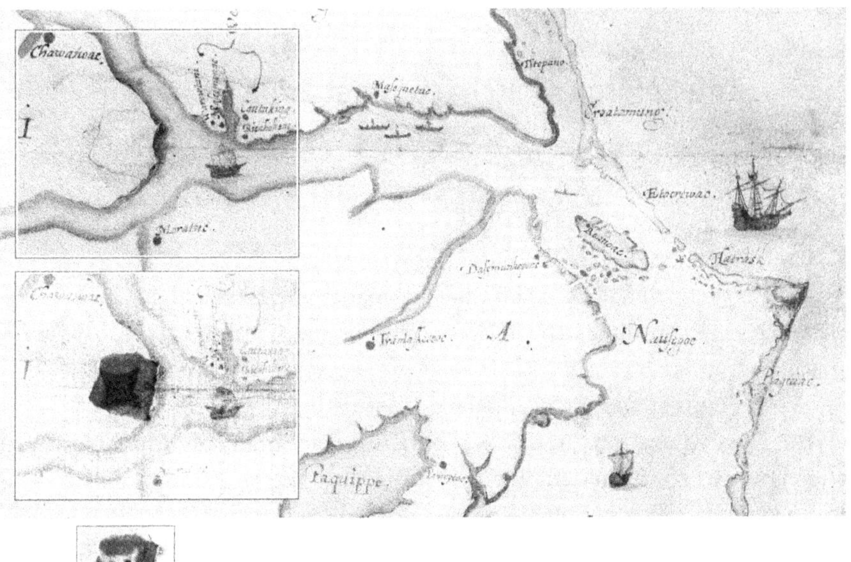

(©UBIQUE American Geographical Society)

The opinion of archaeologist Erika Weinkauf

I'm not a specialist in this period or this geographical area, so my remarks remain very general and based on what I've read in the dossier above, as well as in the articles I've consulted in *National Geographic* and *Sciences & Vie*, two reference magazines.

- Excavations on the cliff overlooking Albermarle Bay in 2020

[In North Carolina, new clues to the Lost Colony of Roanoke, 2020] https://www.nationalgeographic.fr/histoire/2020/11/en-caroline-du-nord-de-nouveaux-indices-sur-la-colonie-perdue-de-roanoke

[The lost colony of Roanoke found? A 400-year-old village sheds light on one of America's great colonial mysteries, 2024] https://www.science-et-vie.com/science-et-culture/archeologie/la-colonie-perdue-de-roanoke-retrouvee-un-village-de-400-ans-eclaire-un-des-grands-mysteres-colonial-americain-135697.html

- Excavations by Mark Horton (University of Bristol) at an ancient Amerindian village on present-day Hatteras Island, formerly Croatoan (2015?).

[United States: The Mystery of the Lost Colony - after 2015] https://www.nationalgeographic.fr/histoire/etats-unis-le-mystere-de-la-colonie-perdue

Based on this, I would tend to agree with the 2024 article and the hypothesis of assimilation for reasons of survival. We always tend to envisage confrontation with the natives, but we're probably wrong to think that in this case. The two communities got along very well.

As for the testimony of the Indians who claim to have killed part of the community integrated into their homes, this obviously needs to be verified, as the idea cannot be dismissed, it seems to me.

The opinion of 1st Commissioner Maillard of the Brussels Judicial Police - Division in charge of crime against property and people.

Obviously I'm not an archaeologist, so I'm going to approach this case as I would a "classic" investigation.

First interesting detail: the authorities leave the island to look for other settlers. Is this to the liking of the local tribes, who may feel gradually invaded? It's well known that when the cat's away, the mice will dance.

What's more, the governor didn't return until three years later, and it's safe to assume that the colonists couldn't have been told the reason for the delay. This raises the question of the colonists' supposed abandonment of the island.

Despite searches on the island, the hundred or so settlers disappeared. The island of Croatan was also visited following the traces and clues found on Roanoke Island, but without success.

There's nothing to suggest a hasty departure: no traces of violence, no buried bodies and all the buildings have been carefully dismantled. But three years is a long time on an island. Everything may have been cleaned up after a massacre, the bodies thrown into the sea or burned. Did the settlers have boats, or is it possible that they built them? Were they far from the American coast?

In 1607, twenty years later, Captain John Smith learned from the chief of the Powhatan Indian tribe that he had ordered his warriors to kill the colonists:

- If this chief can explain that he ordered the massacre of the colonists, why haven't they been able to gather more details about this attack? How did the settlers die? What was done with the bodies? If he can express himself, he can explain that too.

- A hundred people don't just disappear. And, *conversely*, a hundred corpses leave traces.

The possibility of the settlers' assimilation seems quite plausible to me. They undoubtedly made their way to western Roanoke, where their presence was concealed.

Many years later, traces of descendants with similar physical characteristics to the lost colonists were found.

The discovery in January 2020 of remnants of this English colony on Roanoke Island, as well as traces of European artifacts on the island formerly known as Croatan, lends further credence to this thesis.

Let's imagine three groups from the colony of a hundred settlers. One group leaves for the island of Croatan, the other for western Roanoke and the third is decimated by the Powhatan tribe. As far as I'm concerned, the tribal chief has no reason to lie.

At present, DNA research could be carried out on the blond children found on the island to determine whether their origins are indeed English.

For me, the trigger was the settlers' sense of abandonment at not seeing the English return for three consecutive years. At some point, some had to start asserting themselves in order to survive, leading to a split into three groups.

The *Cleveland Torso Murderer* file

15 years after the fact, the epilogue to the Cleveland murders. Will the suspect be found guilty?

A review by Jonathan Latimer, for the Chicago Herald American.

[Eliot Ness's resounding voice, slow and precise, immediately commands attention. His black hair, piercing gaze and attitude give him a dark air, but he is in fact a scholar of the evil that plagues the human race. He's been around it long enough and close enough to bear witness.

Today, in this courtroom, the hero who put Al Capone behind bars utters the words to which every detective aspires: "I think I've solved the case." His eyes light up and his stern face breaks into a smile.

For over a decade, Ness has been investigating the series of murders that terrified Cleveland during the Great Depression of the 1930s. The case severely tested him, the legendary Prohibition agent turned Cleveland security director. His inability to catch the murderer led to draconian measures that belied his heroic reputation.

Now he's getting a chance to restore his reputation, when he's called to the stand to testify at a suspect's trial. Has he solved the murders, fifteen years after the first possible victim washed up on a Lake Erie beach?

The following is an account of his hearing before the twelve jurors assembled by the Honorable Judge Wilkerson].

PROSECUTOR: Mr. Ness, I'm not going to insult you by asking you to identify yourself to the members of the jury, but I believe that your actions and your reputation precede you, so allow me to get to the heart of the matter. Could you give us a brief summary of the facts attributed to the person known as both the *Torso Killer*[12] and the *Mad Butcher of Kingsbury Run*[13]?

ELIOT NESS: Of course. "Torso", as I used to call him in front of my men, is suspected of having killed seven men and five or six women. He dismembered most

---

12. Literally "the torso killer".
13. "The Mad Butcher of Kingsbury Run".

of his victims, cutting them up with a skill that suggests a profound knowledge of human anatomy. He always cut off his victims' heads and had a habit of leaving the bodies in the valley that runs through Cleveland's East Side, from about East 79th Street to the Cuyahoga River.

PROC. What can you tell us about his victims?

E.N.: The oldest victim, referred to as "No. 0", was a woman in her thirties. Her torso, with legs still attached but amputated at the knees, was discovered on September 5, 1934, on the shores of Lake Erie, near Euclid Beach. Cuyahoga County Coroner A.J. Pearse noted that a chemical preservative had made the skin red, hard and leathery. I remember he thought it was rather strange.

Subsequent searches recovered other body parts, but the head was never found and, sadly, the woman was never identified. She was nicknamed "The Lady of the Lake"[14]. However, it's worth noting that it was only two years later that this discovery was included in the official count of Torso-related murders, which is why it was given the number zero.

PROC. I see. What about victim no. 1?

E.N.: It was found on September 23, 1935 at Kingsbury Run. It was a Caucasian male, decapitated and emasculated. Two teenagers discovered him at the foot of Jackass Hill, where East 49th Street leads into Kingsbury Run. The body, naked except for a pair of socks, was clean and bloodless, with rope burns around both wrists. Coroner Pearse determined the cause of death to be decapitation. Fingerprints identified the victim as Edward Andrassy, a twenty-nine-year-old white male who frequented the Roaring Third.

PROC. Could you explain to the jury what Roaring Third is?

E.N.: It's an area east of Kingsbury Run, known for its bars, gambling dens, brothels and vagrants. In fact, some prefer to refer to it as the *Hobo Jungle*[15].

Edward Andrassy was a former nursing assistant formerly charged with carrying an illegal weapon. He was identified by fingerprints.

PROC. While searching the crime scene, the police discovered a second body.

E.N.: A man, also decapitated and emasculated. It transpired that he was covered in the same chemical as the Lady of the Lake and had been dead for several weeks. This white man in his forties has not yet been identified.

---

14. "The Lady of the Lake."

15. In the United States, the term *hobo* refers to a homeless worker who moves from town to town, usually hiding out on freight trains, and makes a living from seasonal manual labor.

PROC. : Then it was 42-year-old Florence Polillo's turn.

E.N.: Half his torso, his upper legs, his right hand and arm were found wrapped in newspaper at the bottom of two baskets on January 26, 1936. The baskets had been abandoned next to the Hart Manufacturing building on Central Avenue, near East 20th Street. The left arm, upper torso and lower legs were found ten days later at another location on Orange Avenue. Identified by fingerprints, the victim turned out to be Florence Polillo, a former waitress known to the police for having been arrested once for prostitution.

PROC. Which brings us to the tattooed man.

E.N.: The famous tattooed man... A young white man of about 25. His head was discovered near the East 55th Street bridge on June 5, 1936, wrapped in pants. The next day, police officers found the man's body dumped in front of the police building on Nickel Plate Railroad. Clean and drained of blood, the corpse was intact except for the severed head.

My colleagues had hoped to identify him by the presence of six distinctive tattoos on different parts of his body, including a butterfly and the cartoon character *Jiggs*, but they were unsuccessful. This death convinced us that all the murders were linked, something that had not been formally established until then.

PROC. Then there was victim No. 5, the man in his thirties found on July 22, 1936 along Big Creek on Cleveland's West Side, also decapitated...

E.N.: Then a man in his twenties, discovered on August 10, 1936 and, finally, victim no. 7, a woman in her thirties whose torso was only partially uncovered on February 23, 1937, at the junction of Lake Shore Boulevard and East 156th Street. All three remain unidentified.

PROC. You say "at last", but this term seems relative in this case, since you were far from having reached the end of your troubles.

E.N.: That's right. The dismembered skeleton of 40-year-old Rose Wallace was waiting for us under the Lorain-Carnegie bridge in June 1937. She was provisionally identified from her dental records.

PROC. Provisoirement?

E.N.: Well, there are a number of indications in that direction. Dental examination, in particular, unofficially identified her as Rose Wallace, of Scovill Avenue. We followed all the leads we had on her, but they came to nothing.

PROC. This is the last victim whose identity you were able to cross-check.

E.N.: Indeed. Bodies n° 9 to n° 12 could never be identified. However, as far as victim no. 9 is concerned, I think it's important to point out that we were able to extract his entire body from the Cuyahoga River.

PROC. : With the exception of his head, of course.

E.N.: Of course... But it's interesting to note that her abdomen had been ripped open and her heart torn out, clearly indicating a new degree of perversion in the killer's approach. The tenth body also told us some interesting things, as for the first time, Coroner Gerber detected the presence of drugs. Were these drugs used to immobilize the victim, or was she a drug addict? The answer might have been established if the arms had been found, but this was not the case. Perhaps the killer took them with him, leaving us in the dark.

PROC. I know you're reluctant to talk about it, but I must mention victims no. 11 and no. 12, and the curious circumstances surrounding their discovery...

E.N.: I see what you're getting at. Very well, then. On August 16, 1938, three scrap dealers rummaging through a junkyard, located at East 9th Street and Lakeside, found a woman's torso wrapped in a man's blue double-breasted blazer, himself wrapped in an old quilt. The legs and arms were discovered in a homemade box, wrapped in brown butcher paper and held together with rubber bands. The head had been similarly wrapped.

Gerber noted that some parts appeared to have been refrigerated. Searching for other parts, my agents discovered the remains of a second body a few meters away. Both bodies had been placed in a position clearly visible from my office window.

PROC. As if to taunt you.

E.N.: That's what I think. This cat-and-mouse game with the police is typical of a serial killer.

PROC. What evidence do you have that all these murders are the work of the same individual?

E.N.: Coroner Samuel Gerber insisted that this was the case, because of the precision of the dismemberment. Whoever did this obviously knew where to make the incisions. They knew the anatomy of the human body.

PROC. What were your main theories at the time about the identity of the killer?

E.N.: We considered the possibility of a hunter, a butcher or a medical intern. For his part, Coroner Gerber argued that the killer had to be highly intelligent, with a deep knowledge of anatomy—perhaps a doctor.

PROC. Is this the basis on which you interviewed Dr. Francis Edward Sweeney in 1938?

E.N.: I'd prefer to come back to Dr. Sweeney's case later, if you don't mind.

PROC. Of course. Tell me the story of the wanderer Emil Fronek.

E.N.: In November 1934, Fronek was walking along Broadway Avenue in search of food. He said he found himself on the second floor of a doctor's office. This doctor allegedly said to him, "I'll give you a meal".

As Emil ate, he began to feel dizzy and wondered if he'd been drugged. So he left the room and ran down the stairs before reaching Broadway Avenue and taking refuge in a train carriage, where he fell asleep. He didn't wake up until three days later, proving that he had indeed been drugged. He said he returned to Broadway Avenue a short time later, but couldn't find the doctor. He then decided that staying in Cleveland had become too dangerous for him and emigrated to Chicago, where he got a job as a longshoreman.

His story didn't reach us until August 1938, and as soon as it did, I sent Detective Peter Merylo to Chicago to bring him back to us. Two of my men then drove Fronek to Broadway Avenue, and when he arrived in the area between East 50th Street and East 55th Street, he said, "It's here somewhere." Nevertheless, despite their wanderings, I regret to admit that they found nothing resembling a doctor's office.

PROC. : Officially, you told the press, and I quote: "We don't think that Mr. Fronek's story has anything to do with the butcher".

E.N.: Indeed, I didn't want to frighten the assassin, as we were convinced that his "laboratory" was close to the city center.

PROC. Tell us a little about Frank Dolezal.

E.N.: Dolezal was arrested in August 1939 by the county sheriff, Martin O'Donnell, for the murder of Flo Polillo. This homeless man worked as a bricklayer and had lived with her for some time.

Upon arrest, he confessed to murdering her, but later recanted and claimed that sheriff's deputies had beaten him. He was found dead in jail a month later, hanged. Coroner Gerber ruled it a suicide.

PROC. Was Frank Dolezal a potential culprit, in your opinion?

E.N.: In my opinion, the main problem is where he could have developed the surgical skills needed to disarticulate bodies. Apart from that, he's a credible suspect, indeed, especially as subsequent investigation revealed that he also consorted with Edward Andrassy and Rose Wallace.

PROC. And Willie Johnson?

E.N.: Johnson was arrested after leaving the dismembered remains of 19-year-old Margaret Francis Wilson at Kingsbury Run in 1942. He was convicted of murder for this act. Witnesses claimed he knew the victim Rose Wallace, but Johnson insisted he was not involved in the *Torso Killer* case. He was executed in 1944.

PROC. Which brings us back to Dr. Francis Edward Sweeney. Earlier you mentioned Peter Merylo, who was one of the lead detectives on the case. What was his reaction to the hypothesis that a doctor could be the killer?

E.N.: I remember he was very open to the idea. But, to tell the truth, Peter was convinced that similar murders had occurred in New Castle, Pennsylvania, and were the work of the same man, and that the killer used the railroad between Cleveland, Youngstown and New Castle to get around, mingling with the homeless population.

To speak more specifically about Dr. Sweeney's suspicions, I base myself on the fact that six doctors practiced together at the corner of Broadway and Pershing avenues, a group to which he belonged along with a few others such as Dr. Edward Peterka.

Dr. Peterka had converted the first floor of a family building into a medical establishment, while the upper floor was reserved for living quarters. My hypothesis is that Emil Fronek probably walked around the back of the house, looking for discarded food, and never saw the front of the building, which is why he couldn't recognize it later. And that's where the staircase to the upper floor would have been.

Was it Dr. Francis Sweeney waiting for him at the top of the stairs and offering him food? I believe so. Any of the six doctors had access to this floor, and his colleagues reported that he was going through a difficult time. His wife had filed for divorce after applying in 1933 to the probate court[16] for him to be taken into care and assessed, as his alcoholism was becoming increasingly problematic. He neglected his practice, was violent towards her and her two sons, and disappeared for days at a time.

The three identified victims of the *Torso Killer*—Edward Andrassy, Flo Polillo and Rose Wallace, if we take her at face value—had at least one thing in common: they all frequented the Roaring Third. In fact, there's a bar there where all three of them drank at one time or another, a popular spot for the down-and-out.

---

16. *Probate court.*

I think Dr. Sweeney could easily have gone into these bars close to the city center and befriended his victims before drugging them, probably in the same way he had tried to drug Emil Fronek.

PROC. The question remains: where did he commit the murders and dismemberments?

E.N.: Not far from Roaring Third is a mortician. This point isn't entirely clear, but it seems that Sweeney enjoyed some sort of privilege at this funeral home, where he could go and perhaps perform surgery on unclaimed corpses.

The icing on the cake is that all these locations cover the area where the first bodies were found in September 1935, and are only a few minutes away by car.

PROC. : So you think Torso, as you call him, is Dr. Francis Edward Sweeney, who was appearing today as a defendant?

E.N.: There's no doubt in my mind that Mr. Sweeney is the killer.

PROC. Thank you, Mr. Ness. I have no further questions.

[Eliot Ness's testimony was not enough to convict Dr. Francis Edward Sweeney of murder, the jury finding that the lack of physical evidence was flagrant, while the body of presumptions was not strong enough to justify a guilty verdict.

To this day, the crimes of the *Cleveland Torso Murderer* remain officially unsolved in the eyes of the law].

The facts

The story you've just read is a mixture of proven facts (all about the victims) and a theory developed by author James Jessen Badal, who has investigated the story for over a decade and written several books on the subject (all of which indict Dr. Sweeney), all told through the medium of a fictional trial. Dr. Francis E. Sweeney never appeared in court as a suspect.

But let's start from the beginning.

Article from the Omaha World Herald, *September 18, 1938, page 37 (©Omaha World Herald)*

Article from The Cincinnati Post, *July 8, 1939, recounting the whole story (©newspapers.com)*

United States, Kingsbury Run neighborhood, Cleveland, Ohio, between 1934 and 1938. Several victims, always decapitated, often dismembered, sometimes with their torsos cut in two or their appendages severed, were discovered. Most of the male victims had been castrated. Some showed traces of chemical treatments applied to their bodies, making their skin red, hard and leathery. Many were found after a considerable lapse of time, sometimes more than a year after their death.

POLICE DEPARTMENT

CLEVELAND, OHIO

DEPARTMENTAL INFORMATION

PRECINCT D.B. DATE July 7, 1937 19

EXAMINED BY RANK DATE 19

FROM: Emil Musil Det. TO: Harvey Weitzel Lieut.

SUBJECT: Torso victim.

COPIES TO: Files-Eastside-Coroner.

Sir:-

    At 11;30 this A.M. on call from this office that two arms of the torso which had been found on July 6th 1937, were floating in the Cuyahoga River, in the upper west 3rd street bridge.

    With Sergeant Hogan responded and upon arrival found the two arms in the river about 100 feet apart, same being recovered from the river by Sergt Hogan and conveyed them to the County Morgue.

    Examination disclosed that they were the two parts of the arms below the elbow of a white man, and were part of the torso which were found on July 6th 1937, in the same vicinity. The right arm showed a small blue scar on the outside just above the wrist.

    Upon examining the left leg of this torso which had been brought to the Morgue yesterday July 6th 1937, we found a scar the shape of the letter X, three inches above the ankle bone on the outside of the same leg. One of the X lines was two inches long, 3/8 inches wide, the other line in the X, was one inch long and 3/8 of inch wide, the same leg showed another mark about half an inch square about 2½ inches back of the ankle bone, both of these scars were blue.

Respectfully

Detective

Police report dated July 7, 1937 (©Cleveland Police Museum)

At a time when forensic science is still in its infancy, these factors further complicate identification, especially as the heads are often not found, further complicating their identification. Thirteen victims, male and female, were officially attributed to the man nicknamed "Torso", and only two of them were formally identified, thanks to their fingerprints: a young man named Edward Andrassy and a woman, Florence Polillo.

A third victim is suspected of being Rose Wallace, but this is never officially established.

The case was entrusted to the famous Eliot Ness, then *Safety Director* of Cleveland. The case proved tricky, as the squalid Kingsbury Run neighborhood was teeming with prostitutes and homeless people with no known family or connections, and took an unfortunate turn when Eliot Ness's teams burned down a large part of the neighborhood in a raid in August 1938.

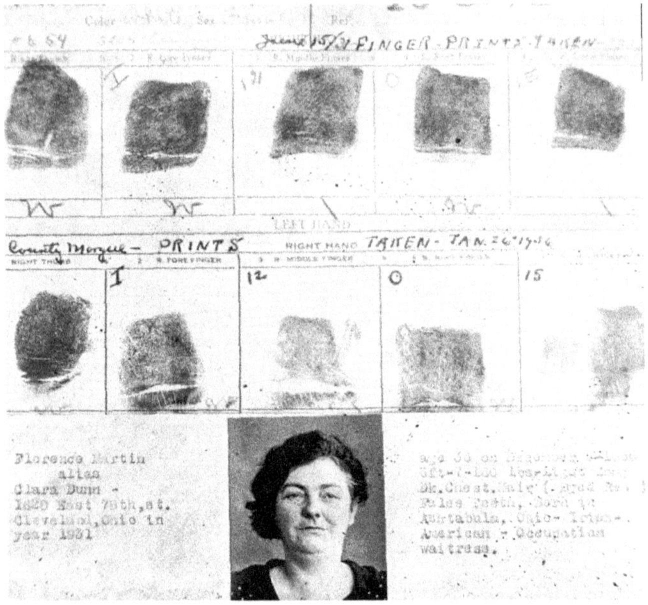

Florence Polillo's fingerprint card (©Cleveland Police Museum)

Eliot Ness (©Cleveland Police Museum)

The Files of the Impossible

This incident coincides with the end of the murder spree, but brings the methods of the police, and Ness in particular, into disrepute. After this episode, Ness claimed that the case had been solved, naming Gaylord Sundheim, described as a homosexual medical student from a wealthy Cleveland family. Questioned by Ness in autumn 1938, Sundheim escaped justice by voluntarily committing himself to a mental asylum, where he died in 1940 or 1941.

MASSILLON OHIO

MONDAY, JULY 19, 1937

America's Strangest Murder Mystery—

. . . . . .

Who Is the "Mad Butcher of Kingsbury Run"?
Why Did He Dismember His Nine Victims?

By ALVIN L. KRIEG
Central Press Staff Writer

CLEVELAND, July 19.—America's strangest murder mystery has Cleveland police baffled.

There have been nine victims in two years—all except two unidentified.

Most gruesome of all—every one of the bodies has been decapitated and dismembered, as if by an expert in anatomy, surgery, or butchering. The heads of some of the victims never have been recovered.

In Mill District

The majority of the bodies have been found in a district that borders industrial mills and railroad yards—a gully that is called Kingsbury run, close by the murky Cuyahoga river.

The district is surrounded by a thickly populated region, and several police stations are within walking distance.

Yet police have found not a single clue.

The unknown murderer has been termed "The Mad Butcher of Kingsbury Run."

Strikes Silently

No one knows when he strikes. The first indication of a new victim is disclosed when a part of a dismembered body is found.

The torso of the last victim was found only the other day, when national guardsmen, called to strike duty, saw the gruesome object floating in the Cuyahoga river.

Police fear that a tenth, and perhaps an eleventh victim, already have met their fates.

(The man is suspected of two or three other slayings in the past in addition to the nine known murders.)

The slayer, police are convinced, is clever. He is a muscular man. (The latest victim was a husky man, about 35, weighing nearly 200 pounds.) He may be a dangerous maniac, or he may be a former asylum inmate discharged as normal (although a check at insane asylums gave no clue.) He may have been or still be a butch-

er, or a surgeon. Or, just as plausible, he may be neither of these.

In "Horror Chamber?"

Perhaps the killer operates in some "horror chamber" in some hidden part of the city. But he may be working normally somewhere, meeting the public daily and deriving sadistic enjoyment from reading newspaper accounts of the slayings.

Literally hundreds of suspects have been questioned since the first of the gruesome killings. Among them have been men with known degenerate tendencies, with various types and degrees of abnormality. Included also have been former patients of mental institutions, others from the fringes of society, some of them dwellers in tiny shacks in "borderline regions."

Many Theories

But never have police been able to link any one of the suspects with the murders, and all the men were released.

Many theories are considered, some of them ranking with creations of

Edgar Allan Poe in their quality of horror.

One theorist has suggested the killer is afflicted with an ailment which destroys the red corpuscles of the blood. This theory was based on the deduction that such a person might possibly seek to replenish his blood supply along vampire lines.

Investigators spurn such fantastic suggestions. But they do give credence to a theory that the slayer does not work alone. They admit, as a bare possibility, that he may have an accomplice.

Detective Inspector Joseph McSweeney believes that the killer is a sex maniac. But Coroner Samuel R. Gerber of Cuyahoga county thinks otherwise.

Dr. Gerber also conjectures that the man is a "lone Wolf". "If there were two or more, one would have told something by this time," Dr. Gerber says. "One man can keep a secret better than two."

His Trademark

The killer has left his "trade-mark" on each of his victims, according to Dr. Gerber, who says the decapitations prove the man has some knowledge of surgery. He believes the bodies are cut and disjointed only as the easiest means of disposal.

Of the slayer's nine known victims, six were men, three were women. All were under 40.

Police say the slayings began some time prior to September, 1935, when bodies of two men were found in Kingsbury run.

Another Link?

The total may be higher than nine. Police also consider the possibility that a woman, parts of whose body were found two years ago in the Lake Erie shallows at North Perry, 25 miles from Cleveland, also was a victim. This, however, has not been established definitely.

Likewise, police here tried to link the murders with several of a similar nature near New Castle, Pa., particularly one where the headless body of a man was found, wrapped in a Cleveland newspaper, in a long-sealed boxcar on a railroad siding. This, too, has not been definitely linked to the Cleveland murders, in the opinion of investigators.

But whether his victims number nine, or 11, or more, the cunning killer remains at large.

BODY OF WOMAN FOUND IN RIVER

CINCINNATI, July 19.—The body of an unidentified woman was taken from the Ohio river Sunday by workmen at the Columbia Park power station. Coroner Frank M. Coppock, Jr., said the woman, about 60, had been in the water "some time."

Article from The Evening Independent, *July 19, 1937 (©newspaper.com)*

Another suspect, Frank Dolezal, was arrested in 1939, charged with the murders of Andrassy and Polillo, to which he had confessed. He was found hanged in his cell, but it was not yet possible to determine whether it was suicide or murder in disguise. To many observers, however, suicide seemed strange, as Dolezal had hung himself from a hook standing at a height of one metre sixty-five, whereas he himself was one metre seventy-two. His body also showed multiple rib fractures.

In December 1938, the *Torso Killer* (or someone posing as him) sent a letter to Ness, claiming that he had moved to California, killed a woman there and buried the head in Los Angeles. In the letter, the killer introduces himself as a "DC" (*Doctor of Chiropractic*). An investigation leads to the discovery of animal bones.

Other enigmatic postcards followed.

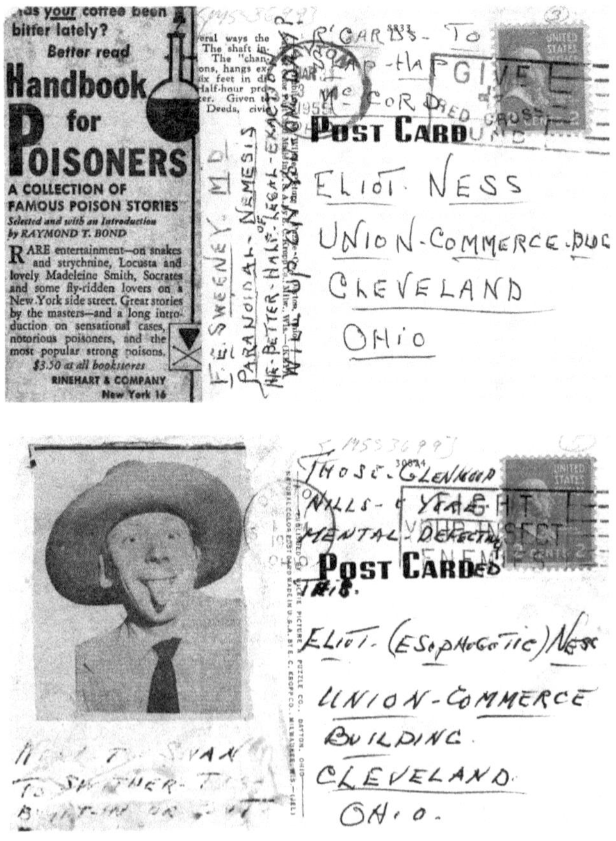

Ten years later, this postal "confession" led authorities to consider the possibility that the *Torso Killer* had a connection with the Black Dahlia case, in which the halved remains of 22-year-old Elizabeth Short were found in the unfinished Leimert Park subdivision in Los Angeles on January 15, 1947.

Inspector Trunk with masks in the Bureau of Criminal Identification laboratory (©Cleveland Police Museum)

Short and the *Torso Murderer* victims had all been thoroughly cleaned after death, and it's thought that a butcher's knife was used in both cases.

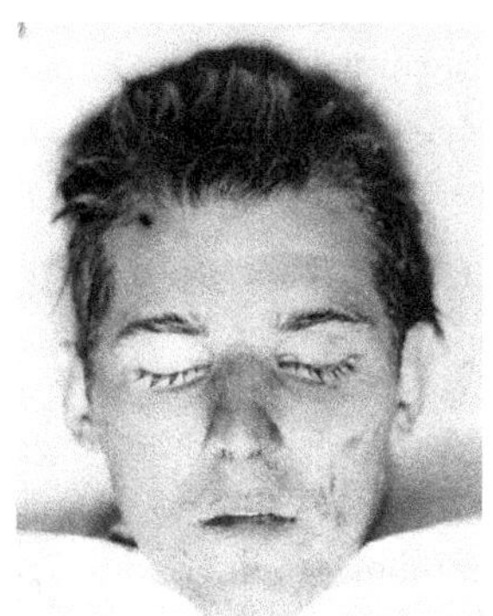

Victim no. 4: the tattooed man (©Cleveland Police Museum)

However, Short was not decapitated, which is the signature of the Cleveland victims. Moreover, the murder took place almost ten years after the letter was received. So, apart from circumstantial evidence and pure speculation, there's nothing to link Short to the *Torso*.

In the final analysis, the identity of this particularly gruesome killer remains unknown almost 100 years after the fact, and will probably remain so forever, even if strong suspicions hang on Dr. Francis Edward Sweeney, who was secretly interrogated by Eliot Ness in 1938 (it would be several decades before his identity was established with virtual certainty).

The main suspects in this case are:

Dr Francis E. Sweeney

Francis E. Sweeney was an intelligent, skilled and highly disturbed surgeon who lived near Kingsbury Run. Sweeney possessed surgical know-how and had access to facilities ideal for dismembering bodies.

He also happened to be the cousin of one of Eliot Ness's political opponents, Martin L. Sweeney. Could this have played a role, one way or another?

Diagnosed with schizophrenia in 1956, Sweeney was secretly questioned about the murders in 1938 by Ness and other top investigators, but never confessed. However, as soon as he was committed to a sanatorium, the murders stopped. He is also suspected of being the author of the enigmatic letters received by Eliot Ness.

He died in 1964, and to this day remains the most credible suspect.

Frank Dolezal

Arrested by sheriff's deputies in July 1939, Dolezal confessed to killing Flo Polillo, but later recanted, claiming that the deputies had beaten him. He was found dead in jail in August 1939, apparently hanged. Coroner Gerber ruled it a suicide, but some thought Dolezal might have been murdered.

Willie Johnson

Arrested after leaving the dismembered remains of 19-year-old Margaret Francis Wilson in Kingsbury Run in 1942, Johnson is convicted of murder. Witnesses claimed he knew the victim Rose Wallace, but Johnson insisted he had not killed any of the victims blamed on the *Torso*. He was executed in 1944.

The opinion of 1st Commissioner Maillard of the Brussels Judicial Police - Division in charge of crime against property and people.

Obviously, it's very difficult to give an opinion on an investigation that took place almost 100 years ago, during the Great Depression of 1930, in Cleveland. Technological developments might have helped investigators if this case had taken place today, but here's how I would have proceeded with this investigation, back then. Of course,

Measures to be implemented

- As soon as there are more than three victims, and the evidence points to a serial killer, a timeline should certainly be established.

- This timeline will enable us to locate the victims in relation to the time of death, the place where they were found and the frequency with which the perpetrator acted.

- It goes without saying that we'll also be able to follow the author's career path or the neighborhood(s) in which he operates.

- What's more, we'll know when it acts most frequently, and we may be able to determine a time slot.

- It's imperative to be meticulous every time, and if possible in the same way, when making findings. This will help us to identify the perpetrator's habits. The laboratory should take as many samples as possible, paying particular attention to detail.

- Victims should be thoroughly researched and, if possible, a link established between them. It's possible that this link will lead us to the perpetrator, who uses this element to find his victims. Is there a physical similarity between the different victims (homosexuals, for example), or is it a particular category of people that is targeted (prostitutes or wealthy people, for example)?

- You need to put together a solid team of investigators, and there have to be enough of them, because you're going to have to investigate a lot of leads while at the same time dealing with the accumulating crime scenes and synthesizing all the cases.

- Systematically carry out a neighborhood survey, as any detail could point us in the right direction.

- Don't let the tracks cool down, and take direct action day and night in the event of new cases.

- Contact the usual informers in the prostitutes' neighborhood. They usually know more than the police.

- Autopsies should be carried out by the same forensic pathologists, to save time and to be able to identify similarities in the remains. The way in which the bodies are cut up is very important, and will tell us a lot about the knowledge and character of the perpetrator. Is he meticulous or violent? Does he know anything about anatomy? Could he have been a doctor or a butcher?

- Draw up a list of missing persons to help identify as yet unidentified bodies, given the lack of information.

- One of the bodies had various tattoos. A visit to one of the tattoo shops in the area can be a great help in identifying the victim. Currently, when a person is arrested, a photograph of the tattoos is taken. In addition, if a body with tattoos is discovered and the person concerned is not identified, a press release is issued with a photograph of the various tattoos.

- The *post-mortem* analysis of corpses is important for their identification. These days, this record would be compared with any *ante mortem* records. (We're thinking here of dental care and possible operations, as well as prostheses).

- As the 11th victim shows signs of refrigeration and his limbs are wrapped in butcher's paper, it would be interesting to start looking at nearby butchers who have cold storage facilities. The butcher's paper could also be analyzed to determine its origin, as well as the different butchers who use this type of paper.

- Victim number 8, Rose Wallace, was known to at least two suspects. We needed to investigate her activities, habits and acquaintances in greater depth. We also needed to find out about all the places she frequented. Where did she stay? etc.

- The essential element in this case is the surgical skill that the perpetrator absolutely must have to make clean cuts in the various bodies. And above all, don't overlook the fact that the perpetrator could in fact be two people.

Items collected for research

Victim 0 (unidentified)

- Woman 30

- Chemical preservative makes skin hard, leathery and red.

- Only the torso, with the lower limbs amputated at the knees.

- Head never found and therefore never identified.

Victim 1: Edward Andrassy

- A 28-year-old white male, naked, emasculated, with rope burns on his wrists.

- Former nurse.

- Identified thanks to his fingerprints following the illegal carrying of a weapon.

Victim 2 (found not far from the body of victim 1) - (unidentified)

- A 40-year-old man, decapitated and emasculated.

- Chemical preservative same as victim 0.

- Dead for several weeks.

Victim 3: Florence Polillo

- 42-year-old woman.

- Half of his torso, his upper legs, his right arm and hand were found.

- The rest of the body, except for the head, was found ten days later in another location.

- Identified by fingerprints following arrest for prostitution.

Victim 4: (unidentified)

- White male, 25 years old.

- The head was first found wrapped in a pair of pants.

- The body was found in front of the police building. Clean and drained of blood, the corpse was intact, but without the head.

- Tattoos failed to identify the body.

Victim 5: (unidentified)

- 30-year-old man decapitated (no further details).

Victim 6: (unidentified)
- Male, 20 years old (no further details).

Victim 7: (unidentified)
- 30-year-old woman.
- Part of the torso was uncovered.

Victim 8: Rose Wallace (provisionally identified from dental records)
- 40-year-old woman.
- Dismembered skeleton.

Victim 9: (unidentified)
- Victim whose body was found in the Cuyahoga River, headless.
- A disemboweled abdomen and ripped-out heart indicate a new degree of perversion in the killer's approach.

Victim 10: (unidentified)
- The victim was found to be under the influence of drugs. Drugs to immobilize the victim, or was she a drug addict? The victim was found without his arms, so this question will remain unanswered. (Traces of injection.)

Victims 11 and 12 (unidentified and found in the same place)
- A woman's torso wrapped in a man's blue blazer, itself wrapped in an old quilt.
- This woman's legs and arms were found in a homemade box, wrapped in brown butcher's paper and held together with rubber bands.
- The woman's head wrapped in the same way.
- Some parts of these bodies appear to have been refrigerated.
- Remains of a second body found a few yards from the first.

Trail of the wanderer Emil Fronek

Fronek was helped by a doctor and found himself on the second floor of a doctor's surgery. He appears to have been drugged when he received a meal from the doctor, and managed to escape to a train carriage where he fell asleep.

Later, an investigation was launched in the neighborhood where the man was allegedly drugged, but to no avail.

Frank Dolezal's runway

Frank was arrested for the murder of the third victim. A confession was obtained, but he later recanted, explaining that he had been beaten to extract it. He hanged himself in prison. His hearing should have been undertaken to question him about the other victims!

The trouble is, it's not clear when he might have acquired the surgical skills to disarticulate a body. However, he also frequented Edward Andrassy and Rose Wallace.

Willie Johnson track

Arrested for the murder of Margaret Francis Wilson, age 19. Convicted of this murder.

He also knew Rose Wallace. Johnson claimed to have had nothing to do with the "Torso Murderer" and was executed.

A hearing with the person concerned might have brought some interesting elements to the case!

Did he have the skills to dismember a body?

Doctor Francis Edward Sweeney's runway

Detective Peter Merylo's opinion

He was convinced that similar murders had been committed in New Castle, and that the killer could have taken the railroad between Cleveland, Youngstown and New Castle, and mingled with the homeless.

As I explained above, in this kind of investigation, you have to take a very broad view, otherwise you may miss the point. It's essential to find out whether other similar cases with an identical *modus operandi* have been committed elsewhere.

It's always a good idea to get the opinion of a colleague outside the survey, to get a different approach. If you're too busy working on a survey, you can end up with your head in the sand and miss the point.

At the very least, we should have familiarized ourselves with Cleveland's files.

The Kholat Syakhl file

1

"I'm obliged to intervene, because neither entrepreneurs nor scientists have seen fit to heed my warnings," said Yuri Yudin, 27, from the podium facing the main auditorium of the Ural Polytechnic Institute.

In front of him, dozens of journalists from all over Russia had made the trip to crowd the bays usually occupied by the Institute's students.

"It's against my better judgment that I'm here today to tell you my reasons for opposing the plan to colonize the Ural Mountains, and I'm all the more reluctant because my warning is likely to be in vain. Faced with the real facts as I must reveal them, your disbelief will be inevitable. And yet, if I were to purge my story of its most inconceivable and/or extravagant elements, there would be nothing left to tell."

Yuri made a discreet sign to his assistant, who plunged the audience into darkness before switching on the projector, which printed a black-and-white shot of an imposing mountain on the wall next to the stage.

"The photographs I'm about to unveil, at once banal and unreal, will bear witness in my favor. In the Mansi language, the name of this mountain, Kholat Syakhl, lost in the northern Urals, some 550 km from Yekaterinburg, means 'dead mountain' or 'mountain of the dead.' Legend has it that nine hunters met their doom here in ancient times. Since then, locals believe it's best to avoid going there in groups. Perhaps we should have heeded this sage advice."

With a nod, Yuri asked his assistant to change the photo, and the Kholat Syakhl gave way to a group of ten people smiling at the lens, eight men and two women, all warmly dressed. They were crammed into what looked like a truck trailer.

"There were eight of us from the university, plus two guides, and if you're wondering about our qualifications, we were all experienced hikers. The Polytechnic Institute, assisted by a few personal contributions, financed our expedition, so our preparations were extremely thorough. Sleds, skis and camping equipment were delivered on time. We were admirably equipped to reach our goal, Mount Otorten, which despite its unappealing name—it literally means 'don't go there'— remains a must-see. No credit to us, we'd simply learned from the example set by our recent predecessors."

A photo of a flag planted in the snow replaced the Kholat Syakhl. On the canvas, the mission's name, Abalakov, spread out in white letters.

"The fame of these prestigious predecessors meant that our expedition, ambitious though it was in terms of archaeology, met with little public response, much to the dismay of Semyon Zolotaryov, our dean, who proclaimed to anyone who would listen that 'the whole world would be talking about our trek'."

A gray-haired man raised his hand to ask a question.

"Yes, sir...?" agreed Yuri.

"Fyodor Gusev, *Izvestia* journalist. Why was Zolotaryov so enthusiastic?"

"To tell the truth, I don't know myself. Sure, we were going to conquer Otorten and bring back plenty of rock and fossil samples, but we were neither the first nor the most illustrious hikers to attack its flanks. That said, to be honest, we were all a little more perky than usual. Lyudmila Dubinina wrote in her diary on January 23: *'It was the last day of preparations and everything was quite hectic. Around eleven o'clock this morning, I was wandering around the stores buying materials, and I was stupid enough to buy five meters of batiste, which cost me 200 rubles. I was in such a hurry to pack that, of course, I forgot my sweater at home. Just before our departure, those who wanted to say goodbye came to wait for us at the Sverdlovsk train station. We were really short of time, but we still managed to get there with only a few seconds to spare, so we were able to say goodbye to everyone. Before we left, we sang a few songs, and once we were in the carriage, we continued to sing together.'* In my opinion, this testifies to the good mood of our group."

"Forgive me, but it seems to me that she also wrote: *'At first, nobody wanted this Zolotaryov, because he's a foreigner, but in the end we accepted him, because we couldn't do without his experience as a guide.'*"

"That's right, but if you've ever been interested, you'll know that it's because Semyon Zolotaryov was the oldest of us. He had also been made a Knight of the Order of the Red Star for his exploits in the army. All this put a certain distance between him and us, but in the end we got on well. Anyway, we got up at half past five on January 25, and after an hour's wait, we managed to catch a bus to the town of Ivdel. The poor twenty-five-seater was forced to accommodate twenty-five occupants plus twenty backpacks filled to overflowing, and as many pairs of skis. In other words, the load was up to the ceiling. The passengers in the first row sat on the seats, on top of a pile of rucksacks, while those in the second row sat between the seats, finding room for their legs on the shoulders of their comrades. We weren't tight enough, however, not to sing."

A smile crossed Yuri's face at the mention of this happy memory, even if a hint of nostalgia crossed his features.

"The trip didn't go without a hitch. The bus took a detour off the highway to the village of Shipichnoye, where we were lucky enough to stretch our legs. The more agile among us made our way to the Talitsa camp, high up in the mountains, to catch a glimpse of the power station (I was one of those four 'agiles'). Suddenly, we heard: *The bus!* We rushed over, but alas, it was already too late—the engine had restarted. It passed us by without seeing us, so we were forced, in desperation, to try and catch it at a run. Have you ever tried running in hiking boots? For me, it was the first time, and the first hundred meters clearly demonstrated the advantages of a fifty-horsepower engine over my poor legs. The gap widened in a matter of seconds, and I have to confess that, at that moment, the prospect of walking thirty kilometers on the highway, without breakfast or lunch, seemed frightfully real to me, when suddenly... divine mercy manifested itself in the form of a young woman going to the same place as us, who hailed the bus, making it pull over to the side of the road. I don't think I've ever been so happy to see brake lights come on."

Polite laughter in the room.

"We reached our stopover at around 2 p.m., where it turned out we would be able to continue our journey by car the following morning. After dinner, which was warm and convivial, we moved into the 'hotel', which was nothing more than a hut with three windows."

Anyway, the car dropped us off in Ivdel on January 25, 1959. For those of you who don't know Ivdel, it's a charming village in the center of the Sverdlovsk Oblast. From here, we took a truck to Vizhay, the last village before the mountains. This is where the photo you saw earlier was taken. Despite our experience as hikers, no one had ventured this far north before, so we relied heavily on our guides —Semyon Zolotaryov, whom we've already mentioned, and Igor Dyatlov, the expedition's initiator. To pass the time, we went to the cinema, leaving Doroshenko and Kolevatov 'at home'. Doroshenko and Kolevatov. For the record, we saw *Symphonie in Gold*, a rather cheesy musical romance that Zina Kolmogorova nevertheless loved. She kept telling us she could see it again and again.

We set off for Otorten on January 27 and soon the landscape changed dramatically, as if we'd entered an unlikely parallel dimension.

As we left the inhabited world behind us, we spotted our first "icebergs"—in reality vertical walls of ice—and just before reaching our resting point, we found ourselves considerably hampered by snow. I'd often suffered from the drop in temperature on previous expeditions, but I was trying to toughen up for the worst to come.

"That's when you injured yourself," commented the graying journalist.

"If you'd like to tell the story for me, I'll leave the podium to you, Mr. Goosev," joked Yuri, triggering another round of polite laughter from the audience. "On the morning of January 28, a clear glimpse of Mount Otorten appeared to the north of our position, and before noon we all felt a thrill of excitement at the sight of this vast, high, snow-covered mountain range stretching as far as the eye could see. If there are any hikers or mountaineers in the room, they'll be able to confirm that, at times like these, you feel very small in the face of Mother Nature's overwhelming immensity. The last part of the trip should have been the most stimulating for my imagination, with the high barren peaks constantly looming on the horizon, while the oblique rays of the northern sun reflected everywhere on the white snow, ice, bluish trickles and black patches of the exposed mountainsides. It was just as we reached the second camp to the north that I was struck by a merciless backache, forcing me to abandon my comrades and set off for home. The journey in the back of the truck, with no brakes and far too many worn shock absorbers, had proved too much for my frail frame. With a heavy heart, I had to let my friends carry on without me. Let it be clear to all that the events I'm about to recount have been recons-tructed from diaries and recordings found at the site of their last camp."

2

"The outside temperature is -8°C," Dyatlov announced to the rest of the team. "We'll have to cover up well. Our friend Yuri is going home today. It's a shame, of course, that he has to leave us, especially for me and Zina, who've known him for a long time, but there's nothing we can do about it. His back hurts too much. It would be very unwise to take on Otorten when he's not in full possession of his powers."

"What's the program?" asked Kolevatov.

"Departure at 11:45 a.m. We'll be heading up the Lozva River, with a relay every ten minutes to lead the group. As the snow cover is much lower than last year, we'll have to stop regularly to scrape the slush off the bottom of our skis. Gueorgui will lead the way and sketch our route. The banks of the river (especially the right bank) are made up of limestone cliffs that rise quite high in places, but on the whole the terrain is flat and entirely covered by forest. Tonight we spend our first night in a tent."

Loud cheers accompanied this announcement. After all, over and above the geological aspect of obtaining sufficient funding for an expedition of this nature, everyone was there to commune with the mountain.

Dyatlov planned to cover as much territory as possible, trekking mainly across the Urals. With frequent changes of camp, and excavating remote areas large enough to be of geological interest, he hoped to unearth an unprecedented variety of material, particularly in the oldest strata accessible via the network of caves and tunnels that criss-crossed the mountain range. His intention was to obtain the widest possible variety of fossiliferous rocks. Research showed that the climate in this region had once been mild and temperate. If a simple drilling revealed traces of fossils, the team would widen the opening with explosives to collect specimens of sufficient size, and in good condition.

In case of failure, Dyatlov intended to fall back on metamorphic rocks containing semi-precious stones of all kinds (rock crystal, serpentine, malachite, jasper, onyx, etc.). The important thing was not to go home empty-handed, in order to satisfy the Institute's top brass.

Using small sleds, the group set off up the difficult Lozva River, making frequent rotations in a movement comparable to that of a peloton of cyclists whose lead changes regularly. After seven rotations, the group decided to take a break, which they did again an hour later. During this time, they covered between six and seven kilometers, following trails laid out by the Mansis, the mountain people. It was not possible to walk on the river, as the water was not sufficiently frozen, despite the layer of snow covering it. They had to be extra careful not to fall and die of hypothermia.

Between the distant peaks intermittently blew the furious gusts of the north wind, whose modulations sometimes transformed the Urals into a gigantic natural flute, whose strangely musical sounds seemed to resonate with deep-seated anxieties in every member of the expedition. Kolevatov couldn't stop shivering. Something about this setting reminded him of the strange, terrifying mountain paintings by Lev Lvovich Kamenev that he had seen at Moscow's Tretyakov State Gallery.

"What's this?" suddenly asked Lyudmila Dubinina.

It referred to a tree trunk whose bark had been stripped to allow symbols to be traced on the light-colored wood.

"A Mansi signpost," replied Zolotaryov.

"And what does it say?"

"No idea, I don't speak Mansi. Does anyone here have any idea what it means?" General denial.

"It doesn't look like a directional pole," observed Alexander Kolevatov.

"Indeed... It looks more like a kind of..."

"A warning," added Lyudmila, a hint of fear in her voice. "Maybe we're entering their territory. We should bypass the area."

"I don't think so," tempered Dyatlov. "The region they live in is much further north. They don't get that close to the cities."

"But this sign suggests otherwise."

"I'm sure we don't need to worry about that."

"All right, you're the boss. But I hope you brought something to coax them with if you need to."

Dyatlov smiled as he resumed his walk.

The young men's first impressions of the slopes of the Urals were both intense and mixed, despite the fact that several expeditions had preceded them to this very spot. The fresh snow crunched beneath their feet, their breath producing small, wispy clouds. They stopped for lunch at the fourth halt. It was here that Zina Kolmogorova announced the good news:

"Today is Doroshenko's birthday!"

The interested party lowered his head, cheeks reddened as much by shame as by cold.

"Is it true?" exclaimed Dyatlov. "I had no idea."

"Let's celebrate!" said Zolotaryov, grabbing one of the bottles of vodka he'd brought along.

"Not now," Dyatlov tempered. "Let's wait until we get to camp tonight. It'll warm us up and help us get a good night's sleep," he added with a smile.

There's probably no need to repeat what the newspapers have already published about the rest of the expedition: their subsequent ascent of the Lozva river, then their fork in the road towards one of its tributaries, the Auspiya; the ice that blocked their passage on several occasions; the successful drilling at various points and the astonishing speed with which the device developed by Yuri Yudin had completed it, even in layers of hard rock; the perilous progress along a snow-covered "deer trail" with sledges and equipment; and, finally, the setting up of the bivouac at the foot of Otorten. Most of the time, the thermometer oscillated between 0°C and -13°C, sometimes even -17°C. Despite this, the team's morale remained remarkable.

This semi-permanent camp was designed to store sledges, provisions, dynamite and other reserves under cover. Only three men were needed to carry the actual exploration equipment. Their health so far remained excellent, the lime juice effectively compensating for their self-imposed diet of canned goods and cured meats around the fire every evening.

"The wind is strong," said Zolotaryov, stirring the embers to create new flames. Direction southwest. The snow will start falling during the night. The clouds are heavy, the temperature is dropping.

"Have you noticed how the forest is getting thinner around here? says Lyudmila. The trees are getting smaller. There are lots of birches and dwarf pines.

"It's the effects of altitude," explained Doroshenko.

"I'd say oxygen depletion," clarified Dyatlov, without looking up from the map he'd been looking at for the last fifteen minutes. "Tomorrow we begin the most complicated part of our journey. Up to now, we've been following the Mansi path, but now we'll be plunging into the unknown."

"Don't be so melodramatic," smiled Lyudmila.

Yet now they were in the far north, a world that had been frozen for an eternity, and just as they became aware of it, they saw the summit of Mount Otorten far above their heads, spreading its titanic height over almost four thousand five hundred feet.

"Well, what's this?" asked Alexander Kolevatov, pointing to an orange-red dot looming behind the ridge.

"Mars?" replied Gueorgui Krivonichtchenko, creating a small cloud of steam in the icy air.

"Impossible," intervened Nicolaï Thibeaux-Brignolles, the most astronomically-inclined of us all. "At this time of year, and at this latitude, we shouldn't be able to see it so well, nor observe it from this direction. Instead, it should be... (he raised his arm and rotated it until he got the desired orientation)... over there! Can you see it? It's right where it should be."

"So what's with the orange ball?"

"No idea, but it's not Mars."

Nicolaï Thibeaux-Brignolles' assertion was confirmed a few moments later when the sphere... split into two, and the two glittering circles engaged in a most astonishing nocturnal ballet. They looked like two fireflies on a love parade. At times, they would disappear behind Otorten's summit, then reappear, before disappearing again. The strange spectacle lasted for almost two minutes, during which the hikers, transfixed, forgot to speak or even breathe.

*

On January 30, 1959, Dyatlov, Zolotaryov and a third fellow by the name of Rustem Slobodin spotted the entrance to a cave. It was, as they reported in their diaries, one of their first objects of excitement. However, exploration proved disappointing on every level, although it did offer some superb examples of the bewildering spectacles to be found in the abysses of our world. They then proposed climbing higher to establish an annex base; the geological specimens collected there would make for interesting comparisons, they believed.

No one but them would have known about their program, but this didn't stop Dyatlov from calling for an extra round of prospecting to the west—or rather, to the northwest—which was strongly opposed by Nicolai Thibeaux-Brignolles and, to a lesser extent, Semyon Zolotaryov. Both seemed convinced that a change of plan was not in the mission's best interests, especially as Dyatlov was unable to explain his interest in this remote area. He claimed to be driven by "irrepressible strength and desire". His team-mates managed to dissuade him, however, and on February 1, the ascent to the pass leading to Otorten began.

The group set off as the first light of dawn struck the mountain summit, which, funnily enough, was not shrouded in mist. Usually, in the morning, the impressive stone spire would be adorned with a wispy crown, which it would only shed by mid-afternoon, but on this particular morning it seemed to be humbly welcoming the hikers determined to unravel its mysteries. To the west, Kholat Syakhl, the "dead mountain", dominated the landscape.

Every incident of this four-and-a-half-hour walk was recorded in Lyudmila Dubinina's diary, as if it marked for her the loss, at the age of twenty-one, of a certain innocence and all the peace and equilibrium enjoyed by a normal mind. The nine hikers ventured into a pristine white world that seemed filled with horrors on the prowl. Thanks to written transcriptions, we can retrace the expedition's uninterrupted climb and their two battles at altitude against treacherous gales. Marching at the rear of the column, Georgi Krivonishchenko beat out the rhythm with military songs that Zolotaryov sometimes took up with a little too much gusto.

"Not so loud, Dyatlov tempera, don't forget the avalanche risk."

"My apologies. These songs bring back fond memories…"

"Because the battle of Stalingrad is a good memory for you?" retorted Lyudmila, whose fiercely anti-militaristic soul couldn't accept that a man should take pleasure in fighting.

"Little girl, you might be speaking German right now if patriots like me hadn't got our hands dirty at Stalingrad. You should be thanking me instead of hassling me."

"Lyuda," intervened Rustem Slobodin, addressing the young woman by her affectionate nickname, "Semyon is right. You know I don't like war very much, but he's talking about defending our country. It's unfair to take it out on him."

"Shut up, everyone," cut in Nicolaï Thibeaux-Brignolles. "You can talk about good and evil later, if you feel like it, but right now, let's focus on our goal."

The young astronomy enthusiast had just caught sight, far ahead of them, of the jagged profile of the gigantic cones and naked peaks that made up the Ural Mountains. They climbed inexorably into the desolate northern sky, white streaked with black. This is where the words in Lyudmila Dubinina's diary fail to convey the bizarre sense of the imaginary that gripped the troupe as they gazed up at this spectacle bathed in brilliant midday light, with the parade of iridescent clouds of ice dust in the background. It was as if these nightmarish spires of rock were the pylons of a formidable gateway to the forbidden abysses of space-time. *I couldn't help feeling they were evil, these mountains whose farthest slopes seemed to watch over unfathomable cursed secrets*", she wrote in her mid-day review of February 1.

"A storm is approaching," observed Rustem Slobodin, surprisingly neutral on the morning of February 2.

The veiled sheen of the increasingly grey clouds suggested the merciless promise of a storm of colossal proportions.

"Damn," grumbled Igor Dyatlov. "The weather forecast predicted good weather for the entire expedition."

"Shall we go back down?" suggested Alexander Kolevatov. "We're only a kilometer from a forest that would offer us better shelter. It would be safer."

"We're only an hour away from our day's destination. It would be a shame to lose this distance."

"Maybe, but will we find enough shelter? Personally, I'd rather not take the risk."

"Maybe we won't have to," said Doroshenko, pointing to a black hole gaping in the side of the nearby Kholat Syakhl, like a gigantic mouth ready to swallow the world.

Lyudmila grabbed the pair of binoculars hanging from her backpack and pointed them westwards.

"A cave!" she exclaimed.

"No way! There shouldn't be anything in this area," commented Dyatlov in disbelief. "The topographical surveys make no mention of it."

"Perhaps other expeditions simply missed it. There's so much to see around here..."

"Very well," sighed Igor Dyatlov. "Let's climb up and pitch our tents. Camping on a slope will give us good exercise. We're going to explore this tunnel and, if need be, we'll be able to take refuge there. Does everyone agree?"

Unanimous assent. However, as they approached the mysterious cavern, another oddity became apparent—other than its incongruous presence there. The geometry of its outline was almost square or semicircular, as if the natural, rough opening had been shaped more symmetrically by some industrious hand.

"A curious geological feature, to be sure," announced Dyatlov, planting himself half a dozen meters from the entrance, hands on hips. "One more to go. Right, let's set up the tents here and here."

In no time at all, the group gobbled up a frugal meal—frugal because excitement was beginning to take precedence over all other considerations. The hikers then divided into two groups: Dyatlov, Zolotaryov, Thibeaux-Brignolles, Slobodin and Kolmogorova on one side; Dubinina, Kolevatov, Krivonichtchenko and Doroshenko on the other. The five would explore the cave, while the four would stand guard outside, collecting samples and standing by to act as reinforcements should the need arise.

The tunnel sloped gently into the heart of the mountain. Observing the many vaulted passages leading off the interior, and sensing the probable complexity of these ramifications, Zolotaryov suggested putting into practice a system of tracing as old as time. Each of them took out a stash of papers from their backpacks, which were cut into pieces and packed into a bag for Dyatlov, who prepared to sow them with as much economy as their safety would allow. This method would undoubtedly prevent them from getting lost in the underground meanders, since there didn't seem to be any violent draughts inside Kholat Syakhl.

3

The absence of precise notes makes it difficult to give a detailed account of the Dyatlov group's comings and goings in the cavernous maze of masonry, both natural and man-made, but undeniably abandoned for ages. Here and there, the rust that was eating away at the metal reinforcements indicated that this cave of ancient mysteries was, for the first time in a very long time, resonating to the sound of human footsteps. And yet, a simple observation of these reinforcements showed an astonishing, if not impossible, level of craftsmanship for the period in which they were supposed to have been installed.

"Are you filming this?" asked Dyatlov.

"I don't miss a thing," replied Slobodin, camera in hand. "I should point out, however, that my film supply will soon run out."

"So cut it out for now. We'll film these strange fixtures on our return if we get the chance. Who knows what awaits us further on!"

After about a kilometer of wandering—distances are hard to estimate indoors, so it may have been two kilometers or barely five hundred meters—the tunnel opened up and...

"Incredible," gasped Dyatlov, dumbfounded. "Film, Rustem, film. Never mind the lack of film, we can't let this go to waste."

The cavern they had just arrived in rivaled the limits of human imagination. Iron-laden water had stained the stalactites, stalagmites and immense limestone candles red, and streaked the walls with innumerable bloody trails. Sometimes, less corrosive flows had polished the rock instead of hollowing it out, and we could make out soft cushions and the curve of "clouds" vying for the available surface on the walls of this ignored geological past. A large hole in the ceiling let in a column of white light, illuminating the place like a divine illumination. However, this grotto and its great beauty were no more than a showcase for the diamond it contained.

At its heart stood an improbable stalagmitic building, whose limestone-based structure looked totally artificial, as if wax had been heated, poured and then shaped into verticality. Dyatlov entered without hesitation, with a lack of caution that could only be explained by his sudden excitement. He had come in search of fossiliferous rocks, and now he was discovering the remains of an unknown, perhaps prehuman, civilization. For one fact was undeniable: this construction had been abandoned when Man was still struggling to articulate intelligible words.

The interior partitions were less massive than the exterior walls, but perfectly preserved in the lower levels. A labyrinthine complexity characterized the whole, and the team would probably have been lost in minutes were it not for the trail of torn papers they left behind.

"Hey ho," said Zolotaryov, whose voice reverberated in throbbing echoes that died a slow death.

No one replied, but for a moment, the former soldier wondered what he'd do if a creature lurking in the shadows suddenly pounced on him. His hand tightened on the handle of his ice axe; inside his glove, the knuckles of his fingers whitened under the pressure.

They decided to explore the most dilapidated, weathered upper sections first, and climbed to the top floor, which was a succession of roofless, snow-covered, ruined rooms opening onto the Ural sky. The ascent was made via steep stone ramps and staircases carved into the rock. Antique, corroded machinery littered the ground, forming snow-covered piles linked by a system of copper cables. It was safe to say that the builders of this place knew electricity. How was it generated and for what purpose? The mystery remains. The images filmed by Rustem Slobodin, though fragmentary, may one day shed light on this mystery, just as they may offer an explanation to one of the city's most incredible enigmas.

While Slobodin filmed a close-up of the cables from which he had removed the snow with the palm of his hand, Thibeaux-Brignolles drew his comrades' attention to the wall above what appeared to be the room's main machine, a kind of mainframe gutted by centuries of weathering. Remnants of peeling paint revealed a symbol that every Russian knew without even meaning to.

"It's not possible," gasped Dyatlov. "It's just not possible."

The sickle and hammer, whose red shadows remained clearly recognizable on the rock, formed the symbol used to represent communism in its Leninist variant. These symbols depicted the sickle of the peasants and the hammer of the working proletariat, and their joining symbolized the union between agricultural and industrial workers. How had they come to be painted inside a thousand-year-old underground structure that no human being was supposed to have trodden since time immemorial?

"Could it be the work of the Mansis?" ventured Kolmogorova.

"Maybe," replied Dyatlov, not believing it for a second. "But why would they do that?"

Indeed, anyone with even the slightest knowledge of the history of the mountain people knew that they had always built themselves "with and against Russia". Over time, there had been periods of peaceful coexistence, interaction and confrontation, but the natives had never embraced communism. What's more, the Mansis had different values and a different relationship to time and space from their neighbors, whose society had embarked on a frantic race that seemed to have no end in sight: everything had to be profitable and profitable, even the passing of time. Conversely, Mansi life was in harmony with that of Earth. Nothing living was taken from it unless absolutely necessary. None of them, except perhaps a rebellious teenager, would have had the idea of painting this symbol on the wall. Not to mention that it didn't change his dating problem.

"Maybe this place was built by the Red Army? suggested Slobodin.

"I doubt it," retorted Zolotaryov. "In my military career, I've never seen anything remotely resembling this kind of infrastructure. On the other hand, it's possible that they discovered it and turned it into an operational base, but that doesn't explain its dilapidated state or why nobody has ever heard of it."

"Come on, it wouldn't be the first time the army hid something," intervened Thibeaux-Brignolles.

"True, but the fact that we had access to it without encountering the slightest resistance, and without seeing any warning signs, tells me that nobody in the Kremlin knows it exists. You can believe me when I tell you that if the army wants to hide information from the general public, it can do so with ease."

"It looks like the control center of a laboratory," observed Kolmogorova.

"Let's keep moving," suggested Dyatlov, "we're bound to get to the bottom of this."

After thoroughly examining the upper levels, the group descended floor by floor to the first floor, where they discovered a second, uninterrupted labyrinth of interconnecting rooms and passageways leading to even more subterranean sectors. The gigantism of what surrounded them was becoming terribly oppressive, for there was something vaguely, but frighteningly inhuman in the architectural proportions and intricacies of this antediluvian masonry, something that the metal patches, as useful as band-aids on an open fracture, failed to conceal.

"There's no way the army could have built this place and kept it secret," asserted Zolotaryov. "A facility of this scale, in such a remote mountain area, would have entailed insane costs, insoluble logistical problems and far too much manpower."

The rooms they visited were generally empty, giving the impression of deliberate abandonment of the place, even if the floors covered in a layer of detritus and debris indicated a certain haste, especially in the living area. Yes, the premises had clearly been used as both a laboratory *and* a home, the two being divided into different sections. What's more, a number of unusual objects, such as tin cans with expiration dates limited to the 1930s, had been left behind. Their packaging, however, appeared to be much older, as the paper crumbled as soon as Dyatlov reached for it.

As the group made their way downstairs, they encountered less and less of this household detritus, which seemed to indicate that the basement had been the scene of laboratory operations. In some of the rooms and galleries below, there was little more than small gravel, cables hanging from the walls and twigs deposited there by some mischievous bird. Skylights, pierced at regular intervals in the ceiling, kept the lower levels from total darkness. Naturally, they had also weakened the structure, causing occasional landslides. In the heart of the mountain, however, the darkness deepened, and in many places, at the level of the cluttered floor, it approached pitch black, so the team had to resort to using their flashlights. From time to time, a communist symbol painted on a wall or ceiling reminded them that they were still on Earth, in Russia, in the Urals, and not in an extraterrestrial structure.

Inevitably, the discovery of this timeless place had changed their immediate objective. Geology had been relegated to the background, as the murky paths dug into the depths of the Kholat Syakhl, the existence of which no-one had previously suspected, were just waiting to be followed and explored. It was now 7 p.m., and the stock of spare batteries to keep the lights on was running low. The camera had given up the ghost an hour earlier—or at least the film supply—forcing the five explorers to be creative in reporting their discoveries, and the last available paper was covered with notes and sketches. When the penultimate electric lamp began to flicker, Dyatlov suggested to his companions that they turn back. If they didn't want to find themselves without light in these disproportionate catacombs, they would have to forego any further progress. Of course, they intended to return the next day, thanks to the batteries held by the other group, and perhaps in the following weeks if supplies were available, but for the time being, they had to leave the area. So they began their ascent of the pieces of paper with eagerness and celerity.

Yet halfway down, Zolotaryov froze at an intersection they hadn't noticed on their descent. At the end of the tunnel, there was a faint glow that they could easily have ignored or explained away as a curious, random reflection on a polished rock, but the former military man found himself astonishingly and instantly fascinated by the beam towards which numerous corroded cables converged.

"We've got to go and see what it's all about," he said in a tone that brooked no contradiction.

Dyatlov nevertheless ventured to challenge his elder's assertion, who took it very badly, even though he wasn't the leader of the expedition.

"We may be on the verge of a breakthrough! We can't give up this close to our goal."

"We'll already have more than our fifteen minutes of fame by revealing the existence of this city to the world, Dyatlov tempered. If we're too greedy, we risk losing everything."

The argument seemed to hit home, for Zolotaryov took a few steps in his direction, then turned on his heels without warning and fled in the direction of the glow, which was faint but sufficient to temper the darkness.

"What's the matter with him?" exclaimed Thibeaux-Brignolles.

"I don't know," retorted Dyatlov.

"Shall we follow him?"

The expedition leader looked back and forth between the corridor at the end of which Zolotaryov had just disappeared and the tunnel leading to the surface. It was during this pause that he perceived a smell in the atmosphere, more pervasive than the mixture of humidity and limestone that had prevailed until then. Paradoxically, it was both more familiar and more frightening, especially in this place and under these circumstances. For the smell was clearly that of ozone, the smell that presides over the arrival of a thunderstorm.

"I can't abandon him," said Dyatlov at last, "but I don't want to risk getting lost in this endless maze either."

"Let me go and get him," suggested Thibeaux-Brignolles. "Go back up there with Slobodin and Kolmogorova, find the others, and if we're not back fifteen minutes after you, come back and get us."

"Are you sure you want to do it this way?"

"I'm the one with the best sense of direction here," smiles the young astronomy buff. "I'll find my way out with my eyes closed."

"All right, then. Fifteen minutes, no more. Take this lamp with you."

"But it's the last one!"

"We won't need them, as the skylights will be sufficient to light the rest of our journey."

"I... All right, thanks. I'll see you later."

Without further ado, Thibeaux-Brignolles turned on his heel and set off in pursuit of Zolotaryov, while his comrades made their way back.

4

Thibeaux-Brignolles shook the flashlight in all directions, casting grotesque shadows on the corridor walls and revealing, three times, adjacent passages, which he overlooked in favor of the one from which the smell of ozone emanated. He sensed that unspeakable horrors had occurred here. The glow at the end of the corridor became more intense with each step, as did the smell of ozone. Thibeaux-Brignolles then noticed that the glow was not uniform; it had small variations in intensity, similar to the pulsations of a human heart. *Mother Nature doesn't conceive of this kind of irregularity*, he thought, which instantly increased all his warning signals. *It has to be artificial, like everything else here.*

The corridor ended in a surprisingly low vault compared to the rest of the megalithic ruins, but Thibeaux-Brignolles saw more before he left. Further on lay a round space some fifty feet in diameter, in the middle of which stood an impressive carved column. A low enclosing wall ran around it, and despite the erosion caused by the weather in this open-air space—the room had no roof—showed a level of artistic finesse superior to anything he'd seen before, as spiral friezes adorned every nook and cranny. The floor, strewn with cables, was lined with a thick layer of ice on which Zolotaryov's footprints had traced a clearly visible path. The most remarkable feature, however, was the stone staircase that wound its way up to the top of the fantastic stone cylinder. The steps were beautifully preserved, which was quite remarkable given their exposure.

For a moment, Thibeaux-Brignolles could only stop and marvel. Then he remembered that his time was running out, all the more so as he could see, through the punctured ceiling, the terrible gusts of the storm sweeping across the Kholat Syakhl. He also noticed, here and there, weapons manufactured in Russia, as well as weathered red flags, totally incongruous in this setting.

The pulsating glow originated at the top of the column, which also seemed to be the point of convergence for the majority of the corroded cables. Thibeaux-Brignolles followed Zolotaryov's footsteps to the top of the tower, and the sight he saw there was to haunt him for the rest of his short life.

At the center of the plateau stood a singular, upright ring of stone. A multitude of cables were attached to it, although it was impossible to say whether their function was to carry electricity to the circle or, on the contrary, to extract a phenomenal quantity of it. Thibeaux-Brignolles immediately leaned towards the second option, for one simple reason: despite the passage of time, and whatever the function of this age-old technological object, it was still in working order. Its interior shone and pulsed with the powerful light that had guided him so far, while reflecting the surrounding scenery. A mirror was the only sensible comparison Thibeaux-Brignolles could think of at the moment. However, he couldn't help noticing minute differences between reality and its reflection. Zolotaryov, for example, who was standing in front of the circle, had removed his right glove to feel the structural rock with his fingertips. The former military man had no tattoos, something he had bragged about over a meal. *"There's no way I'm going to let my skin turn into some kind of ridiculous painting. A man's virility isn't measured by the number of drawings he has on his body."* His reflection, however, bore mysterious symbols on his right hand, including a stylized pictogram resembling a heart, and a strange inscription in an unknown language: "DAERMMOUAZOUAÏA". Apart from this detail, both were identical and reproduced the same movements simultaneously.

Thibeaux-Brignolles was even more frightened when he caught a glimpse of his own reflection in Zolotaryov's back, and saw that Zolotaryov was sporting a finely-trimmed goatee, a hair ornament he had never donned before. This peculiarity frightened him more than anything he'd seen before, instilling in his mind a sudden sense of urgency, which he tried to alleviate by taking a photograph, as if the reassuring *click of* the camera possessed the ability to keep him in a tangible reality.

"Step away from the ring," he shouted at Zolotaryov, who pretended not to hear him. "This thing could be radioactive!"

"Isn't she beautiful?" retorted the latter.

"You're out of your mind. Let's get out of here!"

"Why do you ask? We came to these mountains in the hope of discovering something useful for understanding our past. Didn't I say that the whole world would hear about us? All that's left for me to do is…"

He moved his hand forward to make contact with the reflective surface.

"No!"

A blinding flash of light exploded into the room, filling it with an orange glow. At the same moment, the floor shook and a distant rumble, reminiscent of a thousand drums rolling, was heard.

*

Several hundred meters away, Dyatlov and the two survivors of his group had just reached the surface. The storm was raging outside, kicking up flurries of snow and streaking the sky with thunderous flashes of lightning. It wasn't one of these, however, that startled them, but the roar of the avalanche from the heights of Kholat Syakhl.

"We've got to warn Lyudmila and the others!" shouted Slobodin to cover the sound of the wind.

"It's madness!" retorted Kolmogorova, one hand resting on her hood to keep it in place. "The flow will be here any minute! We'd better stay under cover!"

"Anyway, I can't abandon them," imposed Dyatlov. "It's my responsibility!"

Without wasting a second, he dashed through the trees, close on Slobodin's heels. Kolmogorova cursed and insulted the mothers of her two companions, before rushing back into the midst of the raging elements.

*

Thibeaux-Brignolles came to his senses just moments after losing consciousness. His left arm was dangling over the edge of the tower. A reflex caused him to roll over twice, and he came face to face with Zolotaryov's shoes. Zolotaryov was staring at him with an evil look, but there was no longer the glint of madness in his eyes that had been there just a minute earlier.

"What happened?" growled Thibeaux-Brignolles, helping himself to his feet with his elbow.

"A bolt of lightning struck the mirror while I was touching it," Zolotaryov retorted nonchalantly. "Maybe it's some kind of lightning rod."

"And you're okay? Can we go now? Have you had your fill of thrills?"

"We're good to go. I'll be back tomorrow to study the device. After you."

While grumbling, Thibeaux-Brignolles relit his electric lamp and took the lead of their duo.

It took about twenty minutes to reach the surface. The storm continued to rage, but with less vigour. The avalanche, on the other hand, had swept away everything in its path, toppling the weakest trees and carrying away the weakest rocks.

"Mon Dieu," gasped Thibeaux-Brignolles.

"I'm afraid there's just the two of us left," said Zolotaryov, his tone as icy as the ambient temperature.

"Don't say that. The others are seasoned hikers too."

"I don't want to hurt your feelings, but no one could have survived this."

"I'll bet you anything they've found shelter."

"You've got a bet," concludes Zolotaryov, a sneer on his lips.

But, as they cautiously searched for traces of their companions, a sight appeared which, for a time, put an end to all other preoccupations. Half-buried in the snow were two tents, one of which, badly damaged, had been cut away from the inside and still contained a large quantity of appallingly familiar equipment—walking boots, warm clothes, ski poles.

"They seem to have left the camp barefoot or in socks," said Zolotaryov, vaguely amused.

Thibeaux-Brignolles, on the other hand, didn't seem the least bit entertained. He spotted a series of tracks leading to a nearby wood on the other side of the pass. His friends had certainly judged this to be the best place to hide from an avalanche.

The real shock came at the edge of this wood, when, under a large pine tree, they spotted two forms wrapped in blankets, next to the remains of an extinguished fire: the corpses of Krivonichtchenko and Doroshenko, stiffened by the frost, perfectly preserved, with pieces of plaster where they had been wounded, and wrapped with obvious care to prevent any further damage. Both were barefoot, wearing only their underwear.

The bodies of Slobodin, Dyatlov and Kolmogorova lay some 500 meters away. Their position suggested that they had wanted to return to camp despite the storm.

"How is this possible?" gasped Thibeaux-Brignolles. "How could they let themselves be fooled?"

"I told you: no one can escape an avalanche like that. There isn't enough shelter on the side of this mountain."

"We were only in the cave twenty minutes longer than they were. They look like they've been dead for hours!"

"Are you kidding? You've been missing for more than two days," said a female voice behind their backs.

They turned around sharply. Lyudmila and Kolevatov were standing there, covered in frostbite and freezing, but very much alive.

"What do you mean 'we've been gone for over two days?'" questioned Thibeaux-Brignolles. "What do you mean by that? We were in the cave for three hours at most!"

"It means what it means," Lyudmila spat. "You left almost three days ago. What the hell have you been doing all this time?!"

The young woman's left foot was wrapped in a piece of wool from Krivonichtchenko's pants. For the rest, she wore her usual faux-fur coat and hat. Kolevatov, camera in hand, nodded his approval.

"But... well... that's impossible! I mean... Dyatlov and the others were still with us an hour ago and..."

"They died yesterday morning. Krivonichtchenko and Doroshenko froze in front of the fire the night before last."

"But... this... this is crazy!"

"For you maybe, but I can assure you it's as real as it gets for us, who've been battling the storm for two days."

"Have you been waiting for us all this time?" interjected Zolotaryov.

"No, we didn't. To be honest, we thought you were dead."

"What are you still doing here then?"

"The winds died down less than half an hour ago, allowing us to emerge from our lair. Believe me, we didn't stay hidden for the fun of it. Dyatlov, Slobodin and Kolmogorova tried to brave the snow to get help, but... you saw the result. They all died of hypothermia."

"You say the winds died down less than half an hour ago," said Thibeaux-Brignolles. That's when we came to our senses," he added, addressing Zolotaryov.

"I'll ask you again," Lyudmila continued, "what have you been doing all this time?"

Thibeaux-Brignolles then launched into a brief account of the events as he had experienced them, omitting many details that were unnecessary to the story. When he finished, Lyudmila looked even more skeptical than a few minutes earlier.

"A mirror?"

"I'd describe it as very old technology," Zolotaryov said.

"Who cares? What's it for? Why is it here? You mentioned an orange flash, followed by an earthquake. That's exactly what we observed just before the avalanche started!"

"Are you accusing me of being responsible for this tragedy?"

"I'm not accusing anyone, Semyon. Right now, I'm just trying to understand."

"There's nothing to understand. Dyatlov was reckless and incompetent. As a result, five of us are dead."

"And there'll be a sixth if you don't shut up right away," scolded Kolevatov, who didn't appreciate this lack of respect for his departed friend.

"Boys, this is no time to argue," Lyudmila tempered. "The priority is to stay alive."

"You're absolutely right," agreed Zolotaryov. "You won't blame me for what follows."

With one blow, he turned on Thibeaux-Brignolles and, pressing his head between his hands, fractured his skull. Blood spurted from his nose and eyes, and he collapsed in the snow without realizing that he was about to die. Zolotaryov then threw himself at Lyudmila, knocking her down onto the ice with all his weight, crushing her ribcage in the process, before ripping out her lips, tongue and eyes with his teeth in a truly frightening fit of insanity. The young woman's screams stunned Kolevatov, who only found the strength to move once the beast in Zolotaryov's guise turned its attention to him.

5

"The body of Alexander Sergeyevich Kolevatov was finally found on May 4, under four meters of snow, at the bottom of a ravine, along with those of Lyudmila Dubinina, Nikolai Thibeaux-Brignolles and Semyon Zolotaryov, announced Yuri Yudin from the rostrum of the main auditorium of the Ural Polytechnic Institute. All four victims died very violently, and the bodies were in poor condition when they were discovered. Kolevatov had a broken nose and a deformed neck, but died of hypothermia."

A hand went up among the journalists.

"Yes? Monsieur...?"

"Yaroslav Voïnov, *Komsomolskaya Pravda*. Are you saying that Semyon Zolotaryov assaulted his comrades?"

"That's what the final recordings captured by Kolevatov suggest, indeed."

"In that case, how did he die?"

"That's the question, and we can only speculate on this point. So I'd rather not tell you my theory on the subject, at the risk of appearing even more foolish than I already am."

Yaroslav Voïnov's hand went down, while another went up.

"Yes, Mr. Goosev?"

"These events happened five years ago now. Why did you wait to make these revelations?"

"There are two reasons for this. Firstly, it took me some time to piece together the facts from the fragmentary elements at my disposal. Secondly, their extravagant nature forced me to remain silent in order not to lose credibility. However, as I mentioned earlier, the Ural colonization project, launched jointly by several companies, forces me to leave my reserve."

"How did you come into possession of this information? If I'm not mistaken, none of this was made public at the time of the 1959 investigation."

"That's right, but you should know that I was part of the first rescue team. This enabled me to recover the recordings and diaries of my comrades. Of course, I made copies before handing the originals over to the authorities, who obviously didn't see fit to take them into account."

While Fyodor Gusev was filling in several lines in his notebook, a journalist from the *Ogoniok* asked to speak.

"I read in my notes that the 1959 police report establishes several strange facts. Dr. Boris Vozrojdenny, in charge of the autopsies, states that the traumas were too severe to have been caused by humans, comparing the severity of the injuries with the result of a car accident or the passage of a shock wave. I also read that Semyon Zolotaryov's body was found with his face so badly damaged that his family were unable to identify him with any certainty. Finally, the clothes of some of the victims emitted high levels of radiation."

"And don't forget that, after the funeral, the families said that the victims' skin had a strange brown tint," added Yuri Yudin, before resuming his presentation. "I know all about it. As you know, the investigators concluded that the members of the Dyatlov expedition were killed by, and I quote, *'an unknown irresistible force.*

Given the absence of external wounds and signs of struggle on the corpses, and taking into account the conclusions of the forensic expertise regarding the causes of death of the group members, it must be considered that the cause of their death was a spontaneous force which they were unable to resist'. That's what the official report says, word for word—you can check. All this brings me back to the crux of the matter, the reason I'm speaking to you today: the strange discovery made by Semyon Zolotaryov and Nikolaï Thibeaux-Brignolles in the depths of the Kholat Syakhl."

"According to your theory," continued Fyodor Goosev, forgetting to ask for the floor again, "they unearthed some kind of stone ring, and it was this ring that triggered the storm, wasn't it?"

"As far as the storm is concerned, I obviously can't say for sure, even if the coincidences between its arrival and the activation of the machine, as well as its shutdown, are troubling. What I can confirm, however, is that my comrades have discovered an ancient artifact which, for the safety of all the world's peoples, is best kept hidden. In my opinion, this object is a portal to other dimensions of time and space. The proof is in this photograph."

On the wall appeared the photograph taken by Thibeaux-Brignolles just before Zolotaryov touched the mirror. Despite the backlight caused by the glow emanating from inside the circle, it showed the hikers' doubles, but above all their differences, namely the tattoos on Zolotaryov's hand and Kolevatov's goatee.

"The only explanation for these aberrations is that they are doubles from another universe, or another space-time."

A hubbub ran through the assembly. Yudin raised his voice to put an end to it.

"Nonsense!" replied the *Ogoniok* journalist. "What a load of rubbish!"

"I understand your skepticism. I shared it for a while, but I've come to realize that it's the only logical interpretation of the facts. How else can we explain the dilapidated state of the symbols and electronic devices of Soviet origin scattered throughout these ruins? My theory is as follows: visitors, probably from another dimension, came through the portal to establish a base in the Urals, which they then abandoned to return from whence they came."

"For what purpose?"

"I haven't the slightest idea. Maybe they were looking to colonize another space-time, or maybe they just happened to be there by chance, exploring the mountain, like my friends. Or perhaps they were travelers from the future. I believe that, in some way, this device enables time travel. How is this possible? I don't know. My knowledge of this technology is obviously far too limited, and how it works remains a complete mystery to me."

Yaroslav Voïnov raised his hand again.

"Let's assume that all this is true, Mr. Yudin. Why shouldn't men of science, as you call them, get their hands on this technology and study it?"

"The answer to this question seems obvious to me: it's far too dangerous. I am fully aware of the advantages that our motherland would derive from the use of such a weapon in the face of American imperialism, but it is my duty, in memory of my comrades, to stand in the way of such designs. Their tragic fate should serve as a warning to us all: the laws of the universe cannot be played with impunity. This is why I hope that you, renowned journalists, will help me through your articles to convince as many people as possible to oppose the colonization project that threatens the Ural mountains. Some may find it curious that I'm exposing the existence of this technology today, but making it public is, in my opinion, the best way to protect it. I can't imagine what would happen to us if it were to fall, in the greatest secrecy, into the wrong hands."

Yuri Yudin's lecture concluded with these terrible words and, as the audience emptied of its presentation-stunned public, a bearded man lingered in the aisles, his eyes riveted on the black-and-white clich still adorned the wall; a man who, five years earlier, in the Ural Mountains, had returned to find his double passed out in the Mirror Room, before dragging him out of the Kholat Syakhl, drawing symbols on his skin and murdering him as he had murdered Alexander Kolevatov, Lyudmila Dubinina and Nikolai Thibeaux-Brignolles.

The facts

Russian article from March 9, 2013

The tragic death of the members of the Dyatlov expedition is one of the most talked-about Russian mysteries of the last half-century. The story goes back to January 1959. A group of ten skiers/trekkers led by Igor Dyatlov set off on a high-risk journey. Eight men and two women, all students and graduates of the Ural Polytechnic Institute, set off on a trek classified as "Category III", the most difficult in existence. They died in bizarre circumstances on the eastern slopes of Mount Kholat Syakhl in the northern Urals. The scenario of this tragedy has still not been clearly established sixty years after the fact, which of course has given rise to countless theories, each more original and far-fetched than the last: UFOs, secret agents, nuclear tests, attack by the Mansi people, yeti... As elements were apparently classified as secret defense by the authorities at the time, the public's curiosity and imagination were all the more aroused.

Several books, and even a film directed by Renny Harlin (2013), have been devoted to this subject.

Expedition members crammed into the back of the truck

What we know

The aim of the Dyatlov expedition was to reach Otorten, a mountain some ten kilometers from where the tragedy finally occurred. All its members were experienced cross-country and downhill skiers, so their disappearance raised many questions.

At this time of year and at this altitude, the temperature is close to -30°C. After two stages in mountain villages (Ivdel and Vizhay), the group heads for Otorten on January 27. The following day, Yuri Yudin had to give up due to sciatica. The group was thus reduced to nine members.

On January 31, they began their ascent, leaving some food and equipment in a wooded area for the return journey. On February 1, they start crossing the pass, but due to unfavorable weather conditions, they lose their way and veer off to the west, towards Kholat Syakhl. Realizing their mistake, they decided to stop and camp on the mountainside until the following day. From then on, they were never heard from again.

A page from Zina Kolmogorova's diary

On February 20, a search began for the hikers. Police and military personnel were deployed, and helicopters and airplanes were sent to support the search. On February 26, their camp was found abandoned on the eastern slopes of Kholat Syakhl. The tents were badly damaged, torn from the inside, but still standing. What remains suggests that the hikers were preparing to eat. Their shoes and equipment are still in the camp, which means they left in a hurry, either barefoot or in socks.

In a nearby wood, the rescue team discovered the remains of a campfire and the first two bodies, under a large pine tree: those of Krivonichtchenko and Doroshenko, dressed only in their underwear. Krivonichtchenko has burns on his leg and a self-inflicted bite mark on his hand (the torn skin is still in his mouth). A little further on, they find Dyatlov and Kolmogorova. It wasn't until March 5 that Rustem Slobodin was found in the same spot, and another two months before the bodies of Dubinina, Kolevatov, Thibeaux-Brignolles and Zolotaryov were unearthed, lying under four meters of snow in a ravine further inland. Unlike their comrades, the latter are warmly clothed, but strangely enough, some of them seem to be wearing the clothes of their comrades found earlier, a fact which demonstrates that the hikers didn't all die at the same time. What's more, these new corpses show signs of violent death.

The tents as found by rescue workers

Dr. Boris Vozrojdenny, the forensic pathologist in charge of the autopsies, determined that Dubinina had ten broken ribs, and that her tongue and eyes were missing, as well as part of her lips and a fragment of her skull; Semyon Zolotaryov's face is badly damaged, five ribs are broken and his eyes are also missing, while Nikolai Thibeaux-Brignolles' skull is fractured, and Kolevatov's nose and neck are deformed, although he eventually succumbed to hypothermia like the first five hikers. However, the bodies show no external injuries corresponding to the fractures noted, as if they had been subjected to very high pressure. Dr Vozrojdenny's report, which was published in the press at the time, concluded that the injuries were too severe

Photo of a mansi inscription

The Files of the Impossible

to have been caused by humans. To top it all off, some of the victims' clothing emitted high levels of radiation.

Surveys

On May 28, 1959, the Sverdlovsk Prosecutor's Office closed the investigation, citing as the cause of death *"spontaneous force that these people were unable to overcome"*. On February 1, 2019, however, the Russian government announced that it would be reopened, leading to a different conclusion. On July 11, 2020, Andrei Kuriakov, deputy head of the General Prosecutor's Office of the Urals Federal District, says: *"After leaving the tents, the group set off together, without panic, for about fifty meters. They went up to a rocky ridge, which is a natural limiter for an avalanche. They did everything right. But here's the second reason why the group was, shall we say, condemned to death: they didn't return to camp. When they turned back, they didn't see the tents."* Mr. Kuriakov adds that, that night, visibility was six to sixteen meters.

"The hikers reached a wooded area and lit a fire, which lasted for an hour and a half. Two members of the group subsequently froze to death. The rest decided to split up. One group was led by Igor Dyatlov, the other by Semyon Zolotaryov. Dyatlov's sub-group tried to return to the tents, following in his footsteps. They froze immediately on leaving the forest area; the temperature was -40°C to -45°C, with a penetrating wind."

"The second sub-group also headed for the tents, but they themselves provoked a snow movement by digging a trench for shelter and were thrown into a ravine. As a result, the climbers suffered heavy fractures, covered by tons of snow. It is these mechanical injuries that have given rise to a number of theories. There was no panic, but these young men had no chance of escaping under the circumstances. That's the formal end of the matter. The matter is closed."

Yuri Kountsevich and Yevgeny Chernusov, head and lawyer respectively of the Dyatlov Foundation, nevertheless disagreed with the version of the Prosecutor General's Office, stressing that the Foundation would insist on a resumption of investigations to shed full light on the hikers' deaths.

The opinion of 1st Commissioner Maillard of the Brussels Judicial Police - Division in charge of crime against property and people.

In 1959, an expedition of eight men and two women, all students and graduates of the Ural Polytechnic Institute, undertook a trek classified as "Category III", the most difficult in the world.

Things to consider

1/ These young people are educated and qualified. It's impossible for them to embark on such an adventure without experience and a minimum of training.

2/ I can't imagine they'd start out on a very dangerous expedition without first completing other, less dangerous expeditions.

3/ It is clearly stated that there are ten skiers/randonneurs and that they are led by Igor Dyatlov. Why name the latter if he's just an ordinary person? What's more, all the members have a solid background in cross-country and downhill skiing. This also means that they won't fall into beginner's traps.

4/ I'm already very intrigued by the passage in which it is stated that certain elements were classified as "secret défense" by the authorities at the time! After all, we're talking about missing hikers here. What's there to hide in a place where it's -30°?

On January 31, 1959, they began their ascent and, being organized, acted like the professionals they are, leaving a few supplies and equipment in a wooded area in preparation for the return journey.

One of them leaves the group for health reasons.

Weather conditions being bad, they deviated from their route in the direction of Kholat Syakhl. They realize their mistake and stop to wait for the weather to ease until the next day, camping on the mountainside.

If we're aware of this problem, it's probably because they were in contact with someone to let him know they were on their way, otherwise we'd know nothing at all. Did they have a radio with them?

They were never heard from again.

Twenty days later, with no news from those concerned, the search began.

On 26/02/1959, the camp was found on the slopes of Kholat Syakhl.

Things to note on site

1/ The tents are still standing and are torn from the inside. We can assume that the threat came from within.

2/ Apparently, they were busy cooking when the problem arose.

3/ Despite the cold and a storm, they left the tent in a hurry, barefoot or in socks. The only reason anyone would do this is if they were afraid of dying. Being experienced, they must have known that if they left their gear behind, they'd freeze to death later. Without shoes, they wouldn't get far.

4/ They don't go far, as a fire is found in a nearby wood and two bodies are found under a large pine tree. Both bodies are dressed only in their underwear. A little further on, two more bodies are found.

On 05/03/1959, another body was found, and it would be another two months before four more bodies were found under four meters of snow in a ravine a little further on.

The latter are warmly dressed, but with clothes belonging to their comrades. They show signs of violent death.

Possibilities

- They weren't together when there was a problem in the tent.

- Members of the last group found may have taken their comrades' clothes when they died.

- These four people bear traces of violent death. But we're not told what kind of marks. Fractures, animal bites, traces of knives or firearms—anything is possible.

Autopsy

- After the autopsy, we'll know a little more about the cause of death. The bodies show no external injuries corresponding to the fractures found! It's as if they'd been subjected to very high pressure. The trauma is too severe to have been caused by humans.

- The clothes of some of the victims emit high levels of radiation. It's worth remembering that some of these items have been classified by the authorities as "defence secrets"!

Surveys

- As for the investigations carried out by the public prosecutor's office, these remain only suppositions. No one was on the spot to confirm the claims or to have seen the persons concerned act as the authority claims.

- Cause of death: "a spontaneous force that these people were unable to overcome". We're in the middle of a science-fiction novel.

- It is not explained why the tent is torn from the inside, why they left the tent where they were sheltered in such a hurry and without shoes, but with their underwear on.

- What's most disturbing is the presence of high levels of radiation on the clothing, even though we're in the middle of the mountains. Something must have caused this situation, and only the Russian authorities, who have decreed a "secret defense", can answer.

In this case, there are far too many elements that cannot be explained by natural causes. The only way to explain certain elements is certainly a Russian secret. On this assumption, anything is possible.

Bonus:
The case of the high-school girl
with her hands cut off

Jung So-yoon, the young victim (©그것이 알고싶다 공식계정)

South Korea. March 8, 2001. A worker finds the body of a high-school girl under a bag of cement near a building under construction. The victim's body and the area where she was found show no signs of trauma or struggle. There was also very little blood at the scene. The victim's personal effects are intact and no money has been stolen. Moreover, she has clearly not been raped. The only things missing are her hands.

Identified as Jung So-yoon, the 18-year-old high-school student was working part-time in a clothing store where she was on duty on the evening of her death. The last images of her were taken from the store's surveillance cameras at 8:20 pm.

At 8:35 p.m., someone tried to contact the store, but received no answer, which was strange, as So-yoon should have been there to answer the call. The police therefore believe that the crime took place shortly after 8.20pm. Unfortunately, there are no CCTV images or eyewitnesses to confirm this.

On March 9, the day after the murder, a man makes a strange discovery in a river not far from the scene of the crime. While driving his car, he noticed two white spots on the surface of the water. As they are very pale, he thinks at first of doll's or mannequin's hands. However, he had a hunch that something was wrong and decided to call the police. It is soon confirmed that they are human hands, and the DNA matches that of So-yoon.

(©SBS 뉴스)

The police decide to investigate the construction site and its employees. The only evidence found was an axe stained with the victim's blood (discovered at the crime scene) and a free advertising pen donated as part of a promotion by a car company.

(©그것이 알고싶다 공식계정)

The police are narrowing down the list of suspects to those with access to the construction site, as it seems unlikely that the public would enter, especially at night. The first suspect in the case is none other than the construction worker who discovered the lifeless body, Mr. Lee. According to him, he had started work particularly late that day, but no one had discovered the victim's body before him. Secondly, the police noticed scratches on Mr. Lee's hand that resembled fingernail scratches, as if someone had scratched his hand. Even more disturbing, a shoe print, which seems to match the pattern on the soles of Mr. Lee's shoes, is visible on So-yoon's neck.

However, for lack of evidence, Mr. Lee was not arrested. It was later revealed that the photo of Mr. Lee's hand had been taken a week after the murder, meaning that the scratches could have been caused by something else. The shoe print found on So-yoon's neck was also slightly different from the sole of Mr. Lee's shoes.

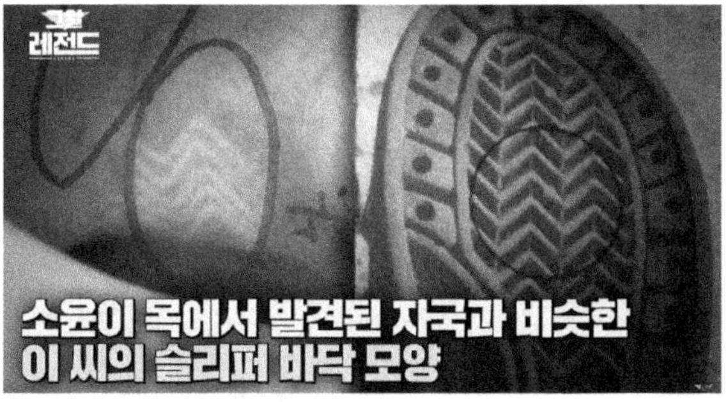

(©그것이 알고싶다 공식계정)

With no other leads, the case was closed.

In 2014, a Korean TV show specializing in the analysis of unsolved crimes, *Unanswered Questions* (그것이 알고싶다), took an interest in the case and decided to recreate the investigation. After the episode airs, 13 years after the fact, a witness comes forward, asking to speak to the production team. The woman was only 10 at the time, but she says she remembers seeing a strange man. As she walked to her mother's car, the man approached her and asked for directions to the nearest toilet. Suddenly, he grabbed her and her screams drew the attention of someone in a nearby store. The man then let go of her and she ran to take refuge in her mother's car.

Shortly afterwards, she noticed that the same man had entered one of the stores to talk to a woman. The woman left with the man and, after a while, the witness said she heard a scream. Later, she saw the man return, holding a black plastic bag.

Unfortunately, as had happened several years ago, this witness was unable to recall the man's face, despite an attempt to recover his memories using hypnosis.

The show's production team took over the investigation and interviewed Mr. Kim, a worker who had never been heard of by the police for health reasons. During an interview, he declares: "I can't imagine someone kidnapping and raping a girl". A member of the production team finds his statement strange and asks him why he thinks rape was the murderer's intention. To this, Mr. Kim replies that this is usually the case when girls are kidnapped. However, So-yoon was not raped. After the interview, the producers point out that Mr. Kim showed signs of nervousness when asked about his statement.

After three interviews with him, the team concluded that Mr. Kim could not possibly be the murderer.

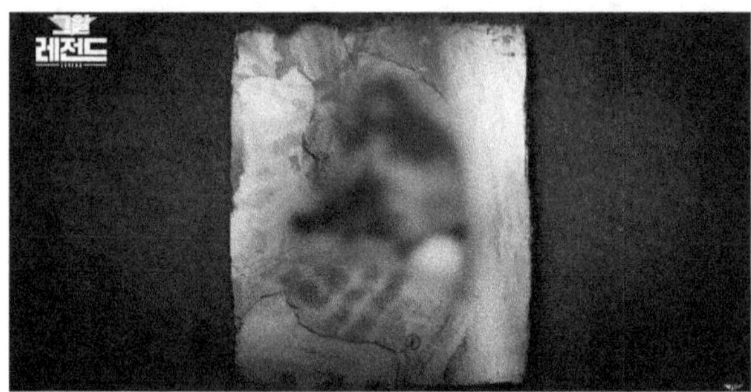

(©그것이 알고싶다 공식계정)

Four years later, in 2018, *SBS News*, in partnership with *Unanswered Questions*, revived the investigation and uncovered new suspects. The hypothesis that the murderer was part of So-yoon's circle of friends began to emerge. One of her friends, known only by the surname "Hwang", called her at around 8.30pm. This means that Hwang was the last person to contact her. At 8:35 p.m., when the store phone rang, So-yoon didn't pick it up. As a result, instead of the 15-minute window that had previously been established, it was now reduced to 5 minutes. Something must have happened in those 5 minutes.

When the investigation began, Hwang left the neighborhood and the school. Hwang had a crush on So-yoon and constantly pestered her to love him back. If So-yoon had indeed rejected him repeatedly, Hwang would have had a motive to attack her. However, the police were unable to find any evidence pointing to him.

Park, another of So-yoon's friends, is also a suspect because of strange messages he wrote online about So-yoon's murder. What's more, he didn't go to school for a few days after So-yoon's death. As with Hwang, the police were unable to incriminate Park despite his strange behavior.

The third suspect is Kim, also friends with So-yoon. After news of his murder broke, Kim left the school, changed his name and disappeared completely from circulation.

Yet the truth about So-yoon's murder is still unknown.

The opinion of 1st Commissioner Maillard of the Brussels Judicial Police - Division in charge of crime against property and people.

In South Korea, a young girl is found dead with both hands amputated. The victim was an 18-year-old high-school student named Jung So-yoon. She can still be seen on the store's surveillance cameras at 8.20 pm.

And at 8:35 p.m., someone tried to contact the store, but no one answered.

It would therefore be logical to assume that it disappeared between 8.20 and 8.35 pm on 08/03/2001.

Now, based on the photograph in the document, all we can make out is a silhouette that could be anyone!

Crime scene

- The victim was obviously not killed on the spot, given the small amount of blood found.

- There's no sign of a struggle.

- Apparently, the victim was neither a thief nor a sexual predator, given the evidence available.

- However, it's hidden under a bag of cement.

- Nor is it a criminal collector as there can be, as the hands were found in a river not far from where it was discovered.

Auditions

- The store owner must be interviewed. Had he had any recent problems? A possible racket or threats? Perhaps the hands had been chopped off to send a message: either you pay up or nobody works in your shop!

- We also need to interview the man who discovered the hands in the river.

- Check both people's alibis and backgrounds.

Neighborhood survey

- It's very important to carry out a neighbourhood survey both near the store and near the place where the body was found.

- Check to see if other stores are having problems with a local mafia.

- Check all nearby cameras to see if the same person is seen in both locations.

Items found at the site where the body was found

- An axe stained with the victim's blood is found. Check whether this is the weapon that may have been used to chop off the victim's hands.

- In-depth analysis of the blood found. It's not out of the question to find blood from the assailant, who may have injured himself when he struck.

- Investigate the pen found and also look for DNA. The pen may belong to the assailant. This would NOT be the first time that a perpetrator has dropped or forgotten something at the scene of a crime.

- Look for the primary crime scene, as the place of discovery is a place where the victim was left after the fact. (The store must be visited, and the building site as well).

Victim autopsy

- Check at autopsy whether the victim has any traces of the substance in his system, because I don't know anyone who doesn't scream when his hands are chopped off, apart from being under the effect of a powerful sedative.

- Compare the marks on the victim's body and hands to ensure that the axe found is indeed the one used to slice the victim's hands.

Several suspects

A/ Mr Lee

- Mr. Lee discovered the victim's body. He claims to have started work late that day. Check whether he usually starts at this time. Why start work when it's almost dark?

- The victim has scratches that appear to be consistent with fingernail scratches. In addition, a shoe tread mark seems to match the one found on the victim's neck. That's a lot of evidence!

- Although the victim's hands had been in the water, I'd still do a nail curage to check for bits of our suspect's skin.

- Perhaps the reason her hands were cut off was to make the marks disappear. Whose axe is it? Could it be Mr. Lee's?

- The same applies to footwear, which requires laboratory analysis.

B/ In 2014, 13 years after the events, a woman testifies (she was 10 at the time). She was also victimized by a man who tried to abduct her and then went into a store afterwards, only to come out with a black plastic bag. She heard screams. It took this person a long time to make that statement!

C/ The Kim worker

- Detailed hearing of worker Kim and background check.

- DNA comparison with his own.

- What were his health problems at the time?

D/ 2018

- A friend of the victim could be a suspect. He goes by the surname "Hwang". He allegedly called her at around 8:30 pm. And it took until 2018 to realize that a friend had called on the day of the incident. Why wasn't this duty carried out at the time of the investigation? Why wasn't the victim's acquaintances contacted? Why didn't the telephone investigation reveal this element?

- The same goes for Park, another friend of the victim, and for Kim, who disappeared afterwards.

It's clear that this investigation has not been conducted with the utmost seriousness, or that we're missing some investigative elements. It's always vital to act quickly after the fact. The victim's entourage must always be studied seriously and precisely.

Bonus:
The Greenbrier file

Buckwheat Cakes

with

ROYAL

Baking Powder

Are delicious and wholesome — a perfect cold weather breakfast food.

Made in the morning; no yeast, no "setting" over night; never sour, never cause indigestion.

To make a perfect buckwheat cake, and a thousand other dainty dishes, see the "Royal Baker and Pastry Cook." Mailed free to any address.

ROYAL BAKING POWDER CO., NEW YORK.

A Weird Story of a Remarkable Crime

On the 22nd day of January, 1897, Trout Shue murdered his wife at his home near Livesay's Mill, in Greenbrier county. The murdered woman was a daughter of Mr. and Mrs. Hedges Heaster, poor uneducated country people, who lived at the foot of Little Sewell Mountain. Zona Heaster was his third wife, it is stated, and was the third one he had murdered. Shue was a rare type of brute criminal and had [illegible] covered up the evidence of his guilt in former cases so as to avoid detection, though not one person. He was arrested and convicted of the murder of his third wife upon the testimony of his mother-in-law, every detail of which was found to correspond with the facts disclosed by the post-mortem. Shue was sentenced to the penitentiary for life and died there. We will state that we knew well the mother of the murdered girl — that she is an [illegible] thoroughly creditable old woman, and that we believe, as the jury in the house believed, that she told the truth in regard to her [illegible] and presentiments. Now will some one explain this case scientifically?

The mother lived nearly twenty miles from the scene of the murder and could have known of it in no way whatever. How could she have told of it in every detail? Was it accident, telepathy or a supernatural revelation? We do not know. The following account of the case was given by our Circuit Judge Hon. Joseph M. McWhorter.

Shue, in November, 1896, married Miss Zona Heaster, of Meadow Bluff district, in Greenbrier county, as his third wife, he being about 34 years of age, and settled at Livesay's Mill to work at the blacksmith trade. He and his wife occupied what once they rented in a two story frame building which had been the residence of the late Wm. Livesay.

On the 22nd day of January, 1897, as he went to his work he called on a colored family who lived a few yards from his house and asked the mother to let her boy, some 12 years of age, go [illegible] up to his house and do some chores there and take some eggs to the store for Zona, his wife. About twelve o'clock he left his shop and went to his colored neighbor and asked if the boy had yet been to his house, and the old woman said he had not, but it was near dinner time. Shue said he was not going to dinner that day and again requested the boy to be sent up. In a short time the boy gave the alarm that Mrs. Shue was dead. She was found in the dining room lying stretched out and her clothes pulled down and apparently had been dead some hours. The doctor was sent for and after making a cursory examination decided that she had died from heart failure, as she had been unwell, and he had been attending her a week or two. It was decided that the remains should be taken for interment to her father's about fourteen miles distant. The remains were kept over night at her father's and buried the following day.

After the burial the friends in talking over the circumstances connected with her death and burial, and recalling the fact that no one ever was permitted to view the remains but in the presence of Shue who always took his place at the head of the corpse, and when she was placed in the coffin, he had a sheet folded and placed alongside of her head and some garment placed on the other side, and her mother stating that her daughter had appeared and talked to her, her parents were not satisfied as to the cause of her death. So after consultation it was decided to exhume the body, which was just one month from the time of its burial.

SOME REMARKABLE EVIDENCE

Here comes the most remarkable part of the evidence introduced by defendant's counsel. Mrs. Heaster, mother of the deceased, who seemed a very pious lady, had told all she knew about her daughter's death and burial and defendant's conduct on the night of the wake.

Counsel for the defendant said to her: "Mrs. Heaster did you not have a dream that caused your suspicions and led you to have the body exhumed?"

She replied: "I had no dream for I was as fully awake as I am at this moment."

"And did you not have a dream or vision that led you to have the body disinterred?"

"Well," she said. "I was not satisfied that my daughter came to her death from natural causes, and I prayed earnestly that it might be revealed to me how she came to her death, and after about an hour spent in prayer I turned over and there stood my daughter and I put my hand out to feel for the coffin, but it was not there. She seemed to hesitate to speak to me, and departed. The next night, after I had prayed again that the manner of her death might be shown, she again appeared and talked more freely and gave me to understand that I should be acquainted with the whole matter and disappeared. The third night she again appeared and disclosed more to me. "And on the fourth night she appeared and told me all about the difficulty, how it occurred and how her death was brought about.

AND HERE IS WHAT ZONA TOLD HER

"He came that night from the shop and seemed angry. I told him supper was ready, and he began to chide because I had prepared no meat for supper, and I replied that there was plenty; there was bread and butter, apple sauce, preserves, and other things that made a very good supper, and he flew mad and got up and came toward me when I raised up and he seized each side of my head with his hands and by a sudden wrench dislocated my neck." She went on and described to me the location of the building and surroundings in the neighborhood where they lived, so that it was fixed in my mind as a reality. I was telling some one whose name the writer has forgotten about the situation of buildings, etc., and he said to me "you have been there," and I replied, I had not, and he said "I have been there many times, and yet I could not describe the place so minutely and accurately as you have."

The attorney then said "Mrs. Heaster, was there not something about a sheet that you could not understand?"

And she replied "There was." She said that when Mr. Shue was leaving from the burial for home, she called his attention to the sheet that had been under the side of her head in the coffin, and he said, "mother, you keep it."

"I kept it for 3 or 4 weeks and while it looked clean and white I imagined it smelled badly and I concluded to wash it. I washed it with my white clothes and when I pressed it down in the tub it turned red, and I concluded I had soiled my other clothes, but when I dipped up water in my hand the water was not colored. I washed it and boiled it and hung it out and from it three or four days, but it still had a reddish color."

Counsel says, "Have you that sheet with you?"

She replied that she had it at her boarding house.

The sheet was brought in and exhibited to the jury, and it was decidedly a reddish color.

When the body was taken up and a post mortem examination made it was found that her neck [illegible] dislocated, which on [illegible] undoubtedly had caused her death.

The trial occupied eight days and the jury found him guilty of murder in the first degree, and that he should be sent to the penitentiary for life.

This murdered woman was his third wife, and he had boasted that he expected to have seven wives. In this, however, he was disappointed. He has passed to the Great Beyond to meet the three he treated so brutally here.

Escaped an Awful Fate.

Mr. B. Haggins, of Melbourne, Fla., writes: "My doctor told me I had consumption and nothing could be done for me. I was given up to die. The offer of a free trial bottle of Dr. King's New Discovery for Consumption induced me to try it. Results were startling. I am now on the road to recovery and owe all to Dr. King's New Discovery. It surely saved my life." This great cure is guaranteed for all throat and lung diseases by Docket Bros. Druggists. Price 50c and $1.00. Trial bottles free.

An article from The Independent-Herald, *dated February 18, 1904, recounting the whole story*

Elva Zona Heaster Shue, known to everyone as Zona, was 23 in October 1896 when she ran an errand in town and met a 37-year-old blacksmith, Erasmus "Edward" Stribbling Trout Shue, known as Trout. The couple married a few weeks later, over the objections of Zona's mother, Mary Jane Heaster, and moved into a house near the blacksmith shop in Lewisburg, West Virginia.

Shortly afterwards, on January 23, 1897, Zona's lifeless body was discovered at the foot of the stairs of her home by eleven-year-old Andy Jones, son of a neighbor who had come to do some odd jobs. The panic-stricken child rushes home to warn his mother, who hurries to the local doctor, Dr. Knapp, while her son informs the deceased's husband of the sad news.

A photograph of the couple

When the doctor arrives on the scene, Edward is already there, weeping loudly as he cradles his wife's head in his arms. Dr. Knapp begins examining the body, but is unable to examine either the skull or the neck, as the husband, who will not let go of his wife's head, violently pushes him away between sobs as soon as he tries to approach it. The latter doesn't dare touch the grief of a man overwhelmed by the loss of his wife, after only a few weeks of marriage. His examination is therefore incomplete, and despite the scant evidence at his disposal, the doctor concludes that the cause of death was a natural heart attack caused by pregnancy complications.

The Files of the Impossible

The tomb of Zona Heaster Shue

Edward leaves no one but himself in charge of dressing and grooming the body for the funeral. He dresses her in a high-collared gown and wraps a scarf around her neck, claiming it was his wife's favorite. Zona's body is taken to his hometown, Big Sewell Mountain, to the home of his mother, Mary Jane Heaster. At the wake, Edward always stays close to the corpse, preventing anyone from going near its head. The funeral takes place and everyone tries to forget this dramatic and brutal death.

Everyone... except the mother of the deceased, Mary Jane Heaster. Mary Jane had never liked her son-in-law, which led her to suspect that he had something to do with her daughter's death. She takes refuge in prayer, hoping to find answers to her questions and, perhaps, confirmation of her suspicions. And against all odds, her prayers are answered...

A month after her daughter's funeral, Mary Jane tells anyone who will listen that Zona's spirit appeared to her four nights in a row to accuse her husband of her murder, giving details of the circumstances: Edward killed her in a fit of anger, provoked by the fact that dinner wasn't ready when he got home from work. He broke her neck by strangling her.

Mary Jane and her brother-in-law John visit the Lewisburg District Attorney, John Preston. At first, he was skeptical, but the two visitors were convincing enough for him to open an investigation. Or perhaps, more likely, he had his own suspicions and found this a good excuse to pursue them. In any case, Dr. Knapp acknowledges that the conclusions of his *post-mortem* examination may have been erroneous, since it was incomplete. In addition, research into Edward Shue's past revealed that he was a notoriously violent man, who had served time in prison, but above all had been married twice and that his previous wives had died in strange, even suspicious, circumstances. One had allegedly killed herself by falling off a haystack, and the other had had her skull bashed in by a falling stone from the chimney her husband was repairing. Of course, both deaths had taken place without any witnesses other than Edward Shue himself.

Portrait of Trout and Zona, drawn by Trout in prison

Despite Edward's vehement protests, Zona's body is exhumed for an autopsy, the results of which are overwhelming: two fractured cervical vertebrae, torn ligaments, a crushed windpipe and strangulation marks on the neck. Despite claiming his innocence, Edward is arrested and charged with his wife's murder.

The trial took place on June 22, 1897. Since the minutes of the hearing have disappeared, all we have today are the newspaper reports of the time, such as the *Greenbrier Independent* of July 1, 1897, which transcribed Mary Jane's deposition, cited by the defense to discredit the prosecution in the eyes of the jury with this supernatural testimony.

Mrs. Mary J. Heaster, the Mother of Mrs. Shue, Sees her Daughter in Visions.

The following very remarkable testimony was given by Mrs Heaster on the pending trial of E. S. Shue for the murder of his wife, her daughter, and led to the inquest and post mortem examination, which resulted in Shue's arrest and trial. It was brought out by counsel for the accused :

Question.—I have heard that you had some dream or vision which led to this post mortem examination?

Answer.—They saw enough themselves without me telling them. It was no dream—she came back and told me that he was mad that she didn't have no meat cooked for supper. But she said she had plenty, and said that she had butter and apple-butter, apples and named over two or three kinds of jellies, pears and cherries and raspberry jelly, and she says I had plenty ; and she says don't you think that he was mad and just took down all my nice things and packed them away and just ruined them. And she told me where I could look down back of Aunt Martha Jones', in the meadow, in a rocky place ; that I could look in a cellar behind some loose plank and see. It was a square log house, and it was hewed up to the square, and she said for me to look right ...

Commencement at Concord.

The Commencement of the Concord Normal School this year was a decided success. The audience was much larger than ever before, and in some respects the exercises were more entertaining.

We were favored by having with use our West Virginia poet and orator, Mr. Butir, whose addresses are always looked forward to with eager anticipation, and remembered with keen appreciation ; and Mr. Trotter, our new State Superintendent, fully met the expectations of every one with his very interesting and encouraging address before the graduating class Tuesday morning.

The exercises throughout were exceptionally good, but by far the most interesting feature of the program and the one longest to be remembered, was the baccalaurate sermon by Rev. T. W. Brown, of Lewisburg, which was delivered Sunday morning, June 20th.— To an unusually large, and very attentive audience. Rev. Mr. Brown preached from James iii, 13 ; "Who is a wise man and endued with knowledge among you ? let him show out of a good conversation his works with meekness of wisdom,"

It was pre eminently a commencement sermon—a sermon for young men and women at the commencement of their careers in life. Never were the ...

STRAY boat hog at my place. Owner come out and get him.

RANDOLPH BAKER.

On Thursday last Mr. J. S. Miller and Miss T. E. Harvey, both of Summers county, were united in marriage at the Methodist station parsonage here, by Rev. T. W. Brown.

THERE will be an excursion to Huntington, Catlettsburg and Ashland, Ky., on the 4th of July. Round trip tickets from Ronceverte will be sold by the C. & O. Ry. for $2.25, which will include a free ride on a palatial steamer from Ashland to Ironton, Ohio. Call on A. B. C. Gray, depot agent, Ronceverte, for particulars.

PERMANENTLY CURED.—"For about two years I suffered with diarrhœa. I used a number of remedies and was treated by physicians, but received no permanent relief. After taking a few doses of Chamberlain's Colic, Cholera and Diarrhœa Remedy, I believe that I am now permanently cured."—JOAB CRITES, Tanner, Gilmer county, W. Va. This remedy is sold by O. P. Sydenstricker & Co.

I HAVE taken personal charge of the Grocery business of Burdett & Co. here at Lewisburg. Will keep on hand a nice, fresh line of groceries, candies, tobacco, cigars, queensware &c., and ...

Extract from the Greenbrier Independent, *July 1, 1897*

Dr. Rucker: I hear you had a dream, or a vision, that led to a *post-mortem* examination of your daughter's body?

Mary Jane Heaster: It wasn't a dream. I was as awake as I am now [...]. I wasn't convinced that my daughter had died of natural causes, so I prayed for the truth. The night after I prayed, my daughter came to see me for the first time [...]. And on the fourth night, she came back and told me that on the night of the murder, her husband had come home from work angry. My daughter had made him something to eat, but he got angry because there was no meat. But there was plenty of bread, butter, potatoes and other things," Zona explained. Trout then got angry, stood up and grabbed my daughter's head between his hands. Then, with a sharp blow, he snapped her neck.

Dr. Rucker: So, if it's not a dream or dreams, what do you call it?

Mary Jane Heaster: I prayed to the Lord that she would come back and tell me what had happened.

Dr. Rucker: Do you think you actually saw her in the flesh?

Mary Jane Heaster: Yes, sir, I think so.

[...]

Dr. Rucker: Don't you think these visions were nothing more or less than four dreams based on your distress?

Mary Jane Heaster: No, I don't think so. The Lord sent my daughter to me to tell me all about it. I was the only one she knew she could trust to talk about it.

Then it was Trout Shue's turn. For an afternoon, he "categorically denied" the accusations against him, reports *The Greenbrier Independent.* "He denied just about everything the other witnesses said [...]. He said he loved his wife dearly and asked the jury to look him in the face and then determine whether he was guilty," reads the local newspaper's archive. But his testimony and defiant demeanor convinced no one.

The verdict finally came down on July 8: Trout Shue was found guilty of first-degree murder, and the jury demanded a life sentence. The verdict was not based on testimony from the beyond, but on the circumstantial evidence of the defendant's violent past and his two previous widowhoods, which were dubious to say the least. Locked up in the West Virginia State Penitentiary, he died there eight years later, apparently of influenza.

Although no one has ever doubted her bona fides, one has to wonder if Mary Jane Heaster really was visited by the spirit of her deceased daughter. Perhaps she has. But perhaps she was also, unconsciously or not, influenced by an article telling a similar story in Australia, which appeared in the very edition in which her daughter's death was announced. Did she read it? It's reasonable to think so, since reading newspapers was one of the few distractions available to small-town folk in the late 19th century.

Even today, the case of the murder of Elva Zona Heaster Shue, known as "the ghost of Greenbrier", continues to cause a stir in the American county. Not far from Soule Chapel Methodist Cemetery, where the young woman is buried, a commemorative plaque reminds visitors of these extraordinary events. It reads:

"Zona Heaster Shue is buried in the nearby cemetery. Her death in 1897 was presumed natural until her spirit appeared to her mother to describe how she had been killed by her husband, Edward. An autopsy on the exhumed body confirmed the ghost's account. Edward was convicted of murder and sentenced to state prison. The only known case in which the testimony of a ghost led to the conviction of a murderer."

The opinion of 1st Commissioner Maillard
of the Brussels Judicial Police - Division in charge
# of crime against property and people.

01/23/1987: Zona's lifeless body is discovered at the foot of the stairs of her home by Andy Jones, 11, son of a neighbor.

The child runs to warn his mother, who fetches the local doctor, and the boy leaves to warn Zona's husband, nicknamed "Trout".

Suspicion of husband

- He refused to let the doctor examine his wife's head and neck.

- The examination was therefore incomplete, but the doctor concluded that the cause of death was natural, due to a heart attack caused by pregnancy complications.

- No one will be allowed near his wife, and the husband will do everything in his power to conceal her neck with a high collar and scarf.

Without a proper examination of the victim, it is impossible to know the exact cause of death. It's obvious that the husband is trying to hide something. Does she even have traces of a possible fall?

Apparitions of the victim to her mother

- Being fairly down-to-earth, I prefer to rely on evidence and material elements rather than on this kind of event. Rarely has anyone been convicted on the basis of a victim's appearance to a loved one.

- On the other hand, the fact that the victim's neck was broken speaks to me even more. Perhaps the victim's mother's subconscious is pushing her in this direction.

Background of husband Edward Shue

- This is a notoriously violent man, who has already spent time in prison.

- Married twice to women who both met tragic ends in strange, even suspicious, circumstances.

A proper autopsy of shingles

Two fractured cervical vertebrae with torn ligaments, a crushed windpipe and, to cap it all, strangulation marks on the neck.

Conclusion, bearing in mind that the events took place in 1897

- A proper medical examination does not take place in the presence of a relative of the victim, even in 1897. A doctor must not allow himself to be influenced by the victim's family.

- Ghost and ghost stories have never condemned anyone. In this case, it was the autopsy and the husband's background that weighed in the balance.

- It's lucky for the doctor that the husband was unable to claim a fourth victim before his arrest.

Acknowledgements

Many people have of course helped me in the conception of this book, and it's only right to thank them, starting with Bob Bellanca, founder and host of BTLV, the No. 1 medium for mystery and the unexplained, without whom this book would never have reached you in this form.

I'd also like to thank my team of proofreaders, as well as those who provided me with information of all kinds: my mom, Sylvie, Mickaël, Adeline, Loïc Holleville and the merciless Simon.

Many thanks also to the excellent proofreader Manon E. Mathieu, for her conscientiousness and attention to detail, as well as Laurent Granier, founder of the specialist site Horreur.net, for believing in the project in the first place, and Alex Rodriguez.

And, of course, a HUGE thank you to the team at Editions Max Milo for all their hard work.

So all that's left for me to do now is to thank you, the readers, for having come this far with me, and to say "see you soon" for even more incredible stories.

Geoffrey Claustriaux

Table of Contents